AA

ILLUSTRATED
WORLD
ATLAS

AA

ILLUSTRATED
WORLD
ATLAS

AA
Illustrated World Atlas

© The Automobile Association
Illustrated World Atlas
1st Edition, August 1990

© Rand McNally & Company
Original Edition, Photographic World Atlas 1989

Maps from the New International Atlas
by Rand McNally & Company, © 1969, 1989

Produced especially for The Automobile Association
by Rand McNally & Company

Printed by L.E.G.O. SpA, Italy

Published by the Automobile Association,
Fanum House, Basingstoke, Hampshire RG21 2EA
ISBN: 0 7495 0165 0

A CIP cataglogue record for this book is available
from the British Library.

Photograph Credits

Christopher Arnesen/Aperture PhotoBank: 24 bottom, 50, 51, 53
bottom right, 74, 79 bottom, 91. David Barnes/Aperture PhotoBank:
39 bottom right, 152 top right. Nathan Benn/Aperture PhotoBank:
35 bottom right, 104 left, 146 top. Campbell & Boulander/Aperture
PhotoBank: 105 bottom, 157 middle left. Byron Crader/Ric
Ergenbright Photography: 47 bottom, 89, 160 bottom left. Chad
Ehlers/Aperture PhotoBank: 135 top right. Ross Ehlert/Viesti
Associates: 125 bottom. Ric Ergenbright/Ric Ergenbright
Photography: cover (Le Mont-Saint-Michel, France), 10, 11, 14
bottom, 15 top, 28 bottom, 29 top left, 32 right, 33 bottom, 35 top,
39 top, 60, 63, 72, 73, 75 bottom, 103, 110, 114 right, 125 top, 126
top, 127. Tim Fitzharris/Aperture PhotoBank: 128 bottom. Ken
Graham/Aperture PhotoBank: 94 bottom. Robert Ivey/Ric
Ergenbright Photography: 88, 90 bottom, 112 top. Wolfgang
Kaehler/Aperture PhotoBank: 95. Stephen J. Krasemann/Aperture
PhotoBank: 81. Greg Lawler/Aperture PhotoBank: 58. Will
McIntyre/Aperture PhotoBank: 28 top left. David Muench/
Aperture PhotoBank: 122. Floyd Norgaard/Ric Ergenbright
Photography: 77. Ken Ross/Viesti Associates: 59, 124, 134 bottom,
156 top. James Randklev/Aperture PhotoBank: 140 top right. Ron
Sanford/Aperture PhotoBank: 25 top right. Kevin Schaper/Aperture
PhotoBank: 101. George Schwartz/Ric Ergenbright Photography:
153 bottom left. Monserrate J. Schwartz/Ric Ergenbright
Photography: 141 bottom left. Masa Uemura/Aperture PhotoBank:
140 bottom. Joe Viesti/Viesti Associates: 13, 18, 19, 34 bottom, 38
top, 42 bottom, 43 top, 46 right, 61, 100, 102 bottom left, 107, 113,
123, 129. Art Wolfe/Aperture PhotoBank: 134 top. Reprinted from
World Atlas of Nations, copyright © 1988 by Rand McNally &
Company, used with permission: 12 bottom, 62. Reprinted from
This Great Land, copyright © 1983 by Rand McNally & Company,
used with permission: 147 bottom left, 156 bottom, 157 top. All
other photographs reproduced from **Rand McNally Pictorial
World Atlas**, copyright © 1980 by Rand McNally & Company, used
with permission. Portions of text revised from previously published
text and used with permission from Intercontinental Book
Productions Limited.

Contents

In this Atlas

Do you know where the nation of Burkina Faso is? How about Vanuatu? And what about Belize?

What does Malta look like? How flat is the altiplano of Peru and Bolivia? And how bright are the lights of Chicago at night?

If you were traveling to Nepal, what kinds of people would you expect to find there? And what if you were going to Melanesia – what would the residents be like?

At any given moment, the minds of most people are concerned primarily with their immediate world: professionals with their budgets, deadlines, and demanding bosses; farmers with their animals, crops, and the weather; and students with their exams, grades, and social lives.

Think, though, of yourself in relation to the earth, with its circumference of 24,902 miles (40,075 kilometers) and diameter of 7,926 miles (12,756 kilometers). That measurement represents a surface area of nearly 200 million square miles (about 500 million square kilometers).

Now think again. Think of the vast expanses of the Pacific Ocean, which, in places, is deeper than Mount Everest is high and covers one-third of our planet. Think of the ancient pyramids of Egypt and the sophisticated culture they represent – a culture that existed thousands of years before humanity harnessed the electric power that could have helped construct those same pyramids. Think of the peoples

in the isolated corners of the world who continue to live as they did in the Stone Age and who worship the airplanes they occasionally see and hear flying overhead. In other words, think of the enormous size, long history, and endless variety of the planet earth.

There's a whole world out there – and it's all here in your *AA Illustrated World Atlas*.

The atlas is divided into sections that cover each major region of the world. In most cases, the regions coincide with the continental divisions of the earth. Thus, you will see sections on Europe, Asia, Africa, South America, and North America.

You will also find, however, sections covering the Soviet Union, Oceania, Middle America, and the Polar Regions. These regional divisions do not fit in with the traditional continental scheme of the earth – a scheme that may no longer be ideal for most purposes.

The Soviet Union, for example, straddles two continents and is of such stature physically and politically that it merits its own section.

Australia alone is a continent, but no atlas would be complete without New Zealand and the widely scattered islands of the Pacific Ocean. This section therefore encompasses all of Oceania.

The two Americas are increasingly divided into three: the largely English-speaking North, the Spanish- and Portuguese-influenced South, and the patchwork of predominantly Latin

mainland states together with the Caribbean and other islands that make up Middle America. Within this atlas, these divisions allow more expansive treatment of each region.

Finally, the most complete of atlases include not only Antarctica but also the vast, frozen expanses of the North Pole.

Following is an overview of what you can expect to find in your *AA Illustrated World Atlas*.

Photographs
This atlas brings you a visual presentation of the world with nearly 175 full-color photographs. As a whole, they work to illuminate the wide variety that is the planet earth.

Captions
An extended caption accompanies each photograph. These captions inform you not only of the location and description of each photograph but also provide some insight into the meaning of each. Browsing the photographs and reading the captions of your *AA Illustrated World Atlas* will educate as well as entertain you.

Maps
The regional sections conclude with full-color maps. These maps represent some of the highest cartographic standards available in print. Mainly on two scales, the smaller (1:12,000,000) presenting the continents as a whole on one or more maps; the larger (1:3,000,000) showing countries or areas in greater

detail. The maps emphasize political features and show the main physical characteristics.

Profiles
The profiles begin each regional section by acquainting you with the location and size; landscape; climate; and history, politics, and economy of the area. They give you the "big picture" of the region.

Countries
Following each profile is an alphabetic list of the countries in the region – except, of course, in the Soviet Union and Polar Regions sections. Here you can find a brief overview of every independent nation and of some major foreign-ruled territories.

Portfolios
In addition to the features described above, your *AA Illustrated World Atlas* presents expanded sections on Europe and the United States – two regions that appeal especially to many travelers. In the portfolios, you will find these two places subdivided into regions, each with a wide variety of photographs to give you a closer look.

Index
Found at the end of the book, the index is an alphabetic list of the names appearing on the maps that gives a page reference, coordinates, and, where applicable, a symbol indicating the nature of the feature.

World Index Map

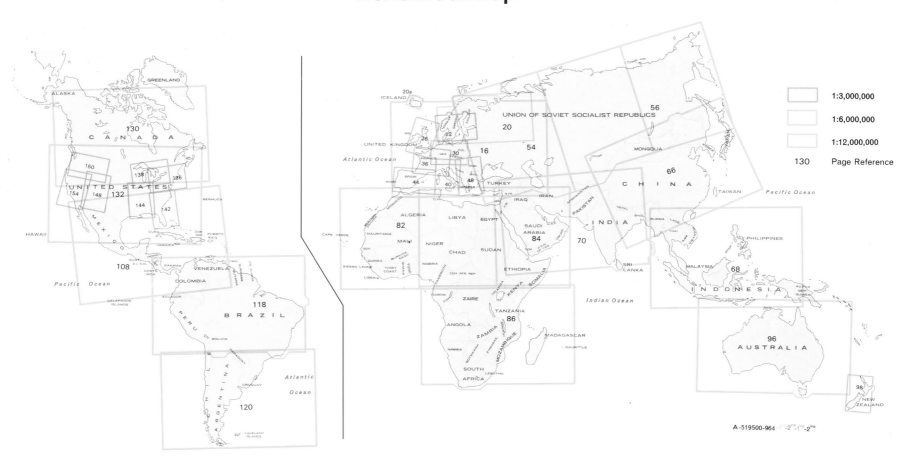

Legend to Maps

Inhabited Localities

The symbol represents the number of inhabitants within the locality

1:3,000,000	•	0—10,000	1:12,000,000	•	0—50,000
1:6,000,000	○	10,000—25,000		⊚	50,000—100,000
	⊚	25,000—100,000		⊡	100,000—250,000
	⊡	100,000—250,000		▣	250,000—1,000,000
	■	250,000—1,000,000		■	>1,000,000
	■	>1,000,000			

☐ **Urban Area** (area of continuous industrial, commercial, and residential development)

The size of type indicates the relative economic and political importance of the locality

Écommoy	Lisieux	**Rouen**
Trouville	**Orléans**	**PARIS**

Hollywood □ Section of a City, Neighborhood
Westminster

Bi'r Safājah ° Inhabited Oasis

Capitals of Political Units

BUDAPEST Independent Nation

Cayenne Dependency (Colony, protectorate, etc.)

GALAPAGOS Administering Country
(Ecuador)

Villarica State, Province, etc.

White Plains County, Oblast, etc.

Alternate Names

Basel	**MOSKVA**	English or second official language names are shown in reduced size lettering
Bâle	MOSCOW	

Ventura	Volgograd	Historical or other alternates in the local language are shown in parentheses
(San Buenaventura)	(Stalingrad)	

Transportation

1:12,000,000	1:3,000,000 1:6,000,000	
		Primary Road
		Secondary Road
		Minor Road, Trail
		Primary Railway
	✈	Airport

MACKINAC BRIDGE — Bridge

GREAT ST. BERNARD TUNNEL — Tunnel

TO CALAIS — Ferry

Shipping Channel

Canal du Midi — Navigable Canal

Intracoastal Waterway

Metric-English Equivalents

Areas represented by one square centimeter at various map scales

1:3,000,000	1:6,000,000	1:12,000,000
900 km²	3,600 km²	14,400 km²
348 square miles	1,390 square miles	5,558 square miles

Meter=3.28 feet
Kilometer=0.62 mile

Meter² (m²)=10.76 square feet
Kilometer² (km²)=0.39 square mile

Political Boundaries

International (First-order political unit)

1:3,000,000
1:6,000,000
1:12,000,000

— — — Demarcated, Undemarcated, and Administrative

— · — · — Disputed de jure

═══ Indefinite or Undefined

— — — Demarcation Line

Internal

═══ State, Province, etc. (Second-order political unit)
GUAIRA

WESTCHESTER County, Oblast, etc. (Third-order political unit)

ANDALUCIA Historical Region (No boundaries indicated)

Miscellaneous Cultural Features

PARQUE NACIONAL CANAIMA ▲	National or State Park or Monument	STEINHAUSEN ⚓	Church, Monastery
FORT CLATSOP NAT. MEM. ▲	National or State Historic(al) Site, Memorial	UXMAL ∴	Ruins
BLACKFOOT IND. RES.	Indian Reservation	WINDSOR CASTLE ♜	Castle
FORT DIX ▪	Military Installation	AMISTAD DAM	Dam
TANGLEWOOD ▲	Point of Interest (Battlefield, cave, historical site, etc.)		

Hydrographic Features

	Shoreline	The Everglades	Swamp
	Undefined or Fluctuating Shoreline	SEWARD GLACIER	Glacier
Amur	River, Stream	L. Victoria	Lake, Reservoir
	Intermittent Stream	Tuz Golu	Salt Lake
	Rapids, Falls		Intermittent Lake, Reservoir
	Irrigation or Drainage Canal		Dry Lake Bed
	Reef	(395)	Lake Surface Elevation
764 ▽	Depth of Water		

Topographic Features

			Lava
Mt. Kenya △ 5199	Elevation Above Sea Level		Sand Area
76 ▽	Elevation Below Sea Level		Salt Flat
Mount Cook ▲ 3764	Highest Elevation in Country	A N D E S KUNLUNSHANMAI	Mountain Range, Plateau, Valley, etc.
Khyber Pass ≍ 1067	Mountain Pass		
133 ▼	Lowest Elevation in Country	BAFFIN ISLAND NUNIVAK ISLAND	Island
		POLUOSTROV KAMČATKA CABO DE HORNOS	Peninsula, Cape, Point, etc.

Elevations and depths are given in meters
Highest Elevation and Lowest Elevation of a continent are underlined

ARCTIC OCEAN

Beaufort Sea

GREENLAND (Den.)

Baffin Bay

Thule

BAFFIN ISLAND

Godhavn

Angmagssalik

ICELAND

FAEROE ISLANDS (Den.)

Reykjavik

Norwe

VICTORIA ISLAND

Godthåb

Davis Strait

UNITED STATES
Arctic Circle

Inuvik

Mackenzie

Hudson

Yellowknife

Glasgow

Bering Strait

Nome

Yukon

Fairbanks

Churchill

Bay

Dublin

UNITED KINGDO

Mount McKinley

Anchorage

C A N A D A

ROCKY MOUNTAINS

IRELAND

LON

Bering Sea

Gulf of Alaska

Edmonton

NEWFOUNDLAND

Winnipeg

Calgary

ALEUTIAN ISLANDS

Lake Superior

Goose Bay

Vancouver

Seattle

St. John's

Portland

Minneapolis

Quebec

L. Huron

St. La

Halifax

NORTH AMERICA

Lake Michigan

Ottawa

Montreal

Toronto

L. Ontario

ATLANTIC OCEAN

CHICAGO

DETROIT

L. Erie

Boston

NEW YORK

Porto

PORTUGAL

SPA

San Francisco

Salt Lake City

Denver

St. Louis

PHILADELPHIA

Washington

APPALACHIAN MOUNTAINS

AÇORES AZORES (Port.)

Lisboa

GIBRALTAR (U.K.)

LOS ANGELES

UNITED STATES

Wi

San Diego

Phoenix

El Paso

Dallas

Atlanta

BERMUDA (U.K.)

ARQUIPÉLAGO DA MADERA (Port.)

Rabat

Casablanca

MOROCCO

ATL
A

MIDWAY ISLANDS (U.S.)

PACIFIC

OCEAN

Tropic of Cancer

Houston

Gulf of Mexico

New Orleans

Monterrey

Miami BAHAMAS

ISLAS CANARIAS CANARY ISLANDS (Sp.)

WESTERN SAHARA

S

HAWAIIAN ISLANDS (U.S.)

Honolulu

CABO SAN LUCAS

MEXICO

Guadalajara

CIUDAD DE MÉXICO

La Habana

CUBA

DOMINICAN REPUBLIC

PUERTO RICO (U.S.)

Nouakchott

MAURI-
TANIA

Tombouctou

MEXICO CITY

Port-au-Prince

San Juan

CAPE VERDE

SENEGAL

JOHNSTON ATOLL (U.S.)

GUATEMALA

BELIZE

JAMAICA

Santo Domingo

GUADELOUPE (Fr.)

Dakar

GAMBIA

Bamako

BUR

HONDURAS

Kingston

Banjul

GUINEA

Guatemala

Tegucigalpa

MARTINIQUE (Fr.)

GUINEA-BISSAU

Conakry

OUAG

San Salvador

EL SALVADOR

BARBADOS

SIERRA

Freetown

IVORY COAST

Yamoussouk

ÎLE CLIPPERTON (Fr.)

Managua

NICARAGUA

TRINIDAD AND TOBAGO

Caribbean Sea

LEONE

Monrovia

Abidjan

San José

Port of Spain

LIBERIA

COSTA RICA

PANAMA

Caracas

VENEZUELA

GUYANA

Georgetown

Medellín

Bogotá

Paramaribo

SURI-
NAME

FRENCH GUIANA

LINE ISLANDS

Equator

COLOMBIA

Equator

PHOENIX ISLANDS

Quito

ECUADOR

Amazon

Belém

Fortaleza

ARCHIPIÉLAGO DE COLÓN GALAPAGOS ISLANDS (Ec.)

Guayaquil

Iquitos

Manaus

CABO DE SÃO ROQUE

Natal

P
O
L
Y
N
E
S
I
A

ÎLES MARQUISES

Trujillo

Madeira

B R A Z I L

Recife

A
N
D
E
S

WALLIS AND FUTUNA (Fr.)

W. SAMOA

AM. SAMOA

ÎLES

TUAMOTU

ATLANTIC OCEAN

Lima

SOUTH AMERICA

Salvador

Apia

FIJI

NIUE (N.Z.)

COOK ISLANDS (N.Z.)

ÎLES DE LA SOCIÉTÉ SOCIETY ISLANDS (N.Z.)

A

FRENCH POLYNESIA

Arequipa

BOLIVIA

La Paz

Sucre

Goiânia

Brasília

Belo Horizonte

P
E
R
U

TONGA

Tropic of Capricorn

Antofagasta

PARAGUAY

SÃO PAULO

RIO DE JANEIRO

Asunción

Santos

PITCAIRN (U.K.)

ISLA SAN AMBROSIO (Chile)

Curitiba

ISLA DE PASCUA EASTER ISLAND (Chile)

CHILE

Co. Aconcagua 6959

Córdoba

Paraná

Porto Alegre

Valparaíso

Rosario

URUGUAY

ARCHIPIÉLAGO JUAN FERNÁNDEZ (Chile)

Santiago

BUENOS AIRES

Montevideo

International Date Line

PACIFIC

ARGENTINA

Concepción

Mar del Plata

Bahía Blanca

OCEAN

CHATHAM ISLANDS (N.Z.)

FALKLAND ISLANDS ISLAS MALVINAS (U.K.)

Punta Arenas

SOUTH GEORGIA (U.K.)

CABO DE HORNOS CAPE HORN

Drake

Passage

SOUTH ORKNEY ISLANDS (B.A.T.)

Antarctic Circle

ANTARCTIC PENINSULA

Ross Sea

Bellingshausen Sea

Weddell Sea

ROSS ICE SHELF

MARIE BYRD LAND

Vinson Massif 4897

A
N
T
A
R

One centimeter represents 750 kilometers.
One inch represents approximately 1200 miles.
Robinson Projection
Scale 1:75,000,000

Europe
Profile

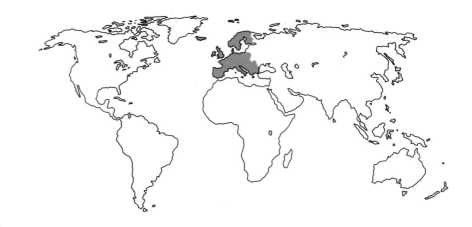

Location and Size

Europe is situated in the Northern Hemisphere. From its northern tip at North Cape, Norway, to its southern point at the island of Crete in the Mediterranean Sea, Europe extends some 2,500 miles (4,000 kilometers). From the west to east borders, Europe extends from the western Portuguese coast to the boundaries of the Black Sea in Romania, approximately 2,100 miles (3,400 kilometers) across. Beyond the mainland, Iceland, the Azores, and parts of Ireland lie even farther west. With over 30,000 miles (48,000 kilometers) of coastline, Europe is an intricate continent with large areas of ocean and sea reaching in everywhere.

Landscape

The three main physical regions of Europe are two areas dominated by uplands – one in the northwest and one in the south – and one lowland area in the east and west. Rarely are found open expanses of monotonous landscape such as are found in some other continents. Not even the lowlands surrounding the Baltic Sea are as expansive as the interior lowlands of North America, the Great Siberian Plain, or Amazonia.

The uplands of the north and west are the remains of a chain of mountains formed in the Caledonian Age about 350 million years ago. Today these mountains reach heights of more than eight thousand feet (two thousand meters) in Norway and more than four thousand feet (one thousand meters) in Scotland.

But not all of this part of the European continent is mountainous. Parts of Sweden and all of Finland, for example, have been reduced over the ages by erosion to their present flat terrain.

The mountains of Iceland were mainly produced by more recent volcanic activity. Iceland is one of the few places in Europe that is still volcanically active.

The largest area of the three major regions is the lowlands that lie east and west across Europe. Geographically they are younger than the northern uplands but older than much of the area to the south. The landscape often has a gently rolling appearance, being a succession of low hills or *scarps* with valleys or *vales* between them. Such landscapes are found in Britain and northern France, generally reaching less than 500 feet (150 meters) above sea level.

The mountains of the south are among the youngest regions of the continent, created less than 100 million years ago. They are a part of a great expanse of mountains that runs west to east from northern Spain, across Italy, Switzerland, Austria and the Balkan countries, and then on into the Soviet Union and Asia. These are the highest mountains in Europe, rising to more than fifteen thousand feet (four thousand meters) at Mont Blanc.

Other older upland areas are also found in southern Europe. The south-central parts of France and parts of central and southern Germany and western Czechoslovakia are eroded mountain systems that were formed about 200 million years ago. In the Massif Central of France, these rise to more than six thousand feet (almost two thousand meters).

In very recent geological times, northern Europe and the higher parts of the southern mountain areas have been covered with ice. Much smaller areas of northern and mountain Europe are glaciated today. At its maximum advance, the ice covered most of the northern continent. It eroded the landscape in many places, and today such features as the Norwegian fjords and the Scottish lochs are evidence of this glaciation. In other places, the ice carried and then deposited much fertile soil that is today the basis of some of the rich farmlands of the central lowlands.

Europe is a continent of comparatively short rivers, and no location in the whole continent is more than about 400 miles (650 kilometers) from the sea. The most important rivers in the western portions begin in the Alps or other central mountains. The largest of these rivers is the Danube, rising in southern Germany and flowing eastward to the Black Sea. Others include the Rhine, Rhône, Saône, Po, Elbe, and Vistula. The major rivers of Eastern Europe flow mostly to the south.

Left: A familiar sight to residents and visitors alike, the many castles of Europe once housed the lords of the land. This small castle is on Loch Linnhe, in Scotland's western coastal region.

Right: One of the Alps' many branches, the Bernese Alps run through south-central Switzerland. Shown here is a peak known as the Eiger.

Europe

Profile continued

Climate

Europe lies on the west side of the world's largest land mass, Eurasia, almost entirely north of 40° – that is, north of southern Italy – and south of the Arctic Circle. Since no mountains run parallel to the Atlantic coast except in Norway, maritime air masses pass well into the central parts of the continent. Thus, most of Europe experiences very temperate climates.

The average temperature in western Europe seldom falls below 32°F (0°C). Rainfall is spread fairly evenly throughout the year with no marked wet and dry seasons. Rainfall totals are almost all above 22 inches (550 millimeters) per year and much higher in upland areas of the west coast.

Southern France also experiences average monthly temperatures always above 32°F (0°C). In some places, particularly in the eastern Mediterranean area, the average monthly temperature in the summer can easily reach as high as 80°F (27°C).

In Eastern Europe and much of Scandinavia, winters are colder, with average monthly temperatures falling below 32°F (0°C) in midwinter. In the north of this region, average monthly summer temperatures may only rise to 62°F (17°C). In Romania and Bulgaria, they may rise to above 75°F (24°C), giving these regions the highest temperature range in Europe – a result of their position farther away from the moderating effects of the ocean.

In the extreme north of Scandinavia and Iceland, polar climates exist where no month has average temperatures higher than 50°F (10°C).

History, Politics, and Economy

Europe has been the birthplace of many major developments in Western civilization from the beginning of recorded history. From the democratic principle originating in Greece to other great concepts such as parliamentary government in the United Kingdom, Europe has contributed many fundamentals that have been adopted by countries throughout the world. The growth of the industrial, and hence, the technological age started in Europe, and it can be argued that Europe's influence in the world has been collectively greater than any other continental area.

Within twenty-five years, Europe was torn apart by two different wars that

Above left: Greek windmills such as this one on Crete pump water to irrigate olive, grape, and grain crops.

Above: Venice, a seaport in northeast Italy, is one of the world's treasure houses of art and architecture.

Left: The changing of the guard at Buckingham Palace, London, is popular with tourists.

Opposite, bottom: Often called the "Land of Fire and Ice," Iceland is an island of contrasting features, as exemplified by the geysers shown here against a backdrop of snow- and glacier-covered mountains. Volcanoes, lakes, a mountainous lava desert, sulfur springs, canyons, waterfalls, and fast-flowing rivers are also found throughout the island, and areas such as these make up almost 80 percent of Iceland's total area. Population is concentrated on the 7 percent of the island that borders the sea.

Left: Historic Aragon, in northeastern Spain, is arid and sparsely populated. The only city of any size in the region is Zaragoza. These women are traditionally dressed for the Fiesta del Pilar, held annually in Zaragoza to honor the Virgin Mary.

Europe

Profile continued

embroiled much of the rest of the world. In the aftermath of the two wars, Communist governments were established in much of Europe, and the continent was divided into Communist and non-Communist nations, or Eastern and Western Europe as we know them today. In 1949, ten Western European nations joined the United States and Canada to form the North Atlantic Treaty Organization (NATO), designed to unify Western countries in defense. Similarly, in 1955, the Soviet Union and most of the other Eastern European countries formed what was called the Warsaw Pact for the same purposes.

In 1958, the European Economic Community (EEC), or Common Market, was established to help integrate the economies of Western Europe by forming common price levels. Although it has not solved all the economic concerns facing its member countries, the Common Market is considered to be a success because much of the economic growth of Western Europe in the decades since its inception can be attributed to the union. In the late 1980s, the Common Market expanded, with Spain and Portugal becoming its newest members.

Although, from the late 1940s through the early 1960s, Europe was engulfed in Cold War tension between the East and West, since then its statesmen have struggled to forge a lasting peace through various trading links and economic agreements. One such agreement involved all of Europe and the United States. Named the Helsinki Agreement, it was signed in 1975. In it, almost every European nation, the United States, Canada, and Cyprus pledged to cooperate on matters of economics, peacekeeping, and human rights.

Since the late 1970s, many European nations have suffered from recession, inflation, and high unemployment.

Opposite, top: Hammerfest, Norway, is sometimes called the world's northernmost town. Here the sun never sets from May to August and never rises from November to February.

Opposite, center: Since the 1600s, northern Bohemia, Czechoslovakia, has been a leader in the craft of glassmaking. Shown here is the Světlá glassworks.

Opposite, bottom: Built in the latter part of the nineteenth century, scenic Kylemore Abbey is in County Galway, Ireland, near the town of Letterfrack.

Above: The Lot River valley in southwestern France is a fertile region dotted with vineyards and small towns.

Right: The glittering nightlife of Monte Carlo draws thousands of tourists to Monaco each year, making this Riviera resort a major contributor to the principality's tourism-based economy.

Kilometers | 0 200 400 600 Km.
Statute Miles | 0 200 400 600 Mi.

Scale 1:12,000,000

One centimeter represents 120 kilometers.
One inch represents approximately 190 miles.
Miller Oblated Stereographic Projection

Countries

Albania
The People's Socialist Republic of Albania established a Communist government in 1944, and since then it has severed ties with one-time allies – Yugoslavia, the Soviet Union, and most recently China. In 1967 religious institutions were banned, and Albania claims to be the first atheist state.

Andorra
Andorra, a duty-free shopping mecca, lies between France and Spain, with Spanish the predominant language. A mild climate complements the mountainous terrain of this attractive and antiquated country. Andorrans have a high literacy rate but no formal constitution, no armed forces, and no political parties.

Austria
Known for its beautiful ski resorts and clean cities, Austria is an attraction for tourists from around the world. With low unemployment, this country has a strong economy. After World War II, the government nationalized some industries; today the economy is a blend of state and privately owned industry. Vienna (Wien), its capital city, is one of the great cultural centers of Europe.

Belgium
A founding member of the EEC, Belgium now plays host to the organization in its capital, Brussels (Bruxelles). Positioned between France and the Netherlands, Belgium borders on the North Sea. The economy and population have been affected by Belgium's central location. Industry was early established as the economic base.

Bulgaria
The mainly mountainous People's Republic of Bulgaria is just south of Romania, bordering on the Black Sea. The climate is similar to that of the American Midwest. A Communist government has been in power since the 1940s.

Channel Islands
Set in the Atlantic Ocean, some 90 miles (140 kilometers) south of the British mainland, the Channel Islands are part of the United Kingdom. English is the predominant language, though a form of Norman-French is also spoken.

Czechoslovakia
An industrialized nation, Czechoslovakia has a centralized economy and one of the highest standards of living of the Eastern-bloc countries. Most people are Roman Catholic, and the government licenses and pays the clergy.

Denmark
Denmark is made up of the Jutland Peninsula and more than four hundred islands, about one hundred of which are inhabited. In addition to these islands, Greenland and the Faeroe Islands are also part of Denmark. Despite limited natural resources, Denmark has a diversified economy.

Faeroe Islands
This group of more than twenty islands belongs to Denmark and is situated 310 miles (500 kilometers) southeast of Iceland in the northern Atlantic Ocean. The name Faeroes is taken from the Danish for "sheep islands," and sheep farming has been a major occupation.

Finland
The most northerly country of mainland Europe, Finland has a low-lying, forested, and lake-filled landscape. The winters are so long and severe that even the capital, Helsinki, in the south of the country, is icebound. Northern Finland has periods of continuous daylight in summer and darkness in winter. Much of Finland's economy is supported by its rich forests.

France
The largest country in Western Europe, France is a major tourist country, famed for its capital, Paris. France has long contributed to learning and the arts. In 1981 France elected a Socialist president. The country is highly developed, and it remains one of the leading powers of Europe.

Germany, East
Also known as the German Democratic Republic, East Germany has a high standard of living, and citizens benefit from extensive educational and social-insurance programs. Postwar economic expansion emphasized industry, and today one of the country is one of the world's largest industrial producers.

Germany, West
Also known as the Federal Republic of Germany, West Germany has about four times the population of East Germany. Despite the destruction of World War II, and Germany's division into two countries, West Germany has one of the world's strongest economies.

Gibraltar
Occupying a narrow peninsula on Spain's southern coast, the British colony of Gibraltar has a mixed population of Italian, English, Maltese, Portuguese, and Spanish. A number of British military personnel are also present.

Greece
This mountainous country at the extreme southeast of Europe relies heavily on maritime trading and tourism. Greece has one of the largest merchant fleets in the world. Greeks are united by a language that dates back three thousand years.

Hungary
This landlocked, Eastern-bloc nation is a socialist republic composed of Magyar tribe descendants. Gypsies and Germans also compose a minority in a country where flat plains dominate and varied terrain is seldom seen. Agriculture is almost completely socialized.

Iceland
Just south of the Arctic Circle, this volcanic island in the North Atlantic was formerly part of the Danish realm. Fish, found in the island's rich coastal waters, is the main natural resource and export. Located in the Land of the Midnight Sun, Iceland has periods of twenty-four-hour daylight in June.

Ireland
The country of Ireland occupies most of an island in the Atlantic Ocean that sits next to the United Kingdom. The north of this island is part of the United Kingdom, and there has been much conflict over its control. Ireland has a long literary tradition and has contributed greatly to world literature. The economy

Right: Tourism has become important to the Mediterranean island nation of Malta. Popular among visitors is the Blue Grotto, situated on the main island, southwest of the town of Zurrieq.

Right: Andalucía, in the extreme south of Spain, is a productive agricultural region. Fruits, olives, tomatoes, wheat, and barley are grown as well as the grapes shown here.

is diversified, but agriculture – aided by fertile, rolling land suitable for farming – continues to play an important role.

Isle of Man

Set in the middle of the Irish Sea, this attractive island relies heavily on tourism as its economic base. The residents raise only a minimum of crops as well as some sheep and cattle.

Italy

The birthplace of the Renaissance, Italy has made substantial contributions to world culture and art. Italy is a long, boot-shaped peninsula that stands in the Mediterranean Sea at the southern tip of central Europe. The islands of Sicily and Sardinia are also part of Italy, and Rome is the capital city. The Italian economy is based on private enterprise, although the government is involved in some industrial and commercial activities.

Liechtenstein

Most of Liechtenstein, one of the world's smallest nations, is covered by Alps, but it features a mild climate. The last few decades have seen the economy shift from agricultural to highly industrialized. Women did not gain the right to vote in this nation until the 1980s.

Luxembourg

The Grand Duchy of Luxembourg is a central European nation governed by a constitutional monarchy. Most Luxembourgers are a blend of Celtic, French, and German stock. German and French are the official languages, as is Luxembourgish, an indigenous German dialect.

Malta

Situated between Europe and Africa, this Mediterranean island is a hilly country. One of the most densely populated places in the world, Malta is home to a diverse group of Arabs, Normans, Sicilians, and English.

Monaco

The Principality of Monaco is found at the southern tip of France, bordering on the Mediterranean Sea. A popular tourist haven, Monaco is famous for it gambling casinos in Monte Carlo.

Netherlands

Often referred to as Holland, the Netherlands is a low-lying kingdom bordering the North Sea. It has one of the highest population densities in Europe. Much of the Netherlands lies below sea level – behind protecting dikes and sea walls – and some of its richest farmlands have been reclaimed from the sea through artificial drainage. A variety of manufacturing strengths – notably the metal, chemical, and food-processing industries – fuel the prosperous economy.

Norway

An independent kingdom since 1905, Norway has been closely linked with neighbors Sweden and Denmark throughout its history. Famed for its mountains and fjords, most Norwegian land is unproductive. In 1967, the government initiated a wide-ranging social-welfare system.

Poland

The Polish People's Republic borders on the Baltic Sea and is surrounded by the Soviet Union, Czechoslovakia, and East Germany. Government policies since the war have transformed Poland from an agricultural nation into an industrial producer. Shortages in consumer goods have been chronic since the 1970s, when debts to the West were compounded by the failure of Polish goods in the market. Poland has a mostly flat terrain, except for mountains in the south.

Portugal

Together with Spain and Gibraltar, Portugal is situated on the Iberian Peninsula. The Atlantic islands of Madeira and Azores are also part of Portugal. A variety of social and political ills have contributed to Portugal's status as one of the poorest nations in Europe.

Romania

When Romania became a Communist country in the 1940s, the government began to turn the country from agriculture to industry. Although Romania remains less developed than many other European countries, it has experienced some post-war growth.

San Marino

Founded in the fourth century, San Marino claims to be the world's oldest republic. Surrounded completely by Italy, it has strong ties to the Italians and combines Latin, Adriatic, and Teutonic roots.

Spain

One of the largest yet least developed countries of Western Europe, Spain, together with Portugal and Gibraltar, occupies the Iberian Peninsula. Despite the effects of recent worldwide recessions, Spain has benefited greatly from an economic-restructuring program that began in the late 1950s. Spain's terrain is mainly composed of a dry plateau area; mountains cover the northern section, and plains extend down the country's eastern coast.

Sweden

The Scandinavian kingdom of Sweden is one of the most prosperous countries in Western Europe. With one of the highest standards of living in the world, Swedish government provides exceptional benefits for most citizens, including free education and medical care, pension payments, four-week vacations, and payments for child care. The nation is industrial and bases its economy on its three most important resources: timber, iron ore, and water power. Most farms are part of Sweden's agricultural-cooperative movement.

Switzerland

This landlocked, central European country is known for the Alps and other mountains that cover nearly 70 percent of the terrain. Most of Switzerland is unsuitable for agriculture, but tourism thrives here. Switzerland is also an international banking and finance center.

United Kingdom

England, Scotland, Wales, and Northern Ireland compose the United Kingdom, which occupies most of the British Isles. The Industrial Revolution developed quickly in Great Britain, and the country continues to be a leading world producer. London is well known as an international financial center. The varied terrain is marked by several mountain ranges, moors, rolling hills, and plains. The climate is tempered by the sea and is subject to frequent changes. The United Kingdom administers many overseas possessions, remnants of its powerful empire.

Vatican City

A tiny sovereign state within the city of Rome, the Vatican provides an independent base for the headquarters of the Roman Catholic church. Governed by the Pope, it has its own coins and stamps, and a radio station that broadcasts in thirty-one different languages. The Vatican City is the smallest independent state in the world.

Yugoslavia

The population in Yugoslavia is one of the most diverse in Eastern Europe. Although Yugoslavia became a Communist republic in 1945, there has been a shift to encourage Western trade and broaden political and cultural exchanges, a result of United States aid from the 1940s to the 1960s. Since 1945, the economy has made a successful transition from agriculture to industry, although agriculture – aided by the moderate climate along the Adriatic – continues to play an important role.

Kilometers 0   100   200   300   Km.

Statute Miles 0   100   200   300   Mi.

Scale 1:6,000,000

One centimeter represents 60 kilometers.
One inch represents approximately 95 miles.

Lambert Conformal Conic Projection

The annexation of Latvia and Eston
in 1940 by the Soviet Union has ne
been officially recognized by the
United States Government.

Copyright © by Rand M?Nally & Co.
Map compiled by Esselte Map Service AB, Stockholm.
Map produced by Rand M?Nally & Co.
A-554400-764

22

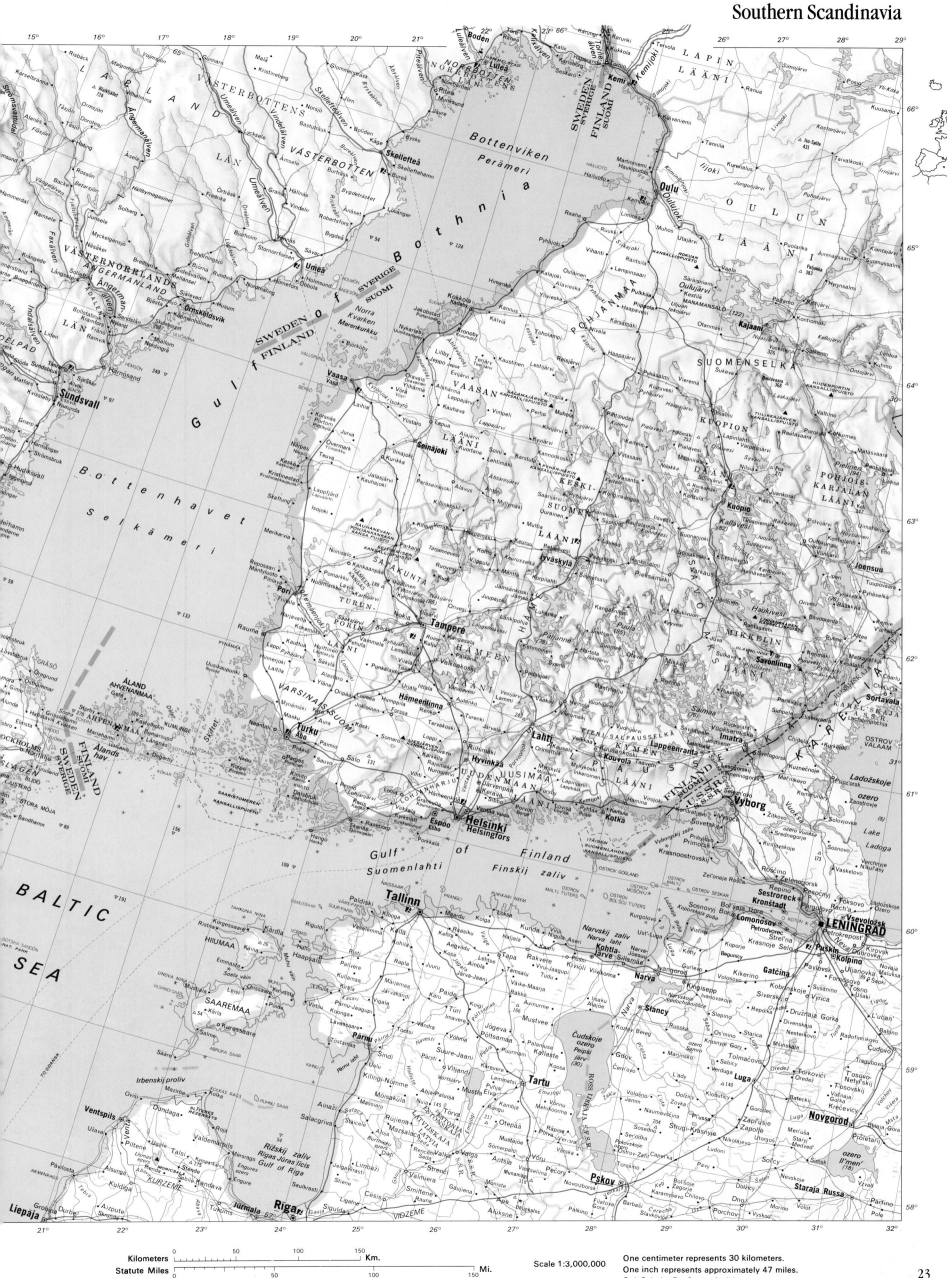

Scale 1:3,000,000

One centimeter represents 30 kilometers.
One inch represents approximately 47 miles.
Conic Projection, Two Standard Parallels

23

Scandinavia

The term Scandinavia has been used for centuries to refer to the northernmost countries of Europe. In the 1980s, Scandinavia has continued to live up to its reputation as a prosperous and innovative corner of the world. Its nations remain world leaders in the search for solutions to such problems as health care, environmental planning, industrial democracy, and the redefinition of age and sex roles.

Visitors might find some contradictions in the nations of Scandinavia. They are alike yet different, sophisticated but simple. Scandinavia boasts vast open spaces and intimate cities; an advanced economic society, yet one that includes a race of nomadic herdsmen.

Think of Scandinavia and you think of the great outdoors, where mountains, lakes and forests combine in one marvelous year-round winter sports center. Water is ever-present, from Sweden's thousands of lakes, to Norway's spectacular fjords and glaciers, from Finland's sailing waters to the sea around Denmark. Trees too stretch away as far as the eye can see, especially in Sweden, the largest country.

In northern Scandinavia, there are prolonged hours of summer daylight and long winter nights. Here the reindeer-herding Lapps cope with the extremes of almost continual summer light and winter darkness. For the most part, however, the populations of Norway, Finland, and Sweden are concentrated in the south.

The Scandinavian capitals are places of warmth and sophistication. Few can resist the charm of Denmark's Copenhagen, a cosmopolitan city with much to offer. Stockholm epitomizes Swedish style and cleanliness, the old town with its narrow streets and cluttered shops contrasting with the modern business center and spacious lakeside suburbs. Oslo, the Norwegian capital, is a major port and the cultural heart of Norway. It is a well-planned metropolis, with wide, straight streets. Helsinki, in Scandinavia's most unspoiled country, Finland, mixes modern amenities with a picturesque setting.

Far left, top: Olavinlinna, in Savonlinna, Finland, is one of the largest castles in northern Europe. Savonlinna is on an island in the Lake Saimaa region of southeast Finland.

Far left, bottom: The area surrounding Sergels Torg in Stockholm, Sweden, is a showplace of contemporary Swedish architecture.

Left: This youthful resident of Turku, Finland, displays the fair skin, blue or gray eyes, and blond or light brown hair of many Scandinavians.

Below: The Romsdal of Norway is characterized by steep, jagged peaks. A beautiful area, it lies on the western coast, south of Trondheim.

Opposite, top: The fjords of Norway are the legacy of the glaciers that once covered the region. After the glaciers melted, their eroded valleys flooded with seawater.

Opposite, bottom: The Tivoli gardens are an entertainment center in Copenhagen, Denmark. Opened in 1843, they feature restaurants, walkways, a concert hall, and a bandstand.

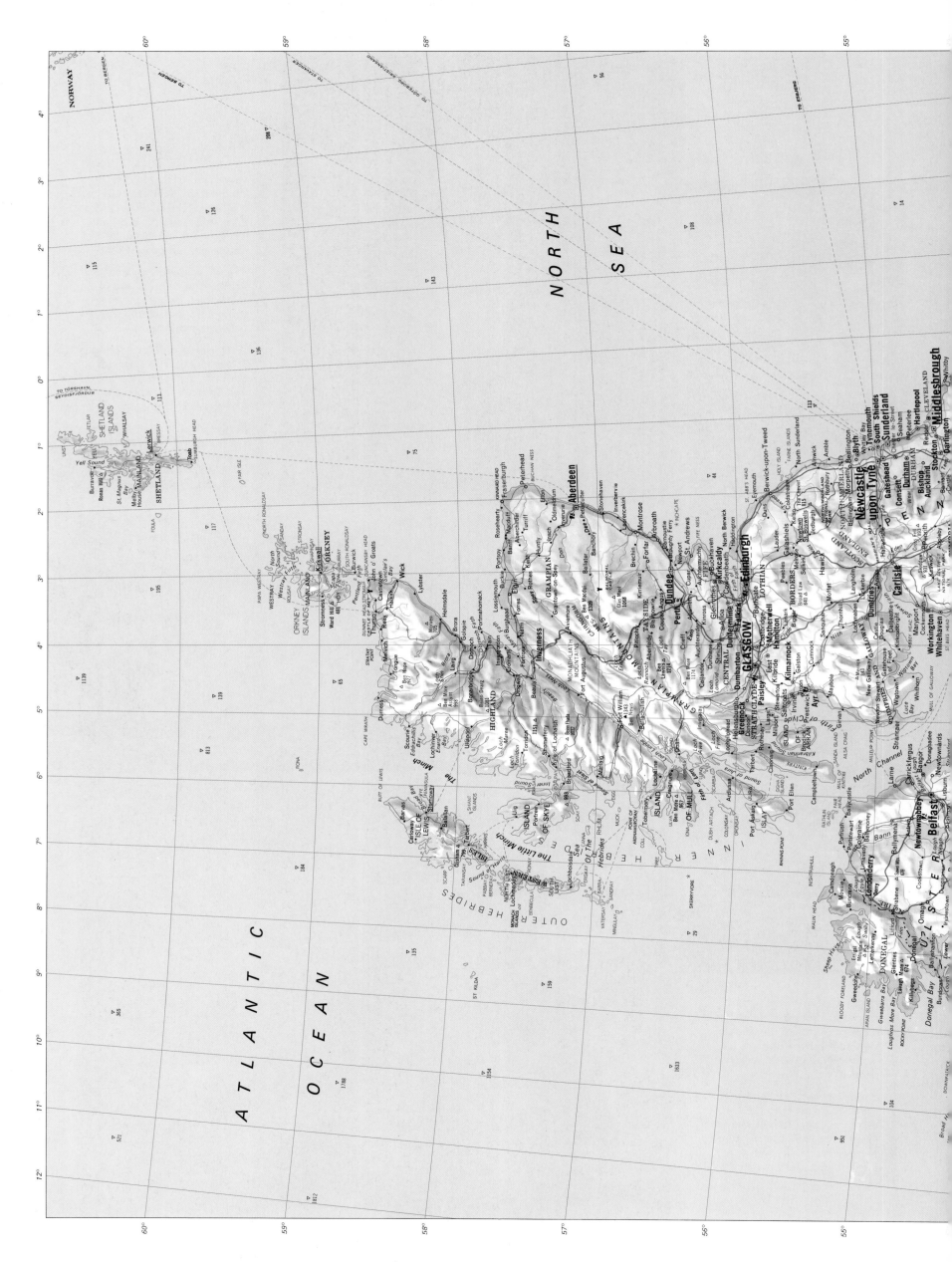

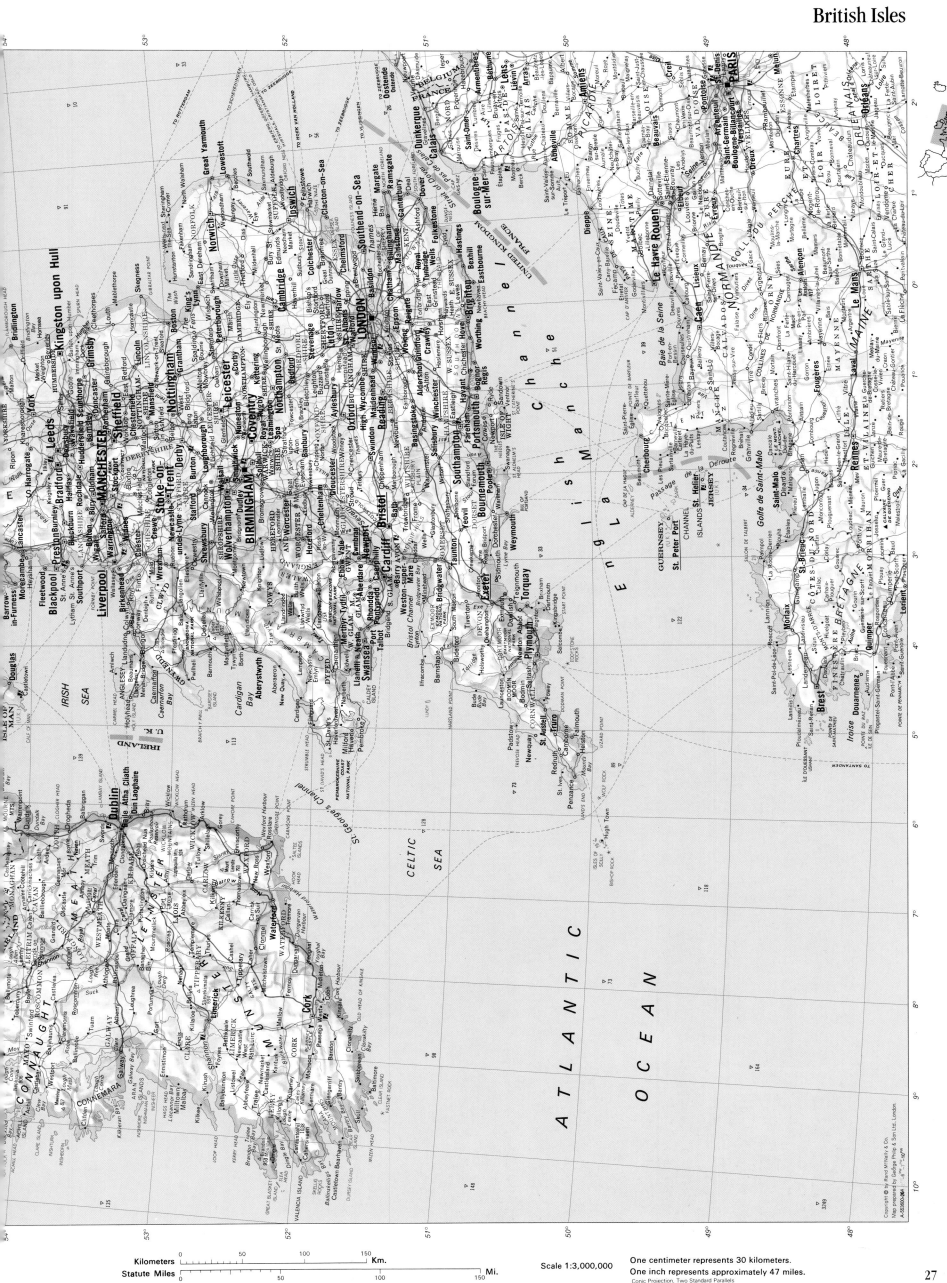

Kilometers 0   50   100   150 Km.
Statute Miles 0   50   100   150 Mi.

Scale 1:3,000,000

One centimeter represents 30 kilometers.
One inch represents approximately 47 miles.
Conic Projection, Two Standard Parallels

British Isles

Many Western nations have experienced sluggish economies in the 1980s, and those of the British Isles are no exception. Visitors still flock to these countries, however, to be charmed by their long histories and rich cultures.

London still represents England to those who have ventured no farther than Piccadilly Circus and the Tower, Buckingham Palace and Westminster Abbey. But England stretches from the glorious West Country coast through soft Cotswold villages and the sweeping landscapes of the Northumberland moors.

In the north, Scotland combines a fierce love of tradition with the modern pace of industrial life. This land of lochs and mountains offers the cosmopolitan delights of the capital, Edinburgh, and the wild beauty of the highlands and islands as typified by remote crofts and grey fishing villages.

Ireland, too, is a place of beauty and contrasts, made all the more apparent and heartbreaking by internal conflict. But everywhere, from the northern loughs to the southern mountains, from urbane Dublin to the comparative poverty of the west, this land of Yeats and Shaw exudes a sense of hospitality and pride.

And in Wales, that same warmth is extended in the Celtic tongue, through Cardiff – the capital and largest city – and the industrial valleys of the south to Snowdonia.

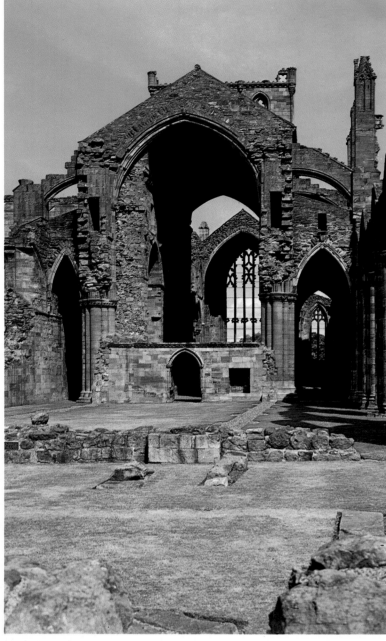

Above, left: An international center for commerce as well as for culture, London is the most populous city in Europe. Two types of public transportation help keep the city bustling: the double-decker bus and the underground train system known as the tube.

Above: Shown here is Melrose Abbey in Roxburghshire, Scotland. Although largely ruined, Melrose is said to be the most picturesque of the Scottish abbeys.

Left: The Houses of Parliament and Big Ben are well-known London landmarks. Situated on the banks of the Thames, this government complex was constructed in the mid 1800s.

Left: County Kerry, in the extreme southwest of Ireland, is a land that features, among other sights, green pastures and rugged coastlines. Shown here is the Ring of Kerry road, which affords the traveler many miles of scenic landscape.

Below: Caerphilly Castle, in Glamorgan, Wales, was constructed in the thirteenth century. It is situated in the town of the same name, just north of Cardiff.

Bottom: Typical of the small towns of the English countryside is Shaftesbury, west of Salisbury, in the southern county of Dorset. Shaftesbury has a long history, and there are a number of sights in the surrounding region.

Kilometers 0   50   100   150
                                        Km.
Statute Miles 0   50   100   150
                                        Mi.

Scale 1:3,000,000

One centimeter represents 30 kilometers.
One inch represents approximately 47 miles.
Conic Projection, Two Standard Parallels.

West Germany, Austria & Switzerland

West Germany's strong economy has persisted, largely because of the nation's cooperation with the EEC. Its recovery after two devastating wars has been remarkable, and today, West Germany not only dominates this part of the map, but it also remains a leader in the world economy.

Yet the industrial landscapes of the Ruhr and Saarland are only as representative of this multifaceted country as the vine-clad slopes of the Rhine and Mosel rivers, the nightlife of Hamburg's famous Reeperbahn, the romance of Heidelberg, and the fairy-tale scenic splendors of Bavaria.

A cultural giant, this country can claim to have produced such writers as Goethe and Schiller and to have an especially powerful musical inheritance in the works of Beethoven and Brahms.

Germany's former traditional capital, Berlin, since 1961 divided by the concrete wall built by the East, retains a particular significance for West Germany and East Germany alike.

Although it is officially neutral, Austria in the late 1980s maintains its position as a prosperous link between Eastern and Western Europe. Also unaligned, Switzerland continues to be one of the most economically and politically stable countries in the world. Its mountainous terrain has caused it to rely on economic contributors other than agriculture, tourism primary among them. Though they may lack size and power in the world economy, West Germany's neighbors offer outstanding scenery, long cultural traditions, and solid worth for vacationers.

Austria's renowned cultural centers of Vienna (Wien), Innsbruck, and Salzburg are equalled in appeal by the mountainous Tirol region, winter sports centers, and health spas. Music lovers are drawn to seasonal festivals held in Austria. Shoppers will appreciate fine Austrian craftsmanship. Porcelain, leather goods, and clothing are fine examples and popular purchases.

In Switzerland – home of financial wizards, precision watch making, and dairying – the scenery is no less spectacular. Beautiful Lake Geneva consistently draws tourists. There are beautiful lakes, lined with palm trees, in the south. Splendid peaks such as the Matterhorn are perhaps more expected sights to visitors. And the ski resorts of St. Moritz and Davos are world famous. Because Switzerland is so compact, a traveler can see many of its different facets in a short time.

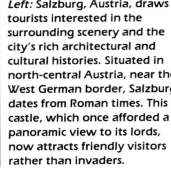

Left: Salzburg, Austria, draws tourists interested in the surrounding scenery and the city's rich architectural and cultural histories. Situated in north-central Austria, near the West German border, Salzburg dates from Roman times. This castle, which once afforded a panoramic view to its lords, now attracts friendly visitors rather than invaders.

Above: Much of West Germany, Austria, and Switzerland is mountainous, but between the peaks of central Europe lie many fertile valleys that are suitable for farming. These countries produce wine, fruits, vegetables, and other crops. Additionally, the raising of livestock and fodder is important. Here, hay is harvested in the region of western Austria called Tirol.

Far left: The Alps of Switzerland have prevented some types of economic development in the small country but have also contributed to the nation's growth: tourism, including outdoor recreation, is second only to manufacturing in importance.

Left: Heidelberg, on the Neckar River in southwestern West Germany, attracts both tourists and students to its historic sites and fine university.

Below: Dominating the landscape of central Europe, the Alps form the youngest and most extensive mountain system on the continent. The range's many arms reach into France, Italy, Switzerland, Germany, Austria, Yugoslavia, and Liechtenstein. Shown here are central Austria's Dachsteins.

The Netherlands, Luxembourg & Belgium

No longer banded together as an economic threesome, the Benelux countries of Belgium, Luxembourg, and the Netherlands remain a delightful entity while retaining their individual charm. Founding members of the EEC, these countries have profited from the coalition, and in recent years, the Netherlands, Luxembourg, and Belgium have enjoyed relative economic stability.

Situated at the mouth of the Rhine, the Netherlands is rightly called "the gateway to Europe." Known the world over as a land of cheese, canals, and bulbs, more importantly it boasts busy seaports, and Amsterdam, the friendly capital, is a world center for diamond cutting.

Among the sights to see in the Netherlands are treasured remnants of the past. Most old city centers are protected from redevelopment, and everywhere there are museums and collections. The Netherlands is a land taken back from the sea, and it is not surprising that marine sports are popular pastimes. The sand beaches and dunes that run nearly the whole length of the coast are well suited for such activities. Shoppers may be interested in the diamonds that are a

relative bargain here; or, for those with less in their budget, Delft china, bearing the official imprint, is also found.

Belgium, now destined to be home to EEC bureaucrats, is notable for its capital, Brussels (Bruxelles), with its magnificent market place, and for the medieval pearl of Bruges (Brugge). The wooded heights of the Ardennes region are a hiker's and a gastronome's delight. Belgium boasts a short, sandy coastline of wide beaches and sand dunes, lined with a long succession of resorts. Traditional festivals are popular and keenly supported in Belgium. Belgian handmade lace, embroidery, and glassware can be found in shops throughout the country, but smart buyers avoid souvenir shops.

Rolling on into Luxembourg, the traveler finds a land of magic castles, rivers, forests, and enchanting towns. This is one of the smallest nations in Europe, but it has one of the highest standards of living on the continent, and it holds its own for the tourist. Popular sights are the ruined fortresses that are scattered throughout the countryside and the narrow cobbled streets and medieval houses of Luxembourg's cities.

Above: Although the Netherlands' use of windmills for power is now minimal, they remain a common sight.

Right: Unlike many other European cities, Bruges (Brugge), Belgium, has remained largely unchanged since medieval times.

Below: Wiltz, Luxembourg, in the north-central region of the country, boasts a twelfth-century castle.

Europe
Eastern Europe

Traveling in Eastern Europe may intimidate some people, but for those who do include Poland, Czechoslovakia, Hungary, and nearby countries on their itineraries, the adventure can be well worth the effort. Rich in history and culture, the nations of Eastern Europe provide a view of the Continent that is slightly different from that offered by Western Europe.

Since the late 1940s, many of the nations of Eastern Europe have been under Soviet influence. Though they lag behind Western European countries, they are developed, industrial nations. In these Soviet satellite countries, the vast rolling estates and artistic splendors that characterized Central Europe before World War I have disappeared.

The Hungarian Magyars, once part of two great empires, still mainly work the land, however, retaining their old traditions and culture. Budapest, Hungary's capital, has been called the most romantic city in Europe.

A land of great scenic attractions, with its extensive Bohemian forests and magnificent Carpathians, Czechoslovakia too is in many ways outwardly unchanged. Many beautiful buildings are now being restored in the capital, Prague (Praha), one of Europe's most charming, relatively undiscovered cities.

Poland, a once mighty nation that was partitioned in the eighteenth century, regained its sovereignty only to lose it to Nazi Germany during the opening weeks of World War II. Warsaw (Warszawa), though devastated in the war, is today a modern, thriving metropolis and Poland's largest city. Cracow (Kraków), on the other hand, suffered little damage during the war and retains many of its fine old structures.

Top right: The old section of Warsaw (Warszawa) was enclosed in walls built in 1380. The city was destroyed in World War II, but much of this section has been restored in its original style. Situated on the Vistula (Wisła) River, Warsaw is Poland's political, financial, and cultural center.

Above: Hungary has had more success with its collective and state farms than have other Eastern European countries.

Right: St. James (Jakuba) church is one of the historic sites in Prague (Praha), Czechoslovakia, to remain intact despite Europe's many wars.

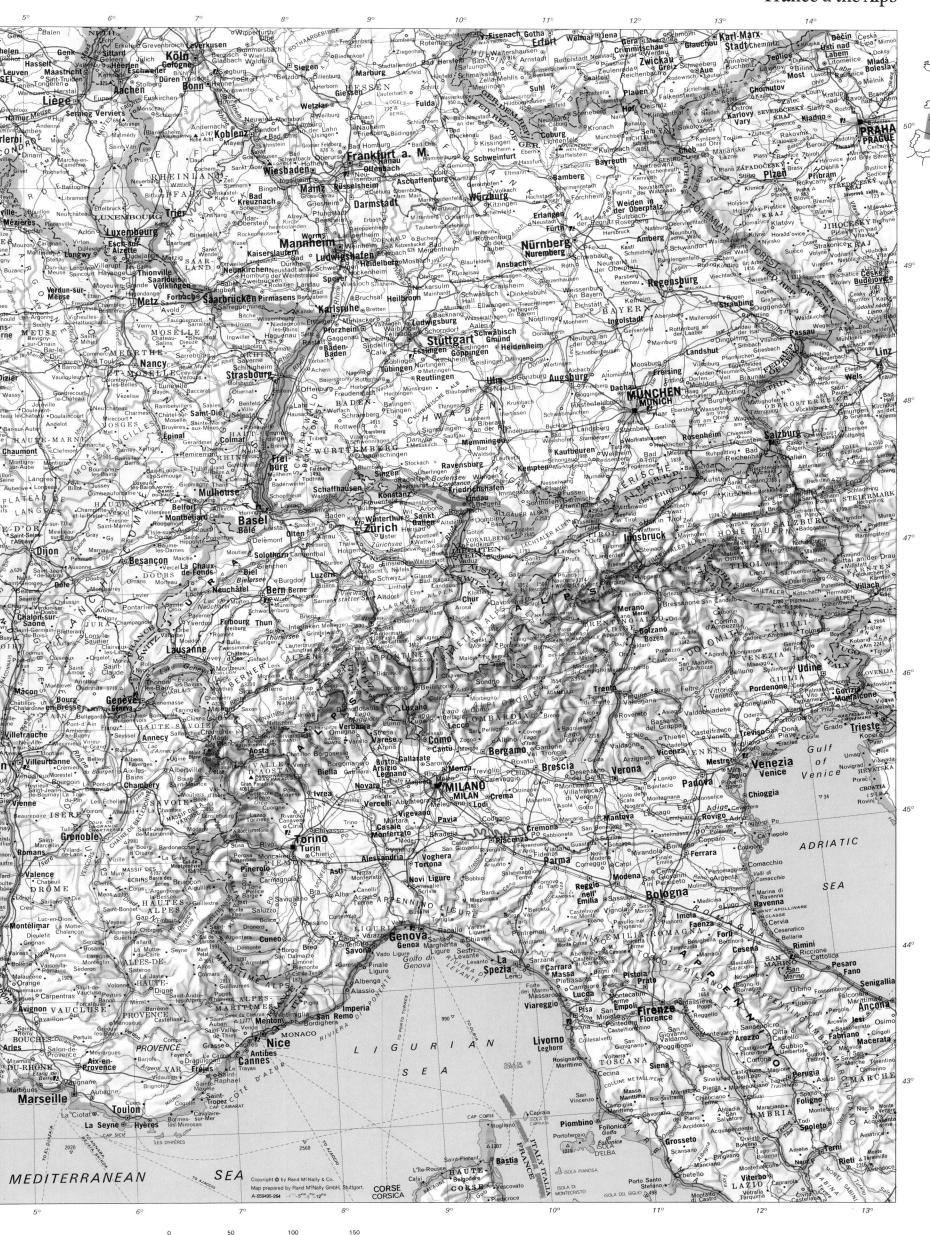

Kilometers 0 50 100 150 Km.

Statute Miles 0 50 100 150 Mi.

Scale 1:3,000,000

One centimeter represents 30 kilometers.

One inch represents approximately 47 miles.

Lambert Conformal Conic Projection

Europe
France

The largest country in Europe, France is also an industrial and agricultural leader. As is the case with many of its neighbors, France's participation in the EEC has contributed much to its success in recent decades. It is not without its share of problems, however, as the inflation and unemployment that trouble other Western European nations persist in France as well.

Yet, France has so much in its favor for tourism that less well-endowed countries might be forgiven a passing resentment at such good fortune. Rich in history and culture, with a pleasing position and climate, it is no wonder that travelers continue to place France high on their lists of places to visit.

Despite its size and wealth, France is predominantly a nation of small towns and villages where home and family, the church, and trade rule supreme.

Is it not strange then, that a land so indisputably rural, with a still large and vociferous peasantry, should be renowned the world over for its enviable chic and its undoubted sophistication? Thus the influence of the capital, Paris, is asserted far beyond its own region. Indeed, its dictates in the world of fashion and the arts are followed more slavishly in London and New York than in its own country.

France has been in the forefront of

true Western culture for centuries, and Paris itself has been the cradle of writers and artists too numerous to mention. Look around at the museums, galleries, artistic treasures and monuments, and you can see the past glory of the mighty French Empire, the golden Bourbons and the military might of Napoleon, all part of an historic heritage that continues unbroken to the present day, despite the major upheaval of the Revolution in 1789.

France in the 1980s is strongly placed on the economic front with its major manufacturing centers at Lille, Lyons, and Paris and the port of Marseille in the south. But it is for its splendid beaches that the Riviera coast is best known; the elegant resorts of Nice and Cannes vying with St. Tropez and its starlet strip. Farther west the wild, swampy Camargue region with its roaming horses and wealth of wildlife is a great attraction for naturalists. Inland, the ancient towns of Arles, Avignon, and Nîmes are much visited.

The southwest also has fine beaches, the forests of the Landes area and, above all, Bordeaux, the greatest wine area in the world. Others may prefer the wilder Brittany coastline, the quiet charm of the Loire region with its magnificent châteaux or the gently pastoral area of the Dordogne.

Above: Paris and its environs constitute the second largest metropolitan area in Europe. The city on the Seine has long been a world center for business, art, religion, education, and tourism. Shown here is the Eiffel Tower, a symbol of French achievement.

Below: The valley of the Loire River, the longest river in France, is famous for vineyards and for the châteaux built during the fifteenth and sixteenth centuries. The Château de Chenonceaux, shown here, is considered by many to be the Loire's prettiest château.

Top: The fields in the foothills of the Pyrenees contribute to France's stature as the leading agricultural nation of Europe.

Above: The Bordeaux area in the southwest is well known for wines. Here grapes are harvested at one of the region's vineyards.

Right: A popular resort area, the subtropical Côte d'Azur runs along the Mediterranean from Cannes to Italy.

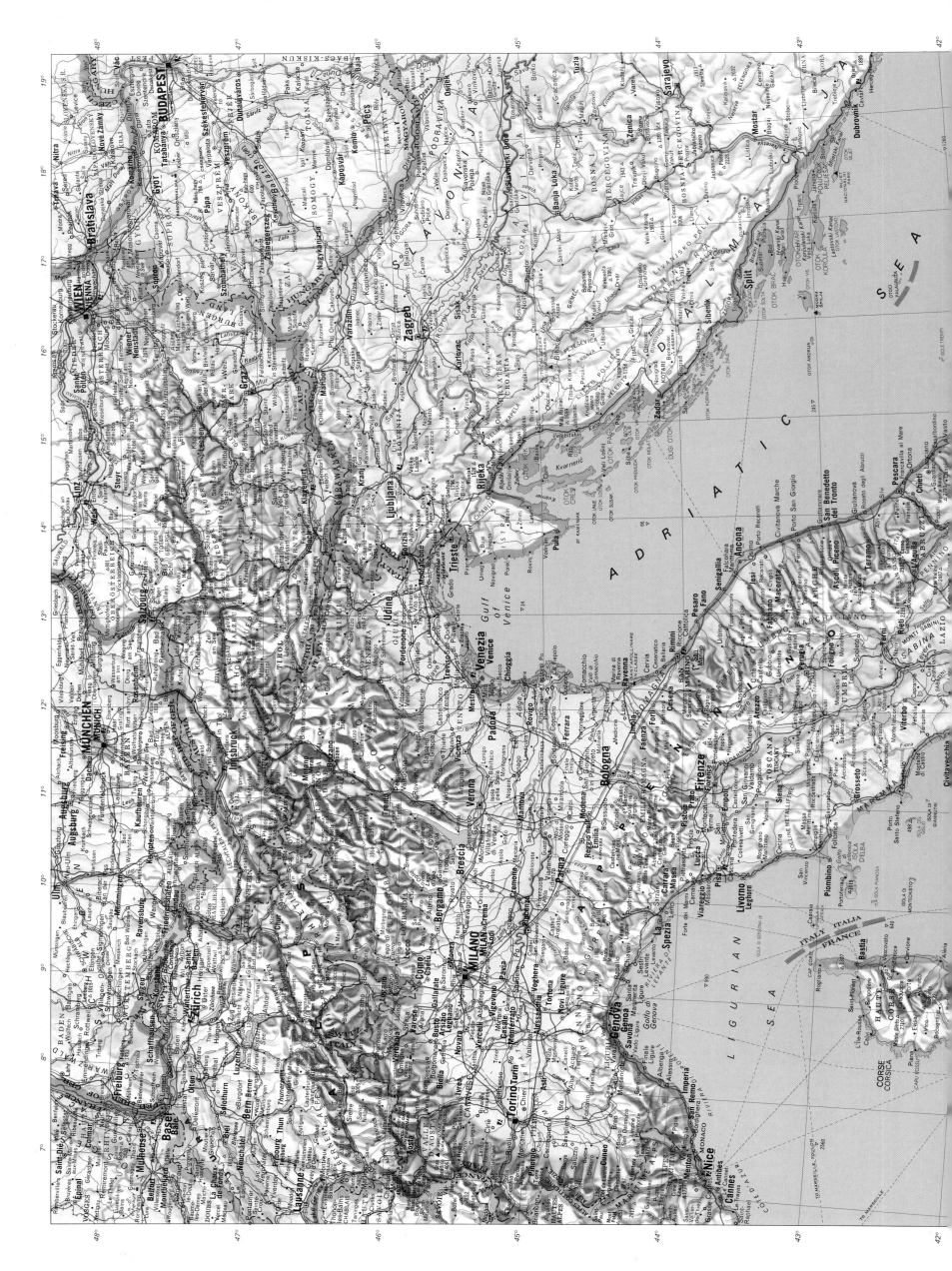

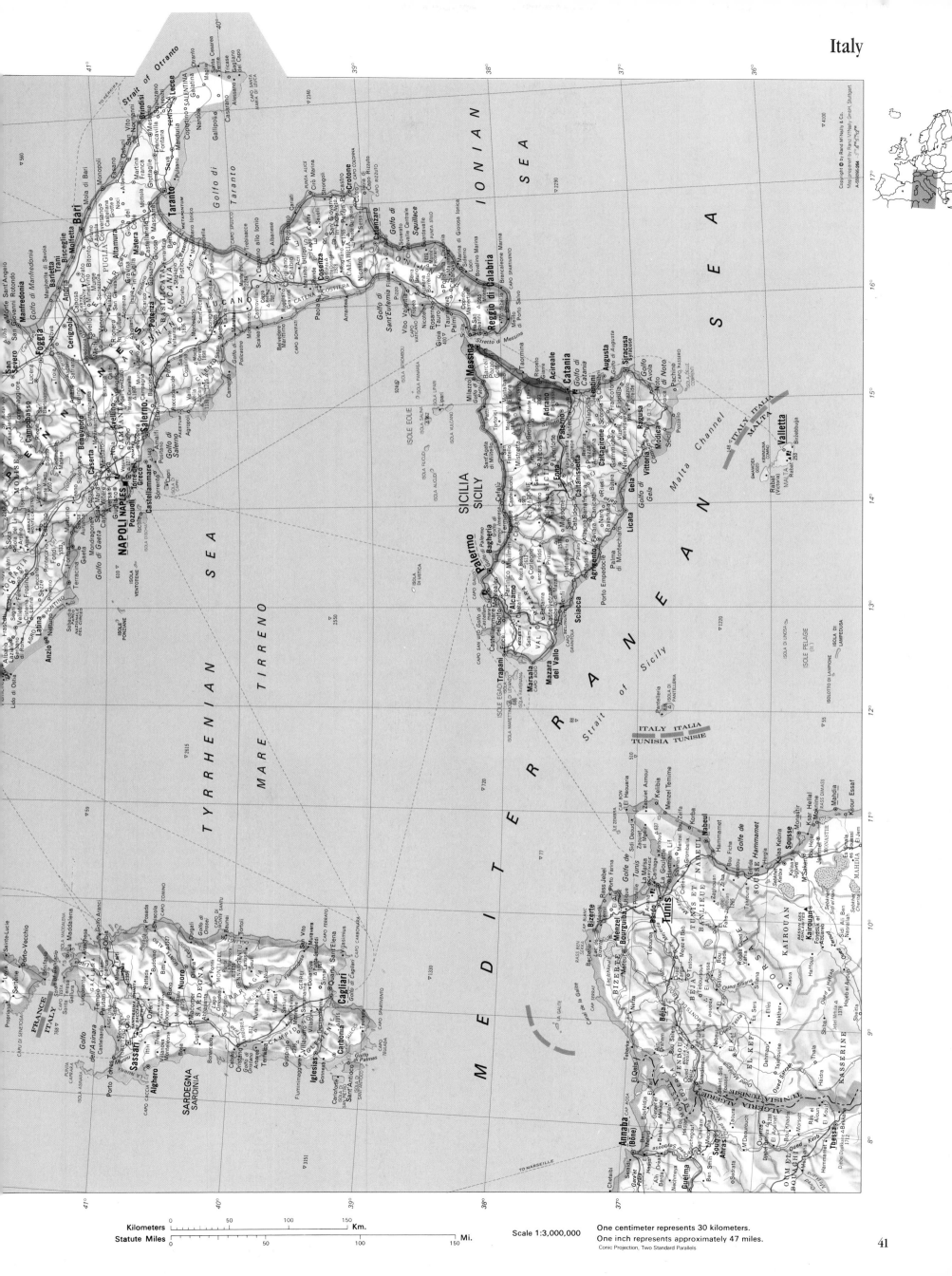

Italy

Italy's skilled and abundant work force has proved to be one of the country's greatest assets. The nation has accomplished something of an economic miracle since 1950, and in the late 1980s, it remains prosperous. Like its people, Italy can be by turns volatile and subdued, extremely wealthy or disturbingly poor, spontaneous and welcoming or difficult to know. It is, above all, a cultural colossus where the influence of the Roman Catholic church is all-pervasive.

At its peak during the Roman Empire, which spread its influence throughout the world, Rome (Roma) itself – the Eternal City – contains more architectural and artistic masterpieces than any other place in the world. At Rome's heart is the Basilica of St. Peter and the Vatican, home of the Roman Catholic church. Rome also has such favorite haunts as the Trevi Fountain and the Spanish Steps.

Golden Florence (Firenze), in Tuscany, birthplace of the Renaissance, combines a wealth of priceless treasures in its buildings and museums with the prosperity of a modern city. Among the sights are classic monuments, like Michelangelo's David, and historic architecture, such as the sixteenth-century Ponte Vecchio.

Venice (Venezia) remains a popular attraction despite its environmental problems. The Grand Canal cuts a backwards S-curve through the city, and modes of travel are limited to motorboats, waterbuses, and the famous gondolas. Tourists can also venture on foot, using the more than four hundred foot bridges that cross the smaller canals. On the many islands that make up the city are found historic squares, the most famous of which might be the Piazza San Marco.

Then there is Milan (Milano), Italy's economic pulse, with much of the new industrial development centered north of the old city. The metropolitan area of Milan is Italy's most populous. The Milan Cathedral is truly awe inspiring, and other attractions include da Vinci's *The Last Supper.* Milan is home to La Scala, one of the world's most renowned opera companies.

And there is more to this country of hot summers and superb scenery. Positano on the fashionable Costa Amalfitina, the artistic haven of Portofino and the Italian coast resorts all have much to offer. Inland, the Italian Lakes lie serenely at the foot of the Alps, while to the northeast are the dramatic Dolomites (Dolomiti) with their famous skiing resorts. To the south is historic Palermo, on Sicily.

Above: Portofino is chief among the resort and fishing towns that line the northwest coastal region known as the Italian Riviera. The beauty and climate of the region draw many visitors.

Left: Umbria – a region in the Apennines – is a land of scenic vistas and medieval cities. Considerable agricultural activity produces grapes, sugar beets, olives, and livestock.

Above: The many eras of Rome's long history are reflected in the buildings, squares, and streets of the city. The Piazza Navona was built in the sixteenth and seventeenth centuries.

Far left: The Dolomites' limestone peaks rise above Cortina d'Ampezzo in northeast Italy. This eastern branch of the Alps is popular with tourists, especially those interested in mountaineering.

Left: Venice (Venezia) consists of more than 118 islands in a large lagoon. The main water thoroughfare is the Grand Canal, but narrow canals separate most of the islands.

MEDITERRANEAN SEA

Golfe du Lion

ILLES BALEARS
BALEARIC ISLANDS

MALLORCA
MAJORCA

MENORCA
MINORCA

BALEARS

ALGERIA

ALGÉRIE

ATLAS TELLIEN

MOUNTAINS TELLIEN

KABYLIE

EL DJAZAÏR
ALGIERS

PLAINE DU HODNA

Kilometers
Statute Miles

Scale 1:3,000,000

One centimeter represents 30 kilometers.
One inch represents approximately 47 miles.

Conic Projection, Two Standard Parallels

Spain & Portugal

Despite their physical togetherness and intermingled histories, Spain and Portugal are two very different countries. Recently, Spain – the larger and more prosperous of the two – and Portugal have become members of the EEC and should benefit economically as a result.

At its heart, Spain remains the land of Hemingway, where bulls still run in the streets of Pamplona – and the land of El Greco, whose magnificent paintings in Toledo are matched by the town's spectacular location. Home to the plundering conquistadors, the civilizing Moors, and the feared Spanish Inquisition, Spain continues to be, above all, a land where holy processions and modern celebrations combine in annual outbursts of gaiety and reverence throughout the country.

The vast hotel blocks on the highly commercialized Costas Brava and del Sol contrast starkly with the unchanged life-style of the interior where hilltop villages and vast plains give way to thriving, historic cities.

But Portugal, with its softer landscape, gentle people, white-walled villages and haunting fado music, has a special appeal. Undisturbed by the last two great wars, Lisbon (Lisboa), the capital, retains much of its past glory, the elegant nineteenth-century buildings and boulevards contrasting sharply with the winding alleys of the old Arab quarter, the Alfama. The city has been the Portuguese capital since 1256.

Close by, the dignified resorts of Estoril and Cascais provided a pleasant exile for many of Europe's deposed ruling families, suitably near to the old royal palaces at Byron's beloved Sintra, and Quelez. Along the coasts, brightly painted small boats, often crewed by men in traditional garments, still go out to fish in the time-honored way.

Above: Fishing has long been one of Portugal's most important industries, and fishing towns such as Sezimbra, shown here, line the extensive Atlantic coast. Sardines, cod, and shellfish are most important.

Left: Barcelona, the second largest city in Spain, lies in Cataluña, on the northeastern Mediterranean coast. The city dates from Carthaginian times and contains many historic sites, including the Barcelona Cathedral, shown here.

Right: Shown here are almond trees in Alicante province, in southeastern Valencia. This part of Spain is a fertile Mediterranean region that produces a variety of crops.

Greece & Yugoslavia

In many ways remarkably different – historically, politically, and ethnically – Greece and Yugoslavia jointly represent southeastern Europe. Economically stagnant for many years, Greece has benefited in recent years from its membership in the EEC. Yugoslavia, a Soviet satellite nation, has a developed economy.

Greece, home of some of Europe's earliest civilizations, relies heavily on tourism. Today, the glory that was Greece is still seen in breathtaking ancient ruins. Placed atop the rock of the Acropolis, the classical architectural simplicity of the Parthenon represents the high point of the great age of Athens (Athínai), the modern capital.

The islands of Greece, with their sunny beaches and blue waters, continue to be popular tourist destinations. Crete (Kríti), the largest of the islands, was home to the Minoans, who represented one of Europe's earliest civilizations. Many ancient ruins still exist.

Tourism is increasing in the less commercially developed yet spiritually resilient Yugoslavia. The largest of the Balkan countries, Yugoslavia has made a successful transition from agriculture to industry. Belgrade (Beograd), its capital, and Zagreb are growing industrial centers.

To the tourist, the country is perhaps best known for its beautiful Adriatic coastline, although Yugoslavia offers much more in a complex medley of peoples, religions, and traditions. Serbs, Croats, Slovenians, Macedonians, Montenegrans – not to mention groups of Albanians, Hungarians, and Gypsies – have maintained their own cultures, providing visitors with fascinating discoveries and endless variety.

Above: The Erechtheion, on the Acropolis in Athens (Athínai), is a symbol of the mastery of Greek architecture. Construction on this temple was completed around 410 B.C.

Top right: In the Julian Alps, near the Austrian border, lies scenic Lake Bled, Yugoslavia. This corner of Slovenija is a popular resort region.

Middle right: The narrow Corinth Canal connects the Gulf of Corinth with Saronikós Bay, thereby eliminating journeys by water around the Peloponnese peninsula of Greece. Freight trains such as this are a regular sight on the canal's bridge.

Right: The Bay of Kotor and the town of the same name are found in Montenegro, Yugoslavia. This inlet on the Adriatic is a prime port and tourist destination.

ISTANBUL

Sea of Marmara
Marmara Denizi

BURSA
Bandırma
Tekirdağ
Çorlu
Edirne
Balıkesir
Edremit
Çanakkale
Bergama
İzmir (Smyrna)
Manisa
Salihli
Denizli
Muğla
Aydın
Nazilli
Ödemiş
Turgutlu
Akhisar

TURKEY TÜRKİYE
GREECE ELLÁS

Ródhos
Rhodes
RÓDHOS
RHODES
KÁRPATHOS

DHODHEKÁNISOS
DODECANESE

Alexandroúpolis
Komotiní
Xánthi
Kavála
Dráma
Sérrai
Thessaloníki
Saloníka
Kateríni
Véroia
Lárisa
Vólos
Tríkala
Lamía
Khalkís
ATHÍNAI
ATHENS
Piraiévs
Piraeus
Pátrai
Agrínion
Ioánnina

KRÍTI
CRETE
Iráklion
Khaniá
Réthimnon

AEGEAN SEA

THRACE

KIKLÁDHES
CYCLADES

LÉSVOS
LESBOS

KHÍOS
CHIOS

SÁMOS

ÍKARÍA

NÁXOS

PÁROS

ÁNDROS

TÍNOS

MÍLOS

KÍTHIRA

Sea of Crete
Kritikón Pélagos

PELOPONNESUS

IÓNIOI NÍSOI
IONIAN ISLANDS

KEFALLINÍA

ZÁKINTHOS

KÉRKIRA
CORFU

ADRIATIC SEA

Tiranë
Elbasan
Durrës
Fier
Vlorë
Korçë
Berat

ALBANIA
SHQIPERI

YUGOSLAVIA

MAKEDONIJA
Bitola
Prilep

BULGARIA

Strait of Otranto

ITALY

IONIAN SEA

MEDITERRANEAN SEA

Kilometers
Statute Miles

Scale 1:3,000,000

One centimeter represents 30 kilometers.
One inch represents approximately 47 miles.
Conic Projection, Two Standard Parallels

49

Soviet Union
Profile

Location and Size

The Soviet Union sits between Europe and Asia and is the largest country in the world – more than twice the size of any other nation. Extending from the Taymyr (Tajmyr) Peninsula in the north to Taškent, next to the Afghan border in the south, the central Soviet Union extends some 3,000 miles (4,800 kilometers). From the west to the east, the Soviet Union stretches from the Czechoslovak border to the Bering Strait, thus wrapping nearly halfway around the globe in the Northern Hemisphere. Beyond the mainland, there are many islands in the Arctic Ocean that belong to the Soviet Union.

The huge distances of the Soviet Union can be envisioned in terms of time. When it is eight o'clock in the morning in Moscow (Moskva), it is six o'clock in the evening in the eastern Cukotskij Peninsula. With a total area of nearly nine million square miles (more than twenty-two million square kilometers), 25 percent of the country is in Europe, 75 percent in Asia. For such a land mass, the Soviet Union has only

limited stretches of coastline that are ice free throughout the year. In the northwest, only a small part of the Arctic coast is free of ice all year. In the west, parts of the Baltic freeze in the winter, but most of the Black Sea coast and its ports remain open all the time. The north-flowing rivers are frozen for up to seven months each year.

Landscape

Most Soviet land borders are in mountainous parts of the country. The south and east are the highest areas, while the northern, central, and western parts are dominated by plains.

European Soviet Union consists in the east of the Great European Plain. Only the Central Russian Uplands, the Valdai (Valdajskaja) Hills – rising to 1,125 feet (346 meters) northwest of Moscow – and the uplands of the Kola (Kol'skij) Peninsula – rising to 3,907 feet (1,191 meters) – stand above this. The lower plains continue eastward through the basins of the rivers Don, Volga, and North Dvina to the Ural (Ural'skije) Mountains, which form the only major

north-south divide in the western Soviet Union.

To the south of this lowland region lies the Black Sea, with its outlet to the Mediterranean, and the Caspian Sea, which is a focus of inland drainage. The Carpathian Mountains on the Romanian border rise to 6,762 feet (2,061 meters), and the Caucasus Mountains (Bol'Soj Kavkaz) between the Black and Caspian seas rise to 18,481 feet (5,633 meters).

East of the Caspian Sea lies the Turanian (Turanskaja) Plain and an area of inland drainage focusing on the Aral (Aral'skoje) Sea. Uplands surround this whole region, particularly to the south and east, where the boundaries with Afghanistan and China lie within the Pamir and the Tien Shan ranges. Here the highest point in the Soviet Union, Communism (Kommunizma) Peak, rises to more than 24,500 feet (almost 7,500 meters). East and northeast of the Turanian Plain are the Lake Balkhash (Balchaš) basin and the Kazakh (Kazachskaja) uplands.

West of the Yenisey (Jenisej) River and east of the Urals is an extensive plain known as the Western Siberian

Lowlands. This has a total area of over one million square miles (2.5 million square kilometers) and constitutes the largest single area of plain land in the world.

The landscape east of the Yenisey is more varied and elevated. The central Siberian Uplands between the Yenisey and Lena rivers is generally above 1,000 feet (300 meters) and in the south reaches to above 10,000 feet (3,000 meters) in the Sayan (Sajany) and Yablonovy (Jablonovyj) mountains. The Putoran (Putorana) Mountains in the north rise to a maximum height of 5,581 feet (1,701 meters). The remote region east of the Lena River is dominated by a series of mountain ranges that reach a maximum of 15,584 feet (4,750 meters) in the Kamchatka (Kamčatka) Peninsula.

The Soviet Union is a land of great rivers draining in four directions. In the west are comparatively short rivers – such as the Don, the Dnepr, and the Dvina – flowing to the Black or Baltic seas. In the east, the Amur and many smaller rivers flow eastward to the Pacific. About half the country is drained northward by the Ob', Yenisey, and Lena

Left: Suzdal', north of Vladimir, was founded in 1028 and is the site of many historic buildings. These women are dressed in the traditional clothing of this region in the east-central Soviet Union.

Right: St. Basil's Cathedral, Moscow, was commissioned by Ivan the Terrible and erected in the mid sixteenth century. This church just south of Red Square epitomizes historic Russia.

river systems. The Volga and Ural flow to the Caspian Sea, and the Amu Darya (Amudarja) and Syr-Darya to the Aral Sea, forming the largest inland drainage basin of the world.

Climate

The Soviet Union is the most extensive west-east land mass in the world. It is a continent surrounded by both land and seas, encompassing huge mountain ranges and massive plains. Overall, the country's climates are characterized by large temperature fluctuations and low precipitation.

The southern parts of Soviet Central Asia experience a midlatitude desert climate. Over a large area, the average monthly temperature in January falls to 14°F (-10°C) but in July rises to 86°F (30°C). Nowhere does annual precipitation rise above eight inches (two hundred millimeters), and it is often far less.

In a broad belt from the southern Ukraine (Ukrainskaja) to the Mongolian and Chinese borders lies an area of dry midlatitude steppe climate. The temperature range here is higher in the east than in the west. Low annual rainfall, less than sixteen inches (four hundred millimeters), comes mainly in the summer.

In the extreme north of the country, polar climates extend from west to east. Most places in this area have at least one month when the average temperature is above freezing, but no month's average rises above 50°F (10°C).

Between these southern desert-steppe and the northern polar climates, most of the Soviet Union has a more humid climate with a wide annual temperature range. In the west, the July average temperature may approach 72°F (22°C) with the winter average going as low as 14°F (-10°C). Precipitation, with a summer maximum, comes throughout the year and may total twenty-eight inches (seven hundred millimeters). This decreases farther east and the temperature range increases.

History, Politics, and Economy

The region that is now the Soviet Union was inhabited as early as the Stone Age. The area has been a changing land that has undergone successive invasions by the Scythians, Sarmatians, Goths, Huns, Bulgars, Slavs, and others.

By A.D. 989, Byzantine cultural influence had become predominant. Various groups and regions were slowly incorporated into a single state. In 1547, Ivan IV was crowned czar of all Russia, beginning a tradition of czarist rule. This tradition lasted until the Russian Revolution in 1917, when the Bolsheviks came to power and named Vladimir Ilyich Lenin as head of the first Soviet government. After the Revolution, the Bolsheviks established a Communist state and weathered a bitter civil war, consolidating their power in 1920. On December 30, 1922, the Union of Soviet Socialist Republics was born. The word *soviet* means *council* in Russian, and it was used because government councils make up the system of government. The word *socialist* was used instead of *communist* because the Russians believed that communism was an ideal political and economic state not yet achieved.

Joseph Stalin succeeded Lenin as head of state in 1924 and initiated a series of political purges that lasted through the 1930s. The Soviet Union later became embroiled in World War II and lost over twenty million people. Suffering widespread destruction of both city and countryside, the Soviets emerged from the war with extended influence, however, having annexed part of Finland and many Eastern European nations. In the late 1940s and 1950s, a period of lasting international tension and mistrust erupted between the Soviet Union and the West. This period is known as the Cold War.

Following Stalin's death in 1953, the Soviet Union experienced a liberalization of policies under Nikita Krushchev. In 1964, Krushchev was ousted from power and Leonid Brezhnev took control. Throughout his reign, Brezhnev worked to consolidate and strengthen the power of the Secretariat and Politburo of the Communist party. He also pursued a policy of détente with the West. In 1982 Brezhnev died, and Soviet leadership was passed on to Yuri Andropov, who died in 1984. Leadership then went to Konstantin Chernenko, who died in 1985. Mikhail Gorbachev, the youngest Soviet leader in decades, took office in 1985 and has initiated many reforms in human-rights policies as well as international diplomacy with the West. In the late 1980s, a period of openness, or *glasnost*, has characterized Soviet society.

As an industrial power, the Soviet Union ranks second only to the United States. Mining, steel production, and other heavy industries predominate. The Soviet Union is self-sufficient in coal, petroleum, natural gas, and iron ore; it is also a world leader in timber production. Although this huge nation is so richly endowed with minerals and other natural resources, the Soviets lag in the development of advanced technology, particularly in availability of consumer goods.

The Soviet economy is controlled by the state, and economic policies are administered through a series of five-year plans, which emphasize industrial and technological growth. The Soviets suffer from low productivity, energy shortages, and a lack of skilled labor, however, and these are problems the government hopes can be eased by greater use of technology and science.

In agriculture, the Soviets produce more wheat, cotton, potatoes, and sugar than any other nation in the world. There are three types of Soviet farms: collective farms, state farms, and private garden plots. Garden plots produce as much as 60 percent of the nation's potato supply. Most bigger field crops are grown on collective and state farms. Though the country contains some of the world's most fertile land, long winters and hot, dry summers keep many crop yields low. This has forced the Soviets to import some farm products from the West, especially feed grains. In 1980 and 1981, the United States refused to sell grain to the Soviets in protest of its invasion of Afghanistan. The Soviet Union is also a leading nation in the fishing industry and the exportation of caviar.

Right: Leningrad, on the Gulf of Finland in the northeast Soviet Union, is the nation's second largest city. Originally named St. Petersburg, the port city was built in 1703 by Peter the Great and served as the Russian capital until 1918. Shown here is Peterhof, formerly the czar's summer residence and now a museum, situated just outside modern Leningrad.

Top left: A basket of caviar is carried for weighing in Ust'-Kamčatsk. The livelihood of many residents of this peninsula on the Bering Sea depends upon world demand for this delicacy.

Top right: State farms are owned by the Soviet government and employ salaried workers. Collective farms are run by their members. These two types of farms account for most of the major crops grown in the Soviet Union. Here, wheat is harvested on a state farm.

Above: Situated in the northwest, southeast of Leningrad, Novgorod is first mentioned in documents dating from the 800s. One of the oldest cities in the Soviet Union, Novgorod has preserved some of its historic sites, including this eleventh-century church.

Right: Jalta, a Ukrainian city on the Black Sea, is a leading Soviet resort. It is situated on a peninsula known as the Crimea – a subtropical region that was first settled by ancient Greeks.

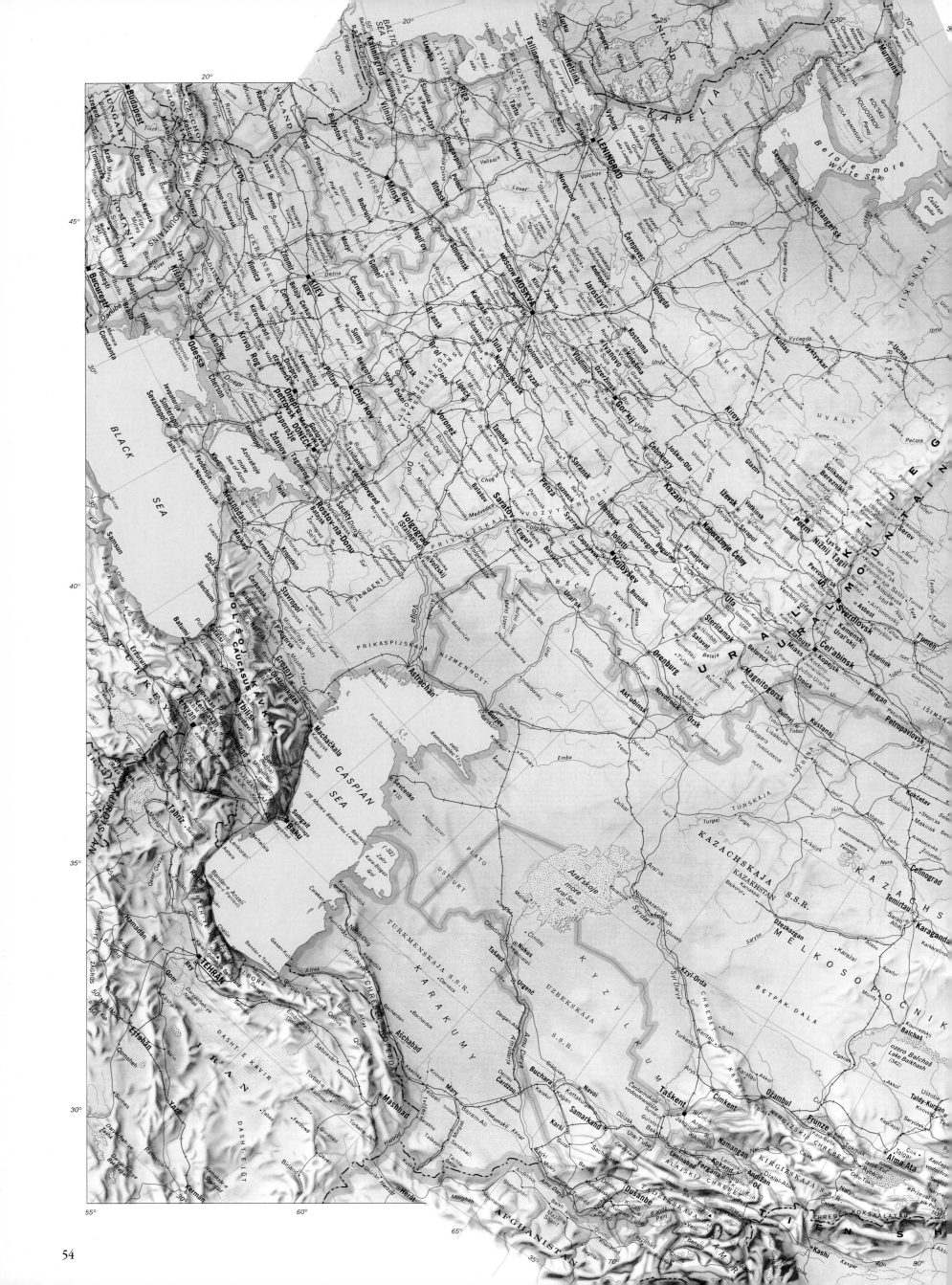

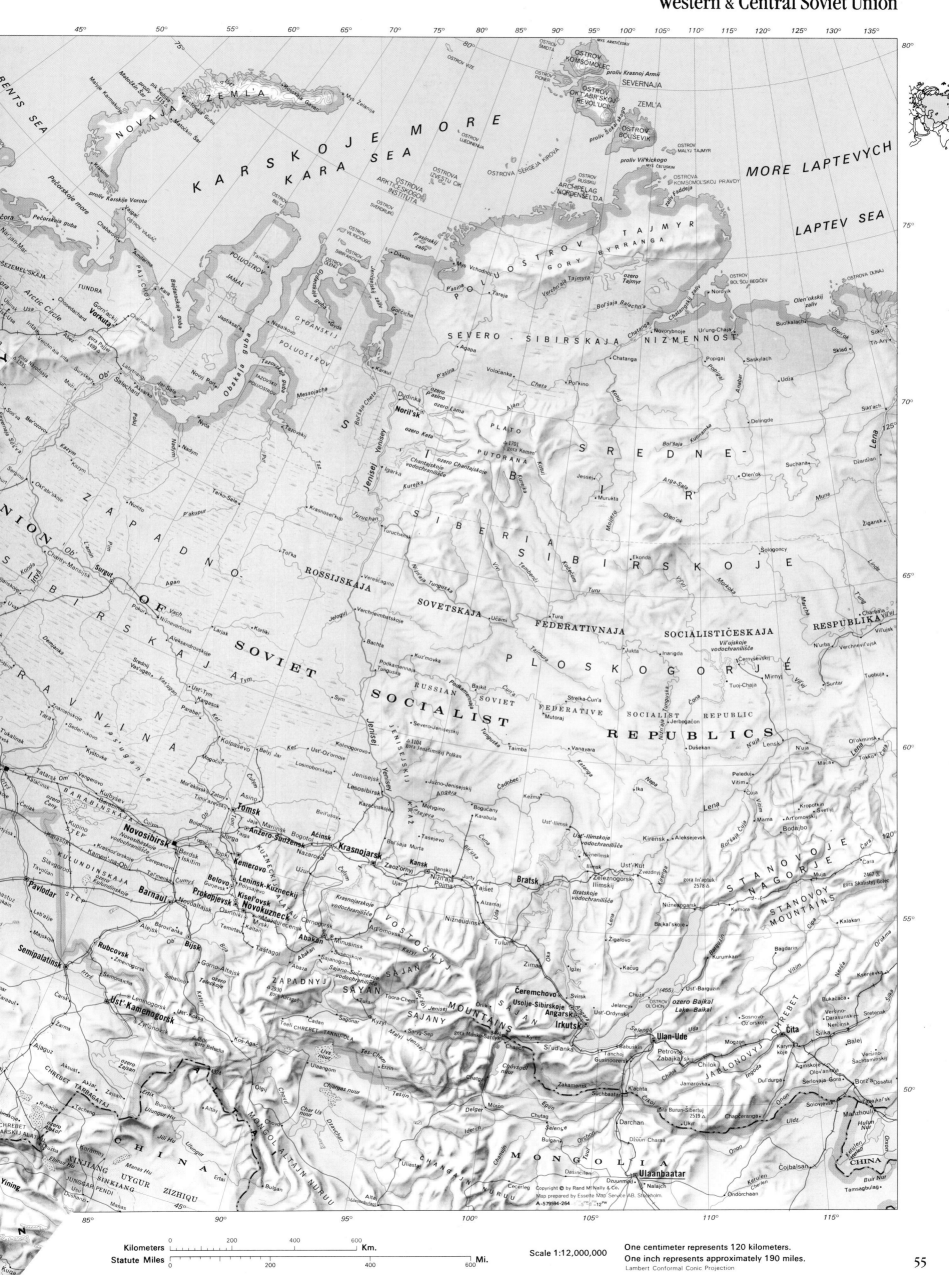

Kilometers | Km.
Statute Miles | Mi.

Scale 1:12,000,000

One centimeter represents 120 kilometers.
One inch represents approximately 190 miles.

Copyright © by Rand McNally & Co.
Map prepared by Esselte Map Service AB, Stockholm
A-579594-264

Lambert Conformal Conic Projection

Kilometers ⊢—————⊣ 200 400 600 Km.

Statute Miles ⊢—————⊣ 200 400 600 Mi.

Scale 1:12,000,000

One centimeter represents 120 kilometers.
One inch represents approximately 190 miles.

Lambert Conformal Conic Projection

Asia
Profile

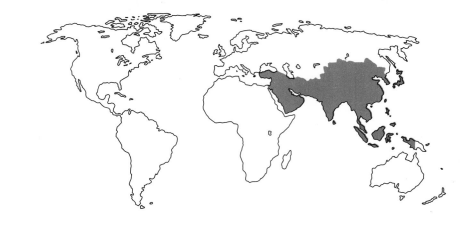

Location and Size

Asia is the largest continent in the world, covering an area of 17,159,995 square miles (44,444,100 square kilometers). It spreads over 33 percent of the world's total land surface and is connected to both Europe and Africa. With the highest population in the world – nearly three billion people – Asia holds about 59 percent of the world's total population.

This vast continent can be divided into six main regions: western Asia, which encompasses Iran, Afghanistan, Cyprus, Iraq, Israel, United Arab Emirates, Yemen, Turkey, Jordan, Kuwait, Lebanon, Oman, Saudi Arabia, and other middle eastern countries east of the Suez Canal; eastern Asia, which includes Japan, North and South Korea, and most of China; southern Asia, including India, Pakistan, Nepal, Bangladesh, Bhutan, Sri Lanka, and Maldives; southeastern Asia, which groups Indonesia, Malaysia, New Guinea, the Philippines, Singapore, Vietnam, Laos, Thailand, Kampuchea, Burma, and Brunei; central Asia, encompassing Mongolia and the autonomous Chinese regions of Tibet and Sinkiang (Xinjiang); and finally, Soviet Asia, clustering Siberia and all the Asian republics of the Soviet Union. Asia is a diverse continent filled with many races, religions, languages, political systems, and cultures.

Landscape

Asian landscape comprises many high mountain ranges, plateaus, basins, island clusters, and lowlands. Mountains predominate, and Asia's tallest peaks are in the Himalayas – the highest of which soar to more than twenty-nine thousand feet (almost nine thousand meters). The lowest point in Asia is 1,296 feet (395 meters) below sea level, at the Dead Sea in Israel.

Southwest Asia tends to be rugged and mountainous, reaching 18,387 feet (5,604 meters) in the Elburz (Alborz) Mountains of northern Iran. Also within this region lie some extensive plateaus, such as the Plateau of Iran. Parts of this region are prone to earthquakes; in 1988, the Soviet republic of Armenia (Arm'anskaja) suffered a devastating earthquake in which more than fifty

thousand people lost their lives.

South of this area is geographically more complex. Its western region is part of the great Rift Valley, which extends from East Africa to Syria. The mountains of the Arabian Peninsula rise to 12,336 feet (3,760 meters). East of these mountains, the landscape falls across the great desert expanse of the Arabian Peninsula to the lowland belt occupied by the Persian Gulf and the southeast-flowing Tigris and Euphrates rivers.

Central Asia is perhaps the most remote and physically brutal area in the world. Bounded in the north by the Tien Shan and the Sayan (Sayany) Mountains, it extends southward across western China, Mongolia, and Tibet to the Himalayas. Within Sinkiang Province, China, the Turfan (Turpan) Depression descends to a level of 505 feet (154 meters) below sea level. In contrast, the highest peaks of the Himalayas are also found here. Encircled by mountains, the area's heartland is a series of plains, predominantly uninviting dry lands including the Takla Makan (Taklimakan) and Gobi deserts, and the Plateau of Tibet.

Farther east lie the large river valleys

of eastern Asia, flanked by the hills and low tablelands of eastern China. The surrounding islands – including Japan and Taiwan – are essentially the tops of a great mountain ridge rising steeply from the floor of the Pacific Ocean. These islands, among others, are in a region known as the Ring of Fire, a zone of active volcanoes and frequent earthquake activity.

South of the mountains of central Asia lies the Indian subcontinent, which is composed of two distinctly different areas. Much of the Deccan Plateau – a triangular-shaped tabletop that occupies

テルモ
医療と歩む

日本ペイント

日本ペ

銀座 ダイアナ

GINZA KOMATSU

信販

ヤマハ家具

築地 玉壽司

銀座ショップ

天元

LOVE Skirt ハ

ユニデン化粧品

国際ロータリー旅行

新潟テレビ21

銀座 大博

銀座 東京羊羹

甘味喫茶

Asia

Left: Erosion of limestone has resulted in unusual conical hills near Guilin in southwestern China. This type of landscape, called *karst,* is often depicted in traditional Chinese art.

the southern parts of the peninsula – lies at 1,650 feet (500 meters) to 2,300 feet (700 meters). Its margins rise in the Western and Eastern Ghāts to greater heights – 8,842 feet (2,695 meters) and 5,512 feet (1,680 meters) respectively. Between the Deccan and the Himalayas are the great valleys of the Indus, Ganges (Ganga), and Brahmaputra (Yaluzangbujiang) rivers.

South of China and east of India lies the intricately shaped peninsula of Southeast Asia and the islands beyond. The northern flanks are mountainous. A large number of rivers flow southward across broad plains in Burma, Thailand, and Kampuchea.

Climate

Asia can be divided into three different climate types: monsoon, dry, and cold. The first climate type, monsoon, is predominant in southern, southeastern, and eastern Asia. In the summer, mainland Asia heats up rapidly. As heat builds up, warm air rises and creates low-pressure centers. High-pressure centers above the Pacific and Indian oceans force humid air inland, bringing heavy rains. This occurs mostly during the summer months. During the season of winter monsoons, the opposite occurs. Because the land cools off much more quickly than the surrounding waters, a high-pressure zone develops, forcing continental winds to blow offshore from inland Asia. Monsoon areas are generally warmer in summer and colder in winter than other areas of similar latitude and geographic type.

Temperatures range considerably within monsoon regions. To the north of the equator, summers tend to be hot and humid, with average temperatures reaching 80°F (27°C), while winters are cool and dry (50°F/10°C). The rest of Asia tends to be fairly temperate with the north being generally cooler than the south.

The second climate type, dry, is found in parts of southeast and central Asia. Here, rainfall varies from less than one inch (twenty-five millimeters) annually in some Soviet Asia desert regions to up to twenty inches (five hundred millimeters) annually in the western regions near the Mediterranean Sea.

The third climate type, cold, is found in most of Soviet Asia, to the north. Here, summers tend to be shorter and rainfall less. In the far northern region of Asia, polar climates exist where the subsoil is permanently frozen year-round.

History, Politics, and Economy

Asia has been the home of many great civilizations: the Sumerians, who thrived in Mesopotamia over five thousand years ago; the great Indus Valley culture, which existed over four thousand years ago; the Chinese dynasties, which culminated in the Chou some two thousand years ago; and the empire of Alexander the Great, at its peak seven hundred years later.

Asia has also been the birthplace of many great religions in the world: Buddhism was founded in India and Confucianism in China in the sixth century B.C.; Christianity began in Palestine and Islam in Arabia in the sixth century A.D.

Great empires have come and gone and centuries of wars have swept the area. The Byzantine Empire flourished in the fourth century. The Mongols, led by Genghis and Kubla Khan, dominated vast regions in the thirteenth century. In the sixteenth century, Ottomans ruled parts of eastern Asia. These empires were followed by those of the British, French, and Dutch, and other invaders, who moved in to establish outposts. Today, the remnants of foreign domain have crumbled, and the continent is made up of independent countries.

The people of Asia differ greatly in their life-styles, languages, religions, and politics – more so than in any other single continent. As evidenced by the Tibetans who never leave their mountain aeries and the Arab teenagers who commute by jet to shop in Europe's capital cities, Asians experience very different existences.

Asia's politics are equally diverse. In India, the great leader Mahatma Gandhi preached a doctrine of religious tolerance and civil disobedience that changed his nation forever. Gandhi is regarded as the founder of India's independence movement, and in 1947 he prevailed upon Great Britain to grant India its autonomy. This event changed the course of history for India.

The Chinese Revolution in 1911 brought the downfall of the Manchu dynasty and set about a Nationalist government. This revolutionary force, also called Kuomintang, was aligned with the Chinese Communist party and led by Sun Yat-sen and later by Chiang Kaishek. Tension grew between the Communists and Nationalists until fighting broke out and many Communists were executed. Remaining Communists reorganized under Mao Zedong, and the Communist-Nationalist conflict continued, along with Japanese invasion and occupation. By 1949, Communists controlled most of the country, and the People's Republic of China was proclaimed. Mao died in 1976, but his legacy lives on.

After over two centuries of isolation from the West, Japan began to adopt Western technologies and legal systems, stressing industrialization and education in 1853. After a military expansion that included the annexing of Korea in 1910, Japan became a British ally in World War I. Japan invaded China in 1937, then attacked United States military bases in Pearl Harbor, Hawaii, in 1941. After the United States dropped atomic bombs on Hiroshima and Nagasaki in 1945, Japan surrendered. Since the war, however, Japan has flourished economically and has become a model of the West.

Because the nations of the region are so diverse, the economic outlook for Asia in the late twentieth century is a varied one. Asia now includes a new, rising economic generation in the Middle East and in Japan, South Korea, Taiwan, Singapore, and Hong Kong. China and India embrace rich histories yet have unrealized economic potential in the modern world. Many Asian countries are still Third World nations, clinging to a minimal existence.

Countries

Afghanistan

Formerly a kingdom, Afghanistan has been a republic since 1973. A terrain of mountains and valleys separates the desert region of the southwest from the more fertile north. Increased development has made natural gas an important export. Since the Soviet invasion in 1979, continued conflict and guerrilla fighting has plagued the nation, and in 1988 the Soviets agreed to remove military forces. Political factions make it unlikely that social and economic conditions will improve quickly.

Bahrain

Composed of thirty-three small islands in the Persian Gulf, this Middle Eastern country has a fierce desert climate. Many of the country's islands are barren and the population is concentrated in the capital city. The oil economy has resulted in an influx of foreign workers and considerable westernization. Friendly international relations and political allegiance to the Arab League characterize the current government.

Bangladesh

The people, mostly peasant farmers, are among Asia's poorest and most rural. With a relatively small area and a high birthrate, the country is also one of the world's most densely populated. The country has yet to recover from damage sustained in a 1971 civil war and a 1985 tidal wave. Farm output fluctuates greatly, subject to frequent monsoons, floods, and droughts. Partially a result of this, the nation's food shortages have not been assuaged.

Bhutan

This small landlocked Himalayan state is independent, but neighboring India officially guides its foreign affairs. The mountainous terrain of Bhutan has long isolated the nation from the outside world. The population is largely rural, with small villages that have grown up around monastery fortresses. Partially due to its physical isolation, Bhutan has one of the world's least developed economies and is dependent on foreign aid. Mining and tourism are developing.

British Indian Ocean Territory

Formed in 1965 from a number of scattered islands in the western Indian Ocean, this British colony today comprises the Chagos Archipelago, some 1,000 miles (1,700 kilometers) southwest of Sri Lanka. The small population mainly fishes and grows food crops.

Brunei

Independence was gained from Britain in 1984. Today the nation is ruled by a sultan, who, as a result of significant oil and natural gas income, is generally regarded as the wealthiest person in the world. Situated on northeastern Borneo, Brunei is generally flat and covered with dense rain forests.

Burma

A Socialist republic since 1974, Burma left the then British Commonwealth in 1948 to become an independent federal country. The terrain is marked by mountains, rivers, and forests; the climate is tropical. Sporadic uprisings continue, often carried out by ethnic minorities.

Burma has been beset with economic problems, caused mainly by the significant destruction it suffered during World War II and by postindependence instability. Agriculture continues as the economic mainstay.

China

One of the oldest civilizations on earth, China has a very long history and has contributed much to world culture. The People's Republic of China has been a Communist state since 1949. China's terrain is varied: two-thirds consists of mountainous or semiarid land, with

Below: The desert and semiarid regions of northwestern India contrast with the rest of the mostly tropical country. Here, near Pushkar, Rājasthān, camels and other animals are traded during a religious festival held since the fourth century.

Asia

Countries continued

fertile plains and deltas in the east. China has the largest population of any country in the world. Since Communist leader Mao Zedong's death in 1976, foreign trade and contact have expanded. A current economic plan focuses on growth in agriculture, industry, science and technology, and national defense. In 1979, the United States recognized Beijing – rather than T'aipei on Taiwan – as China's capital.

Christmas Island

Lying 210 miles (350 kilometers) south of Java in the eastern Indian Ocean, Christmas Island is now under Australian sovereignty. The extraction of phosphates is the island's major industry.

Cocos Islands

These islands lie six hundred miles (one thousand kilometers) west of Christmas Island. Their control was passed from Singapore to Australia by the British government in 1955.

Cyprus

This eastern Mediterranean island became independent from Britain in 1960. Since then, its history has been marked by Greek-Turkish conflict. Cyprus is marked by a fertile central plain bordered by mountains in the southwest and north. Relocation of Greek Cypriots in the south and Turkish Cypriots in the north has severely disrupted the economy. Greek Cypriots have made progress, expanding agriculture to manufacturing and tourism. Turkish Cypriots remain agriculturally based and dependent on Turkey.

Hong Kong

One of the world's most densely populated areas, Hong Kong is a British colony that was leased from the Chinese in 1898 for a period of ninety-nine years. Low taxes, duty-free status, an accessible location, and an excellent natural harbor have helped make Hong Kong an Asian center of trade. The islands are hilly and tropical.

India

India has a history of civilization that dates back to about 2,500 B.C. The population is composed of two main ethnic groups: the Indo-Aryan and the Dravidian. Hindus are the religious majority, but the country has one of the world's largest Muslim populations. Hindi is the official language. Although economic conditions have improved since India became independent in 1947, poverty, unemployment, underemployment, and civil strife continue to plague the nation. In 1984, Prime Minister Indira Gandhi was assassinated, and conflicts continue.

Indonesia

Java (Jawa), Sumatra (Sumatera), Sulawesi (Celebes), and most of Borneo (Kalimanatan) are the largest islands in this independent republic, which is the fifth most populous nation in the world. Overpopulation threatens the economy and food supply. Economic and political instability led to an attempted Communist coup in 1965, and the government has since outlawed the Communist party, cut its ties with China, and strengthened relations with Western powers.

Iran

Set between the Persian Gulf and the Caspian Sea, Iran (formerly Persia) has a history dating back several thousand years. Nearly all Iranians are Aryan and Muslim, mainly of the Shiite sect. The country is an Islamic republic, with law based on Islamic teachings. Aridity and a harsh mountain-and-desert terrain result in population concentrated in the west and north. Iran's previously rapid economic development has slowed as a result of a 1979 revolution and ongoing war with Iraq. Small-scale farming, manufacturing, and trading appear to be current economic trends. Oil remains the most important export, and trade of Persian carpets continues.

Iraq

This former kingdom became a republic in 1958. It is centered on the fertile basin of the Tigris and Euphrates rivers, where civilizations such as the Sumerian, Babylonian, and Parthian once existed. Oil is the mainstay of Iraq's economy. Despite its wealth, the Iraqi economy, like the Iranian, has been drained by the continuing Iran-Iraq war.

Israel

Israel comprises much of the region of Palestine, the site of most biblical history. Most Israelis are Jewish, and the non-Jewish population is predominantly Arab and Muslim. Hebrew and Arabic are the official languages, and both are used on documents and currency. Despite drastic levels of inflation and a constant trade deficit, Israel has experienced economic growth. Taxes are a major source of revenue, as are grants and loans from other countries and

Right: The Bhote, an ethnic group related to Tibetans, comprise many different populations whose cultures have developed in isolation from one another. These Bhote come from Yakba, a village in western Nepal.

income from tourism. The nation of Israel was established in 1948. Torn by war since then, Israel remains steeped in conflict with many of its neighbors over territorial rights.

Japan

One of the world's leading industrial powers, Japan is remarkable for its economic growth rate since World War II, especially considering its lack of natural resources. After Japan surrendered to the United States at the end of World War II, industry became the country's chief occupation. It has since become famous for its innovative technology. Japan's mountainous terrain includes both active and dormant volcanoes, and earthquakes sometimes occur. Japan's culture blends East and West, with karate, tea ceremonies, and kimonos balanced by baseball, fast food, and business suits. Japan has gained much attention as an economic power, but lack of military might could stifle its authority in the world marketplace.

Jordan

The modern Arab kingdom of Jordan was established in 1949. A nation of few natural resources, Jordan has suffered further economic damage from an influx of refugees and the chronic political instability of the Middle East. In a 1967 war with Israel, Jordan lost the economically active West Bank, which made up about half the country's farmland. Agri-

culture remains the most important activity, however, and tourism has helped the weak, foreign-aid-dependent economy.

Kampuchea

The Khmer, one of the oldest peoples in Southeast Asia, constitute the major ethnic group in Kampuchea, formerly known as Cambodia. The population has declined significantly since the mid-1970s as a result of war, famine, human-rights abuses, and emigration; the nation has suffered economically for the same reasons. Several insurgent groups, including the Khmer Rouge, have continued guerilla warfare against the Vietnamese-installed government.

Korea, North

The northern part of the Korean peninsula is a Socialist republic and maintains one of the world's largest armies. Despite its ties to the Soviet Union and China, North Korea strives for an independent foreign policy based on self-reliance. The government discourages religious activity. The division of the Korean peninsula after World War II left North Korea with most of the industry and natural resources but little agricultural land and few skilled workers. The country has succeeded in becoming one of the most industrialized nations in Asia and is overcoming its agricultural problems. The Soviet Union and China have contributed aid.

Korea, South

The southern part of the Korean peninsula is officially known as the Republic of Korea. Its economy is more evenly based than that of the north, and most trade is with Japan and the United States. Population is much more dense in the south than it is in the north, as a result of massive migration to the south after World War II. Internal unrest has led to demands for wider democracy and reunification of Korea. South Korea has recently gained attention as a growing economic force.

Kuwait

Kuwait is one of the world's largest oil producers, a fact that has transformed it from a poor nation into an affluent one. Poised at the tip of the Persian Gulf, Kuwait must always be sensitive to the interests of its many neighbors. Though it strives to remain politically neutral, the ongoing Iran-Iraq war has created problems for Kuwait. The nation's prosperity has drawn emigrants from the Persian Gulf and beyond, giving it a diverse population.

Laos

Formerly part of French Indochina, this landlocked country is now an independent Socialist republic. It is one of the least developed countries of Southeast Asia, and agriculture remains the mainstay of the economy. Many Lao, opposed to the Communist rule, have fled the

Above: **The highest mountains in the world, the Himalayas dominate central Asia. Extending roughly 1,550 miles (2,500 kilometers), they cut through Pakistan, India, China, Nepal, and Bhutan. Their formidable terrain and climate limit settlement, but in some places, humans manage to grow crops such as these apricots, laid in the sun to dry in northern Pakistan.**

country for refuge in Thailand and the United States.

Lebanon

This small republic borders the Mediterranean Sea and has long been a center of commerce; however, prolonged fighting, beginning with the 1975 civil war, has greatly damaged all economic activity. Islam is the majority religion, although Christianity continues to be a strong presence. Palestinian refugees have settled in Lebanon since the creation of Israel in 1948, many of them living in refugee camps. International attempts to reconcile warring factions, including a peace agreement signed by faction leaders in 1986, have been unsuccessful.

Macao

Two islands and a part of a peninsula form this Portuguese territory on China's coast. Tourism, gambling, and light

63

Asia

Countries continued

Right: Shown here is the Marble Temple (Wat Benchamabophit), a Buddhist temple in Bangkok (Krung Thep), Thailand. Buddhism, Hinduism, and Islam are the principal religions of Asia.

industry help make up Macao's economy. Although the government is nominally directed by Portugal, any policies relating to Macao are subject to China's approval. Macao is the oldest European settlement in the Far East.

Malaysia
Malaysia's location at one of Southeast Asia's maritime crossroads has left it with a diverse population, including Malays, Chinese, Indians, and native non-Malay groups. Composed of the Malay Peninsula and parts of northern Borneo in the South China Sea, Malaysia has one of the healthiest economies in the region, supported by multiple strengths in agriculture, mining, forestry, and fishing. The nation is one of the world's leading producers of rubber, palm oil, and tin, and one of the Far East's largest petroleum exporters.

Maldives
Now an independent republic, this collection of 1,200 coral atolls lying southwest of Sri Lanka was a British protectorate until 1965. Tourism and fishing are the main activities. Nearly all residents are Sunni Muslims.

Mongolia
This Socialist republic is a sparsely populated, landlocked country lying between the Soviet Union and China. Situated in the heart of Asia, Mongolia supports the Soviet Union, and Soviet

troops are stationed throughout the land. The traditional nomadic way of life of many Mongols is becoming less common as recent government policies have led to urbanization and settled agriculture. Mongolia's economy, long based on the raising of livestock, has been shaped by the ideal grazing land found in most of the country.

Nepal
Landlocked between Tibet and India, Nepal is a Himalayan kingdom. This nation has one of the least developed economies in the world, with agriculture the most important activity. Most of Nepal is covered by the Himalayas, the tallest mountains in the world – a fact that hinders it economically by curbing agriculture and that helps it by encouraging tourism. There are no political parties in Nepal.

Oman
Situated on the Persian Gulf, Oman's land borders are undefined and in dispute. Oil production is the economic mainstay, but oil supplies in Oman are not as vast as those in other Arab states, and the government is seeking to diversify. Oman is a moderate, pro-Western Arab state, and a desert climate prevails over most areas.

Pakistan
The Islamic Republic of Pakistan remains an agricultural economy.

Spurred by poor living conditions and a lack of jobs, many Pakistanis work abroad. Pakistan remains troubled by population growth, unskilled labor, a trade deficit, and an influx of refugees fleeing the war in Afghanistan. Subsequent political activity in Pakistan has included martial law and accusations of government corruption.

Philippines
Only one-tenth of the seven thousand islands in the Republic of the Philippines are inhabited. The Philippines is primarily an agricultural nation, relying on rice, sugar, coconuts, and wood. Manufacturing is developing through government incentives. A dependence on imported goods, along with inadequate but growing power and transport systems, has hampered growth. Since the election of Corazon Aquino, the country has been plagued by coup attempts, leftist insurgency groups, and unresolved social and economic problems.

Qatar
The State of Qatar relies on oil to fuel its economy, and extensive reserves of natural gas await exploitation. Qatar became independent in 1971 after failing to agree on the terms of a union with eight Persian Gulf sheikdoms. Despite a political trend toward a modern welfare state, Qatar retains many elements of a traditional Islamic society.

Saudi Arabia
Saudi Arabia is inhabited primarily by Arab Muslims, but some Bedouin tribes roam this hot, arid region. Agriculture is severely limited, and the country must import nearly all its food. A dominant member of the Organization of Petroleum Exporting Countries (OPEC), Saudi Arabia is the world's leading exporter of petroleum. It possesses the largest concentration of known oil reserves in the world. The country maintains strong diplomatic and economic ties with Western nations.

Singapore
Singapore is one of the most densely populated nations in the world, with most of the population living in the city of Singapore on Singapore Island. The island nation at the tip of the Malay Peninsula is a leading Asian economic power and a world leader in petroleum refining. Cool breezes and a tropical climate make Singapore an attractive spot for tourists. Singapore's society is characterized by a mixture of Western and traditional customs and dress.

Sri Lanka
Formerly known as Ceylon, the Democratic Socialist Republic of Sri Lanka is an island off India. The economy is based on agriculture, which employs nearly half the people. Sri Lanka is sponsoring several internal-development programs; however, continuing high

government subsidy and welfare policies threaten economic growth. Tensions between ethnic groups have often erupted in violence.

Syria

Syria is a developing country with great potential for economic growth. Oil is the major natural resource. The majority is Sunni Muslim, and Islam is a powerful cultural force. Tensions over land disputes between Syria and Israel erupted in war in 1967 and 1973 and remain unresolved.

Taiwan

Taiwan – or the Republic of China – is an eastern Asian island off the coast of mainland China in the South China Sea. Since World War II, Taiwan's economy has changed from agriculture to industry, and today technology and heavy industry are emphasized. T'aipei, Taiwan, has been proclaimed the capital of Nationalist China, a separate nation from mainland China, but nearly all nations view Taiwan as part of the People's Republic of China.

Thailand

Formerly called Siam, Thailand is a southeastern Asian kingdom with a tropical climate. It has been under military rule since 1976. With an economy based on agriculture, Thailand exports large quantities of rice each year. The cost of caring for thousands of refugees from the Vietnam war has been a major drain on the economy. Thai society is rural, with most people living in the rice-growing regions. The government has sponsored a successful family-planning program, which has greatly reduced the annual birthrate.

Turkey

The Republic of Turkey was restored to civilian rule in 1983 after control by Turkish generals. Military rule came about as a result of a fledgling government and years of terrorism, flared by disputes with Greece over Cyprus. The government owns and controls many important industries, transportation services, and utilities. Most people are farmers and the population is mainly Sunni Muslim.

United Arab Emirates

Most residents are not U.A.E. citizens, but Westerners and Asians attracted by jobs in the oil industry. With one of the highest per capita incomes in the world, this small urban federation situated on the Persian Gulf provides free medical and educational facilities. The nation is divided into seven independent states. Because each emirate has a great deal of control over its internal affairs and economic development, the growth of federal powers has been slow.

Vietnam

Vietnam is a war-torn nation composed mostly of ethnic Vietnamese. The official language is Vietnamese, but a history of foreign intervention is reflected in wide use of French, English, Chinese, and Russian. Communist Vietnamese gained control over North Vietnam in 1954, and in 1975, they were victorious in unifying the north and south into a Socialist republic. Economic problems have increased since the Vietnam War, and the country remains dependent on Soviet and Eastern-bloc aid.

Yemen

At the southwest tip of Arabia, the Yemen Arab Republic – or North Yemen – has a terrain suited for agriculture, the backbone of the nation's economy. Border clashes have erupted with South Yemen, but the governments of both North and South Yemen want to unify Yemen.

Yemen, People's Democratic Republic of

Formerly controlled by Britain, the People's Democratic Republic of Yemen – also referred to as South Yemen – was established in 1970 after a Marxist takeover. Petroleum products are South Yemen's major industrial export. Military leaders assumed control of the country in 1974.

Below: The Troglodyte dwellings shown here are found in Turkey's Cappadocia region. The Troglodytes were a primitive people who inhabited the caves and tunnels of rocky hillsides. They were given their name by the ancient Greeks.

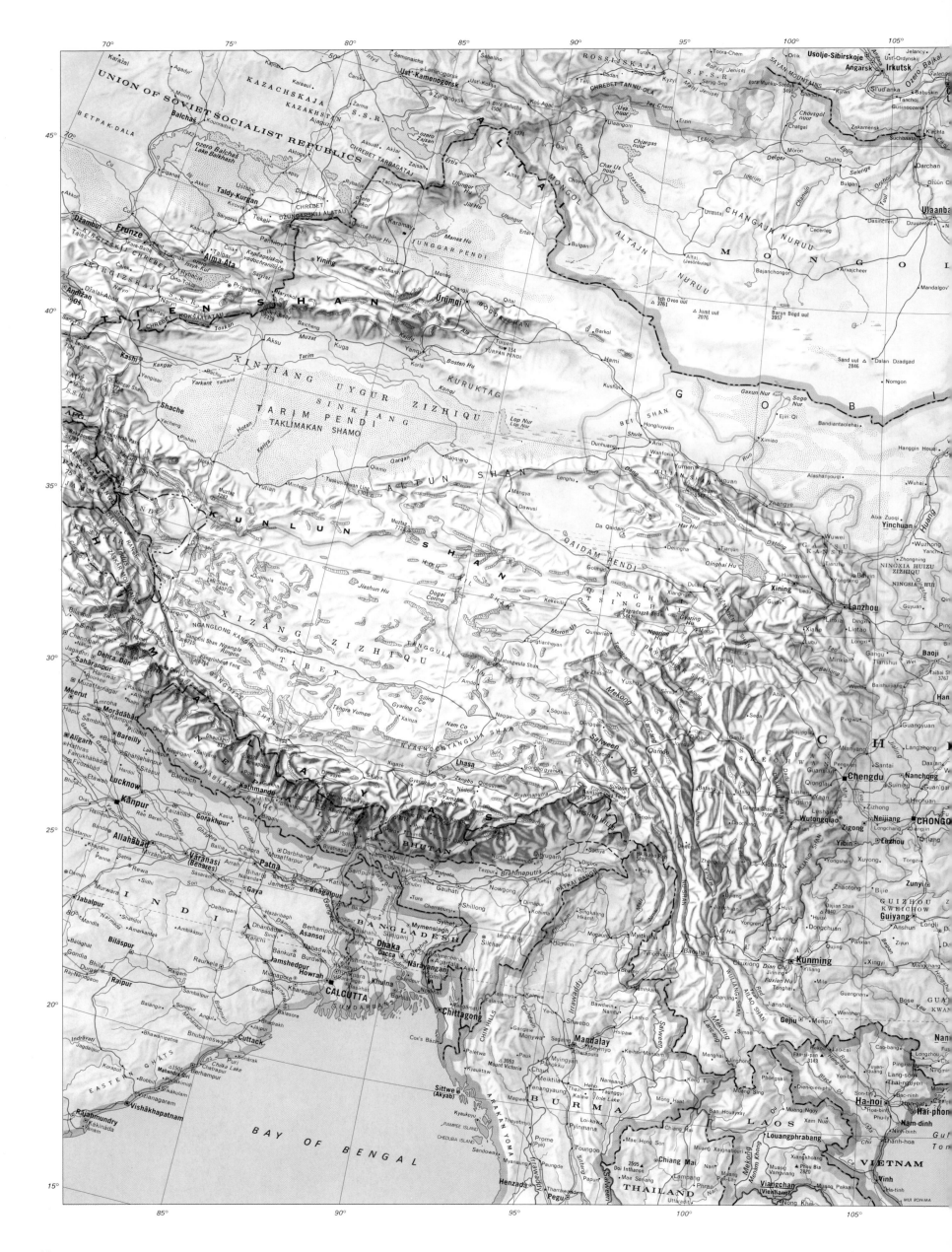

PACIFIC OCEAN

SEA OF JAPAN

EAST CHINA SEA

SOUTH CHINA SEA

PHILIPPINE SEA

Yellow Sea

Kilometers 0 200 400 600 Km.

Statute Miles 0 200 400 600 Mi.

Scale 1:12,000,000

One centimeter represents 120 kilometers.
One inch represents approximately 190 miles.

Lambert Conformal Conic Projection

Copyright © by Rand McNally & Co.
Map prepared by Esselte Map Service AB, Stockholm.
A-569700-264

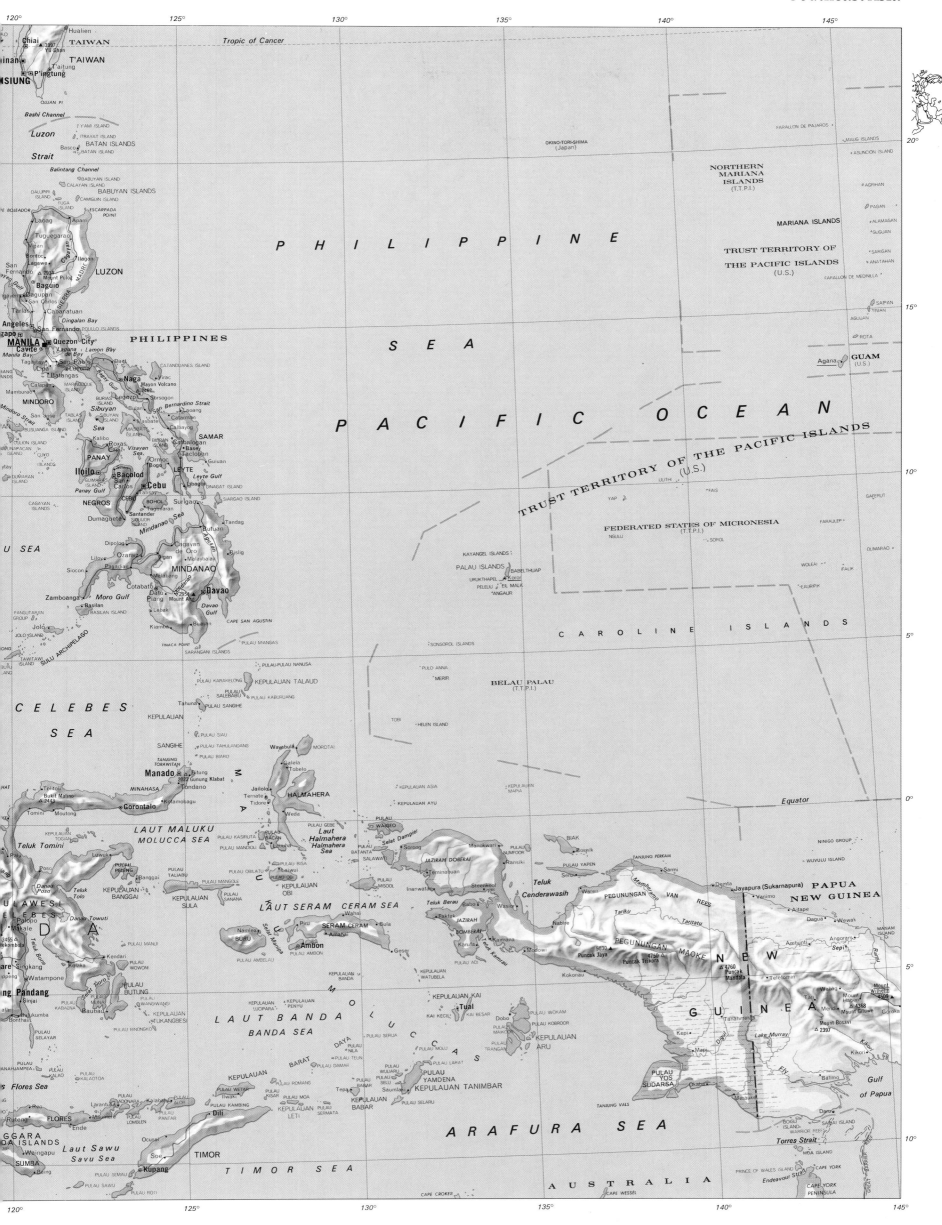

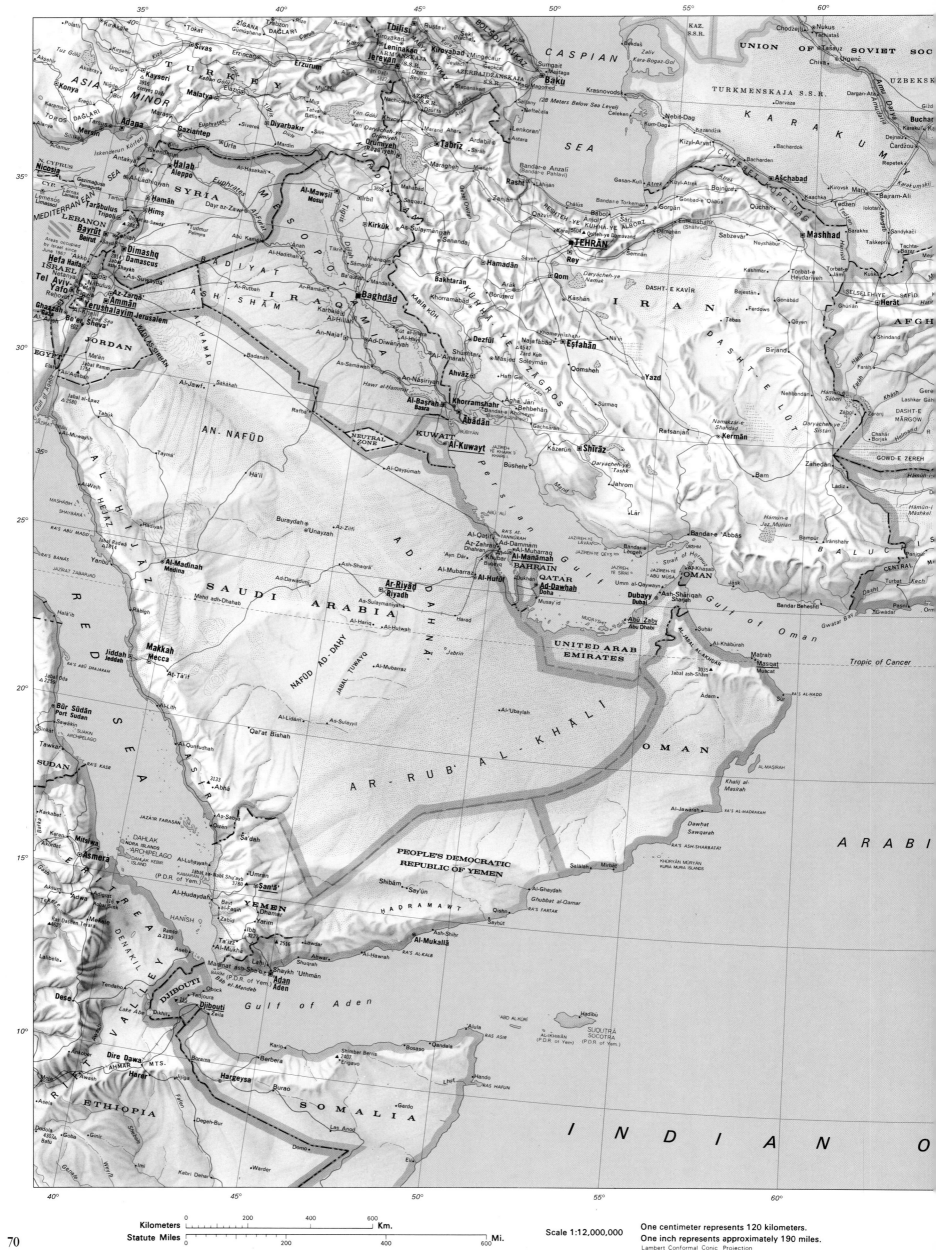

Kilometers |0   200   400   600| Km.

Statute Miles |0   200   400   600| Mi.

Scale 1:12,000,000

One centimeter represents 120 kilometers.
One inch represents approximately 190 miles.

Lambert Conformal Conic Projection

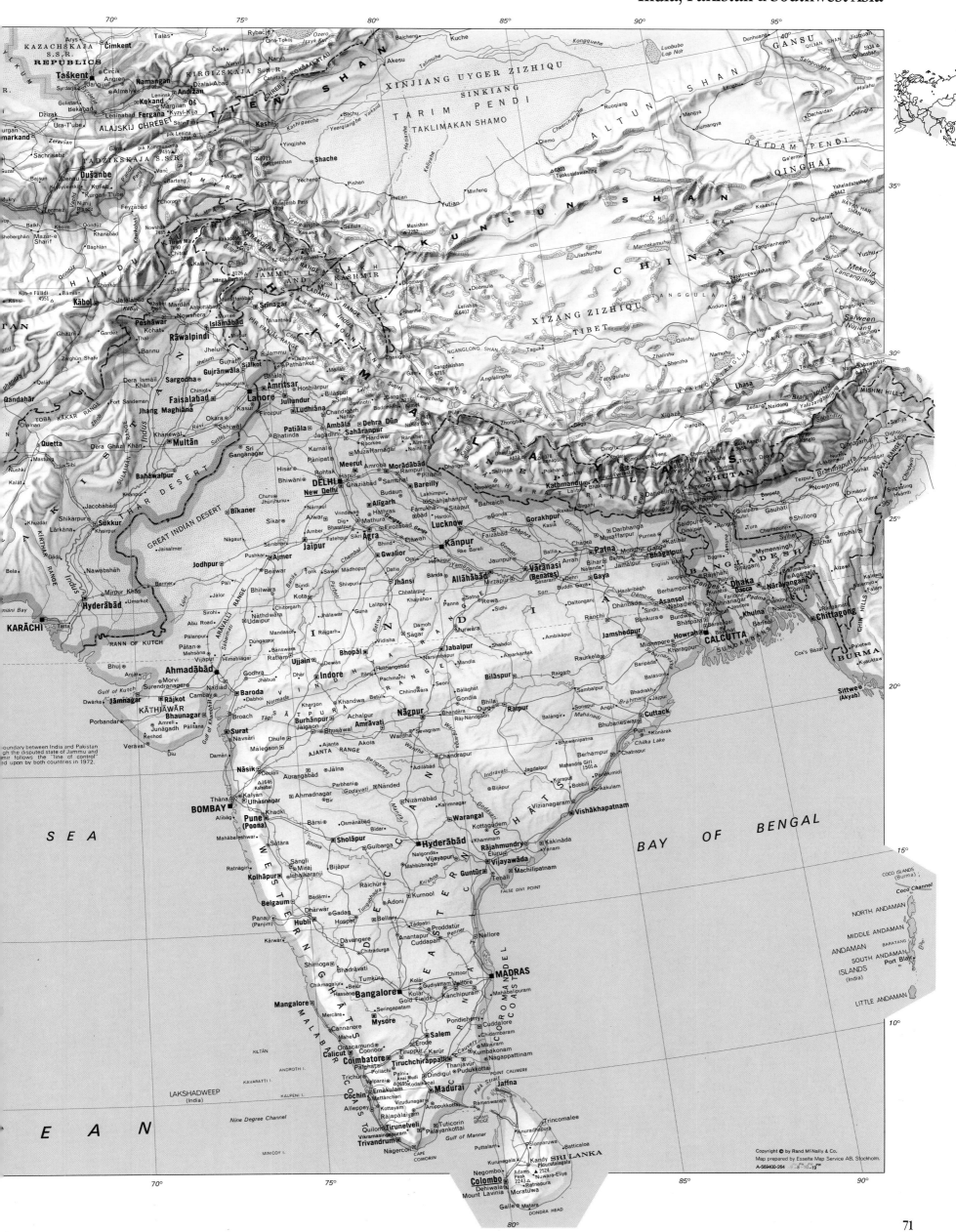

Africa
Profile

Location and Size

Africa is the second largest continent – after Asia – and constitutes 22 percent of the earth's land area. Yet it seems that few people realize just how huge Africa is. The entire United States could be placed in just the Sahara Desert, which extends 3,200 miles (5,150 kilometers) across northern Africa. The continent sits astride the equator and reaches north-to-south distances of some 4,900 miles (7,900 kilometers) and, at its widest, east-to-west expanses of about 4,450 miles (7,100) kilometers.

Africa is geographically connected to Asia by the Suez (Suways) Canal and to

Europe by the Strait of Gibraltar. The waters surrounding Africa include the Atlantic Ocean to the west, the Indian Ocean to the east and south, and the Mediterranean Sea to the north. Africa includes not only the mainland area, but it also comprises a number of large and small islands in these surrounding waters. Madagascar is the most significant of these.

At the northernmost point of mainland Africa is Cape Ben Sekka, Tunisia, while at the southernmost point is Cape Agulhas, South Africa. At its farthest eastern border is found Cape Hafun, Somalia, and to the west is Cape Vert, Senegal.

Landscape

Africa is an ancient, mammoth plateau of crystalline minerals dating back over 3.2 billion years. On top of this platform sits a vast area of mountains, deserts, rain forests, and plains that is mostly lower in the north and west and higher in the east and south.

It is easy to see how some of Africa's outstanding landscape features have influenced its history and development by preventing human migration and exploration. For example, Africa has remarkably straight coastlines with very few harbors, inlets, or bays – a fact that hindered seafaring explorers. The

world's largest desert, the Sahara, dominates the landscape in northern Africa, preventing penetration from that direction. The majority of African rivers are largely unnavigable, and coastal swamps, mountain ranges, and forests have further discouraged foreign conquerors.

Africa lacks the huge mountain ranges of most other continents; the spectacular Rift Valley in the eastern third of Africa provides the greatest land relief. This majestic trough cuts into the earth from the Dead Sea in the Middle East southward to Mozambique and Swaziland, extending approximately 4,300 miles (6,900 kilometers). In the deepest spot of the Rift Valley, the walls rise up more

Left: The nomadic, cattle-herding Masai people of East Africa forage over the lands of southern Kenya and Tanzania, paying little attention to national boundaries and resisting permanent settlement and integration into the economy. Trade among the Masai is based on cattle, which provides food and leverage for other types of exchanges. These young Masai women are dressed in typical garb.

Right: Contrary to popular belief, Africa is more a land of plains and deserts than it is of jungles. Grassland containing scattered trees and other hardy plants, or savanna, covers much of eastern, central, and southern Africa. Here the sun sets behind an acacia tree on the East Africa savanna.

than 10,500 feet (3,200 meters).

Most of the continent's great natural lakes are found in or around the Rift Valley. Lake Victoria, lying between the two main valleys, has a surface area of nearly 26,830 square miles (69,500 square kilometers) and is second only to Lake Superior as the world's largest freshwater lake.

Close to the Rift Valley are a number of mountainous areas, some of which contain active volcanoes. Here is found Africa's highest point: Mount Kilimanjaro, at 19,340 feet (5,895 meters). The mountainous Ethiopian Plateau contains some of the highest elevations in Africa.

The north is marked by semiarid, mountainous regions. In the northwest, the barrier of the Atlas Mountains of Tunisia, Morocco, and Algeria, rising to 13,665 feet (4,167 meters), effectively divides the coastal strip from the Sahara.

Finally, at the bottom of the continent, the Drakensberg Mountains of Lesotho and South Africa reach heights of more than ten thousand feet (three thousand meters). This range is part of the escarpment that forms the southern edge of the continental plateau.

In many parts of Africa, comparatively short rivers flow to the Atlantic and Indian oceans. The major exception in both size and destination is the Nile, the world's longest river, which flows northward for 4,160 miles (6,700 kilometers) from the East African lakes to the Mediterranean Sea.

In West Africa, the Niger follows a circuitous course for 2,595 miles (4,190 kilometers) between the highlands of Sierra Leone and its delta in Nigeria. The Congo (Zaire) is the main channel of equatorial Africa. In the southeast, the Zambezi (Zambeze) flows for 1,615 miles (2,600 kilometers) from Angola eastward to the Indian Ocean, cascading over the Victoria Falls en route. All African rivers contain similar waterfalls and cataracts, where they drop from one plateau to another.

Climate

Since Africa sits on the equator, climatic conditions are mirrored on the opposite sides of 0° latitude. In the extreme north of Morocco, Algeria, and Libya, as well as the southern tip of South Africa, the climate is subtropical. Summers here are dry, with the highest monthly average temperature above 72°F (22°C) and no winter average monthly temperature below 50°F (10°C). The South African plateau has a cooler subtropical climate with no dry season and most of its rainfall in summer.

In a belt of central and western Africa close to the equator, and on the east coast of Madagascar, rain falls throughout the year with total accumulation in excess of 60 inches (1,500 millimeters) and often more than 100 inches (2,500 millimeters). Monthly average temperatures never fall below 64°F (18°C) and reach just above 80°F (27°C) at their maximum.

Tropical savanna lands are found in much of eastern and south-central Africa. Here, precipitation is less and, although temperatures never fall below 64°F (18°C) in any month, they show a greater seasonal range than in other parts of Africa.

North and south of the savanna lands lie semiarid and true desert climates such as that of the Sahara Desert. Average monthly summer temperatures in the arid regions may reach 98°F (37°C), while winter temperatures average 59°F (15°C). Precipitation, often negligible, rarely exceeds an average of five inches (125 millimeters). When rain does fall, it is brief but torrential.

Overall, two factors influence African climates. First, 75 percent of the continent has a water supply problem. Average rainfall amounts throughout the continent seem sufficient but, except in equatorial areas, rainfall varies from year to year and creates great difficulties. Second, because so much of Africa – outside of the deserts – is of mid- to high-level elevation, consistent high temperatures are more the exception than the rule. Thus, while the temperature on the Kenyan coast may be unpleasantly high, regions that are farther west – still on the equator but 5,000 feet (1,500 meters) above sea level – the temperature is lower.

History, Politics, and Economy

Modern humankind's research has uncovered evidence suggesting that Africa may well have been the birthplace of the first humans. Sites in East Africa, especially in Tanzania and Kenya, have produced the oldest human remains, some of them thought to be more than two million years old. Many civilizations and empires have flourished and disintegrated during the long course of Africa's history.

The Stone Age probably began in Africa. Many Stone Age peoples were hunter-gatherers; that is, they foraged the land, without engaging in organized agriculture. Some hunter-gatherer societies still exist in remote regions of Africa, the most well-known of which might be the San of the Kalahari Desert.

The culture of ancient Egypt was one of the world's first great civilizations. Although the valley of the Nile has been inhabited for more than twenty thousand years, the classic period of the ancient civilization began about 3100 B.C. and reached its peak about 1400 B.C. The rise of Rome eventually ushered in the demise of ancient Egyptian power.

Elsewhere in Africa, other agricultural civilizations sprang up. About the time of Christ, a huge north-to-south migra-

Right: Africa is the least urbanized continent, and in many nations, the capital city is the only sizable urban center. Harare, shown here, is the capital and largest city of Zimbabwe, a subtropical republic in southern Africa.

Above: The native section of North African cities is sometimes referred to as the Casbah. These women in the Casbah of Tétouan, Morocco, are veiled in accordance with the ancient Islamic custom of purdah, which assures the seclusion of women from public observation. Some North African Muslims have abandoned purdah.

Top, right: Mount Kilimanjaro, in Tanzania, soars above these giraffes in nearby Amboseli National Park, Kenya. Africa's highest peak, Kilimanjaro is always covered with snow.

Right: Ngorongoro Crater lies in the volcanic region of northeastern Tanzania. In the crater is found one of the heaviest concentrations of wildlife in Africa, including these zebras.

Africa

Below: Table Mountain, shown here, rises behind Cape Town, South Africa. The mountain is sometimes covered by a gray-white cloud, referred to locally as "the tablecloth."

tion of black Africans began, bringing agriculture to central Africa.

In the seventh century, Islam began to spread from the Middle East across northern Africa and down into East Africa. Later on, after about 1100, Arab traders began to settle along the eastern African coast, in what is now Kenya, Mozambique, Somalia, and Tanzania. They thrived on trade with China, India, and Indonesia.

By about 1000, West African society had emerged. Early West Africans were generally governed by single chiefs, often men who were thought to hold divine rights or special powers. They lived in autonomous, tightly knit groups that were close to each other and fought often. The kingdom of Ghana dominated West Africa by 1000; it was succeeded by the Mali Empire in the 1200s and the Songhai Empire by 1500.

Portuguese exploration of the western African coast began in the 1400s. Soon, trade was established with Africans, with several commodities exchanged, among them European guns and African slaves. After the New World was discovered and then colonized, the demand for slaves accelerated.

By the nineteenth century, about ten million Africans had been forced from their homeland and placed into slavery in the New World. Many died on the long and crammed voyages to America; others resisted and were killed. Areas known for slave trade – such as Ghana with its powerful Ashanti kingdom – flourished

economically, and the slave trade was dependent upon the toleration and cooperation of these African entrepreneurs. For those who remained in Africa, the slave trade brought new sources of revenue and technology from the West. Britain abolished slavery in 1807, and other countries followed suit soon thereafter.

There were other groups, however, that refused to tolerate slavery. Additionally, large regions of Africa experienced little or no European influence until after 1800.

During the nineteenth century, exploration of the African interior increased, as did European involvement in African economic affairs. A great rivalry began among the European nations in the opening up of the Dark Continent. By 1900, Britain, France, Portugal, Spain, Germany, and Italy laid claim to most of the land.

African nationalism rose greatly after World War II. In 1951, only three African countries were independent. From 1956 to 1968, thirty-eight independent countries emerged, many changing their colonial names to African names. Most African nations won their independence peacefully, unlike many nations in other parts of the world.

Today, most African governments are marked by the problems that face many developing nations: poverty, illiteracy, disease, and food shortages. Additionally, unstable governments and ethnic tensions have led to dictatorships, military

takeovers, and civil unrest. Most African nations remain agricultural, Third World countries, with South Africa having the only developed, industrial economy on the continent.

South of the Sahara, widespread famine is a most serious issue, and it is accompanied by the related problem of overpopulation. In the early 1980s, a widespread and long-lasting drought struck the middle of Africa. Its effects were felt most by the already poverty-stricken nomadic and seminomadic peoples of the area. Accustomed to living just above the starvation level even in the best years, these people died by the hundreds of thousands. Worldwide efforts to rush relief to the famine victims resulted in vast amounts of food finding its way to mid-Africa, but it is believed that inefficient government agencies slowed food distribution.

In southern Africa, racial tensions continue, especially in South Africa. Despite efforts of the government to set up black "homelands," and constitutional reforms that allow a minimum political role for nonblack minorities, the large black majority has become increasingly restive. Strikes, job actions, demonstrations, and other forms of civil disobedience are widespread, and the death toll of blacks is growing amid increasing international scrutiny.

Namibia and Angola continue to suffer from problems left over from colonial days. Angola, long a Portuguese colony, is finding it difficult to achieve

and maintain its status as an independent republic, while Namibia has been trying to free itself from imperialism since World War I.

To the north, Nigeria – with its enormous oil deposits – made what appeared to be great economic strides in the 1970s. But the collapse of the world market for oil in the 1980s made it especially vulnerable; it suffered from the same kinds of problems faced by industrial nations in economic recession while trying to cope with the strains present in a developing nation.

Despite North Africa's cultural link with the Middle East, its colonial past ties it to the rest of the African continent. As in other parts of Africa, colonies were demarcated by artificial borders that had more to do with foreign treaties and agreements than with indigenous ethnicity or tribal allegiance. The land of the region has fostered a nomadic life-style, and the foreign-imposed boundaries prevented people from following their traditional way of life. When independence was finally achieved, the artificial boundaries remained, sometimes uniting diverse peoples into a single nation, and sometimes separating a single people by an international border. Dissension was often the result; many borders were finalized only recently, and many remain in dispute. Libya's Bedouin tribes, for example, long presented a unified resistance to the imposition of what they viewed as artificial borders.

Countries

Algeria
Algeria is the second largest country in Africa, but 90 percent of it lies in the Sahara Desert. A French possession until 1962, Algeria's oil and natural gas provide most of its revenue. The nation enjoys political stability, free medical care, and a greatly improved educational system.

Angola
Situated on the southwest coastline of Africa, Angola was a Portuguese territory until 1975. It is now a Socialist republic. A civil war, the resultant departure of skilled European labor, and continuing guerilla activity have taken their toll on Angola's economy. Most people are subsistence farmers, although Angola is also a large oil producer.

Benin
Lying on the Gulf of Guinea, Benin was formerly called Dahomey. It is now a Socialist republic, having gained independence in 1960. Political instability has been both the cause and effect of Benin's economic problems. The agricultural economy remains largely undeveloped.

Botswana
Botswana is a landlocked republic in southern Africa that gained independence from Britain in 1966. Though limited by the Kalahari, agriculture and the raising of livestock are the primary activities. Since the early seventies, the economy has grown rapidly, with diamond mining the focus.

Burkina Faso
Landlocked Burkina Faso – formerly Upper Volta – is under military rule. The West African nation became independent from France in 1960. The agricultural economy suffers from frequent droughts and an underdeveloped transportation system. Most people are subsistence farmers.

Burundi
Set in the highlands of East Africa, Burundi is a small, densely populated land where subsistence farming is most important. The nation became an independent monarchy in 1962 but is now a republic. Tourists are drawn to Burundi's pleasant climate and hilly terrain.

Cameroon
Cameroon, once controlled by France and the United Kingdom, claimed its independence in the early 1960s. Most of the people in the central African republic live by subsistence farming. Recent economic plans have focused on agriculture, industry, and the development of oil deposits.

Cape Verde
These islands off the west coast of Africa have been independent from Portugal since 1975. The volcanic, mountainous terrain features few resources and low rainfall; thus the economy remains underdeveloped. The tropical climate, however, has helped tourism.

Central African Republic
This republic was once called French Equatorial Africa and remained under French rule until 1960. Fertile land, extensive forests, and mineral deposits provide adequate bases for agriculture, forestry, and mining. Economic development remains minimal, however, impeded by poor transportation routes, a landlocked location, lack of skilled labor, and political instability.

Chad
The Republic of Chad has one of the lowest population densities in Africa. Nomadic Arab herdsmen roam the dry lands with their animals in the north. In the south, black Africans grow some commercial crops. Independence from France was gained in 1960; conflicts between the north and south have marked Chad's politics since then.

Comoros
An Islamic republic, Comoros is an island nation situated between Madagascar and southwestern Africa. The nation was formerly ruled by France and gained independence in 1975. The economic mainstay is agriculture, and most Comorans practice subsistence farming and fishing.

Congo
The Congo is a Socialist republic that sits on the equator and is largely clothed in equatorial rain forest. Brazzaville was the commercial center of the former colony of French Equatorial Africa; the Congo became independent in 1960. It now benefits economically from the early groundwork laid for service and transport industries.

Djibouti
Set on the Gulf of Aden in East Africa, the Republic of Djibouti is mainly a stony desert. Traditional nomadic herding continues as a way of life for many Djiboutians. Formerly under French control, the nation became independent in 1977.

Egypt
Occupying the extreme northeast corner of Africa, Egypt is a Socialist republic that is mostly desert. The nation has a very long and rich history but today suffers from wars, shifting alliances, and limited natural resources. Agriculture, centered in the Nile Valley, remains an

Right: Most Ethiopians are subsistence farmers who live in small villages such as this one. These villages range in size from a few people to several hundred and feature small stone houses or mud huts with thatched roofs.

Africa

Countries continued

economic mainstay. Offshore petroleum will most likely continue its economic role, and tourism is a contributor as well.

Equatorial Guinea

On Africa's west coast near the equator sits Equatorial Guinea. Previously a Spanish colony, the republic gained independence in 1968. The economy is based on agriculture and forestry.

Ethiopia

Formerly known as Abyssinia, Ethiopia has a very long history. Until 1975, it was a kingdom ruled by a house said to be descended from King Solomon and the Queen of Sheba. Today, Ethiopia is a Socialist republic. Political instability and drought have taken their toll on Ethiopia's agricultural economy. Subsistence farming remains a major activity, though much arable land is uncultivated.

Gabon

Covered with dense rain forests, Gabon is a republic that sits on the equator in West Africa. Formerly controlled by several European nations, Gabon gained independence from France in 1960. The most important activities are oil production, forestry, and mining, although many people continue subsistence farming. The economy depends on foreign investment and imported labor.

Gambia

This narrow strip of land stretches along either bank of the Gambia (Gambie) River in West Africa. Formerly under British rule, the nation achieved independence in 1965 and became a republic in 1970. Gambia's economy relies on peanut production, but fishing and tourism have expanded in recent years.

Ghana

Formerly known as the Gold Coast, Ghana was one of the first countries to achieve independence from Britain in 1957. This West African country is predominantly agricultural, but its natural resources are diverse. Periods have unrest have resulted in the present military government.

Guinea

Ruled by France until 1958, Guinea is West Africa's most mountainous country. Agriculture is important, along with mining. In recent years, the military set up a provisional government and banned political parties.

Guinea-Bissau

Formerly a Portuguese province, this Atlantic coast republic has been independent since 1974. The economy is underdeveloped and dependent upon agriculture.

Ivory Coast

Until 1960, Ivory Coast was under French rule, but it is now an independent republic. It is potentially one of the richest countries of West Africa. Once solely dependent on the export of coffee and cocoa, Ivory Coast now produces and exports a variety of agricultural goods. Petroleum, textile, and apparel industries contribute to the strong economy.

Kenya

Straddling the equator in East Africa, Kenya became independent from Britain in 1963. Scenic terrain, tropical beaches, and abundant wildlife have given this republic a thriving tourist industry, and land has been set aside for national parks and game preserves. Agriculture, including the raising of livestock, is the leading economic contributor. Recent administrations have pursued a policy of Africanization, under which land and other holdings have been transferred from European to African hands.

Lesotho

Lesotho is a small, landlocked constitutional monarchy that is dependent economically upon South Africa, which surrounds it. Agriculture remains at the subsistence level, and livestock raising is important.

Liberia

This is the oldest independent country in West Africa, having been established in 1822 as an American settlement for freed slaves and granted independence twenty-five years later. The nation is a republic but is currently under martial rule. Liberia owes its healthy economy largely to an open-door policy, which has made its extensive resources attractive to foreign nations.

Libya

This North African nation is a Socialist republic that is under the leadership of Colonel Mu'ammar al-Qadhafi. The discovery of oil in 1959 propelled Libya from the ranks of the world's poorest nations to one of its leading oil producers. Most of Libya is covered by the Sahara Desert, and the limited agriculture has been further hurt by Libyan farmers migrating to the cities. Libya's support of terrorist activities led to a controversial United States air strike against the country in 1986, and several nations have instituted economic sanctions against the nation.

Madagascar

Lying some 240 miles (400 kilometers) off the southeastern African coast, Madagascar is an island in the Indian Ocean. It gained independence from France in 1960 and is now a republic.

Above: Ghana was one of the first African countries to become independent from European rule. A variety of crops are grown and traded here, as this street market shows, but cocoa is the most important export.

Right: The oasis town of Béchar, Algeria, is situated in the foothills of the Atlas Mountains. These coastal mountains prevent moisture from reaching inland and thereby contribute to the arid conditions of the huge Sahara Desert.

Below: The city of Aswān marked ancient Egypt's southern frontier. Now known for the nearby Aswān High Dam (As-Sadd al-ʿĀlī), this city on the Nile River has a hot, dry climate and is a popular winter resort.

Right: These Nigerians are fishing in the Niger River, an important activity in this region. Though relatively small in area, Nigeria is the most populous African nation.

Africa

Countries continued

Madagascar is chiefly an agricultural nation, with the majority of the work force engaged in farming or herding.

Malawi

This landlocked republic in East Africa became independent from Britain in 1964. Malawi relies almost entirely on agriculture, though production is limited.

Mali

Formerly under French control, the Republic of Mali gained independence in 1960. One of the world's poorest nations, Mali depends primarily on agriculture but is limited by a poor climate and a desert terrain. Mali is a landlocked nation in West Africa.

Mauritania

This largely dry desert faces the Atlantic Ocean in West Africa. Mauritania was ruled by France until 1960; it is now under provisional military rule. The economy is based on agriculture, with many farmers producing only subsistence-level output.

Mauritius

This group of islands in the Indian Ocean five hundred miles (eight hundred kilometers) east of Madagascar is a parliamentary state, having gained independence from France in 1968. Sugar remains fundamental to the economy.

Mayotte

One of the Comoros Islands situated in the Mozambique Channel, Mayotte is a territorial collectivity of France. Unlike the mostly Muslim population of the other islands, most residents of Mayotte are Roman Catholic descendants of Malagasy immigrants.

Morocco

The Kingdom of Morocco has been independent from France since 1956. The nation is situated at the extreme northwest of the continent, on the Atlantic Ocean and Mediterranean Sea. Although agriculture employs much of the work force and is an important activity, the nation depends on mining for most of its income. Severe drought,

rising dependency on imported oil, and a costly war in Western Sahara have slowed productivity, while investment by Arab countries has bolstered the economy.

Mozambique

This former Portuguese territory is now a Socialist republic that has been independent since 1975. Stretching along the southeast coast of Africa, Mozambique has an underdeveloped economy that is centered around agriculture and transport services. Continued guerrilla fighting, severe drought, and subsequent food shortages have created a crisis situation in Mozambique.

Namibia

Situated on the southwest tip of Africa, Namibia is governed by South Africa. The economy rests on the mining of diamonds, copper, lead, and other minerals. Agriculture makes a marginal contribution. South Africa has refused international orders to withdraw from the nation; negotiations for independence continue.

Niger

This landlocked nation in West Africa is now under a provisional military government, but it became independent from France in 1960. Niger's economy is agricultural, although arable land is scarce and drought common. Civilians now take part in the political system.

Nigeria

Africa's most populous nation, Nigeria was under British rule until 1960. The West African nation has suffered from civil war and political instability since independence and is now under a provisional military government. Nigeria's economy is based on mining and agriculture; petroleum is very important, but oil revenues have been declining.

Réunion

Réunion – an island in the Indian Ocean some 560 miles (900 kilometers) east of Madagascar – is an overseas department of France. Réunion's traditional sugar crop continues as its economic mainstay, although commercial fishing and shellfish are also important.

Left: The pyramids at Giza (Al-Jīzah), Egypt, were constructed between 2650 and 2550 B.C. and remain one of the wonders of the ancient world. The pharaohs for whom they were erected employed vast numbers of people and primitive tools to create these architectural wonders and such others as the tomb of Tutankhamen and the huge temples at Luxor (Al-Uqṣur) and Karnak (Al-Karnak).

Left: Olduvai Gorge, Tanzania, has been the site of numerous archaeological digs. After World War I, animal fossils were discovered here, but it was not until the Leakeys found evidence of human remains that investigation of the gorge began in earnest. Since then, Olduvai Gorge has yielded many fossils and artifacts that evidence thousands of years of prehistoric habitation. The earliest remains at Olduvai are estimated to be about two million years old.

Rwanda

This landlocked East African republic was under Belgian rule and became independent in 1962. Agriculture is the major activity, although plagued by the erosion and overpopulation of arable land. Tourism is small but growing.

St. Helena

This small volcanic island 1,200 miles (1,900 kilometers) west of the African mainland is a British colony. A number of other islands are associated with it, particularly Ascension Island, 700 miles (1,100 kilometers) to the northwest.

São Tomé and Príncipe

These islands off western Africa were formerly under Portuguese administration, having gained independence in 1975. Cocoa dominates São Tomé and Príncipe's economy.

Senegal

Senegal, situated on the western coast of Africa, was under French rule. It became an independent republic in 1960. The mainstays of the economy are petroleum, agriculture, fishing, and mining. Tourism is a rapidly growing new industry.

Seychelles

This group of more than one hundred islands in the Indian Ocean, some 1,000 (1,600 kilometers) east of the Kenyan coast, was formerly a British colony. Seychelles achieved independence in 1976. The basis of the economy is tourism, with foreign visitors attracted by the tropical climate, white-sand beaches, and exotic flora and fauna found on the islands.

Sierra Leone

Sierra Leone is a West African republic that was under British domination until 1961. The nation is one of the world's largest producers of industrial and commercial diamonds. Poor soil, a fluctuating tropical climate, and traditional farming methods keep crop yields low.

Somalia

Jutting along the northeast corner of Africa, Somalia is a Socialist republic. The economy is based in agriculture, though activity is restricted to the vicinity of the rivers and certain coastal districts. The region was once under British and Italian domination, and it became independent in 1960.

South Africa

The discovery of gold and diamonds in South Africa in the late 1800s shaped this republic's prosperous economy. Mining remains a mainstay, as does agriculture; the nation is almost self-sufficient in food production. Today, South Africa is one of the richest and most developed nations in Africa, yet, in spite of increased racial tension and violent conflicts, the white-run, Afrikaner government continues to suppress the black majority population with its apartheid system.

Sudan

A republic in northeastern Africa, Sudan overcame British administration in 1956. A series of military coups since that time has burdened the country with economic and political instability. The economy is based on agriculture. Irrigation has made arid Sudan a leading producer of cotton, although the land is vulnerable to drought.

Swaziland

The Kingdom of Swaziland is a small, landlocked country in southern Africa, which became independent from British rule in 1968. Most Swazi are subsistence farmers. Europeans own nearly half the land and raise most of the cash crops.

Tanzania

Independent since 1961, Tanzania is an East African republic. Agriculture accounts for most export earnings and employs 80 percent of the work force. Yet two-thirds of the land cannot be cultivated because of lack of water and tsetse-fly infestation.

Togo

This West African republic has suffered internal strife and a military dominance since separating with France in 1960. Togo has one of the world's largest phosphate reserves. Although Togo is an agricultural nation, farmland is scarce.

Tunisia

The Republic of Tunisia sits at the tip of northern Africa. It became independent from France in 1956. The economy is based in agriculture and oil. Tourism is growing despite an unemployment problem.

Uganda

This East African republic sits on the equator. Political instability has marked the government since independence from Britain came in 1962. Despite attempts to diversify the economy, the country remains largely agricultural.

Western Sahara

Occupied by Morocco, Western Sahara sits on the northwest corner of Africa, facing the Atlantic Ocean. Most of the nation is desert, with a rocky barren soil that severely limits agriculture. In Western Sahara are found valuable phosphate deposits – the source of most export income.

Zaire

This central African republic was under Belgian domination until 1960. Mining has supplanted agriculture in economic importance and now dominates the economy. Agriculture continues to employ most Zairians, however, and subsistence farming is practiced in nearly every region. The government has stabilized under the present administration.

Zambia

Landlocked in southern Africa, Zambia became an independent republic in 1964. The economy is based in copper, which is the major export. Declining copper prices and a severe drought are problematic.

Zimbabwe

Zimbabwe is a landlocked republic in southern Africa that became free of British rule in 1980. Despite Zimbabwe's move toward stability since independence, some internal unrest continues. The nation's natural resources have played a key role in its sustained economic growth. The subtropical climate supports the exportation of many agricultural products and makes large-scale cattle ranching feasible.

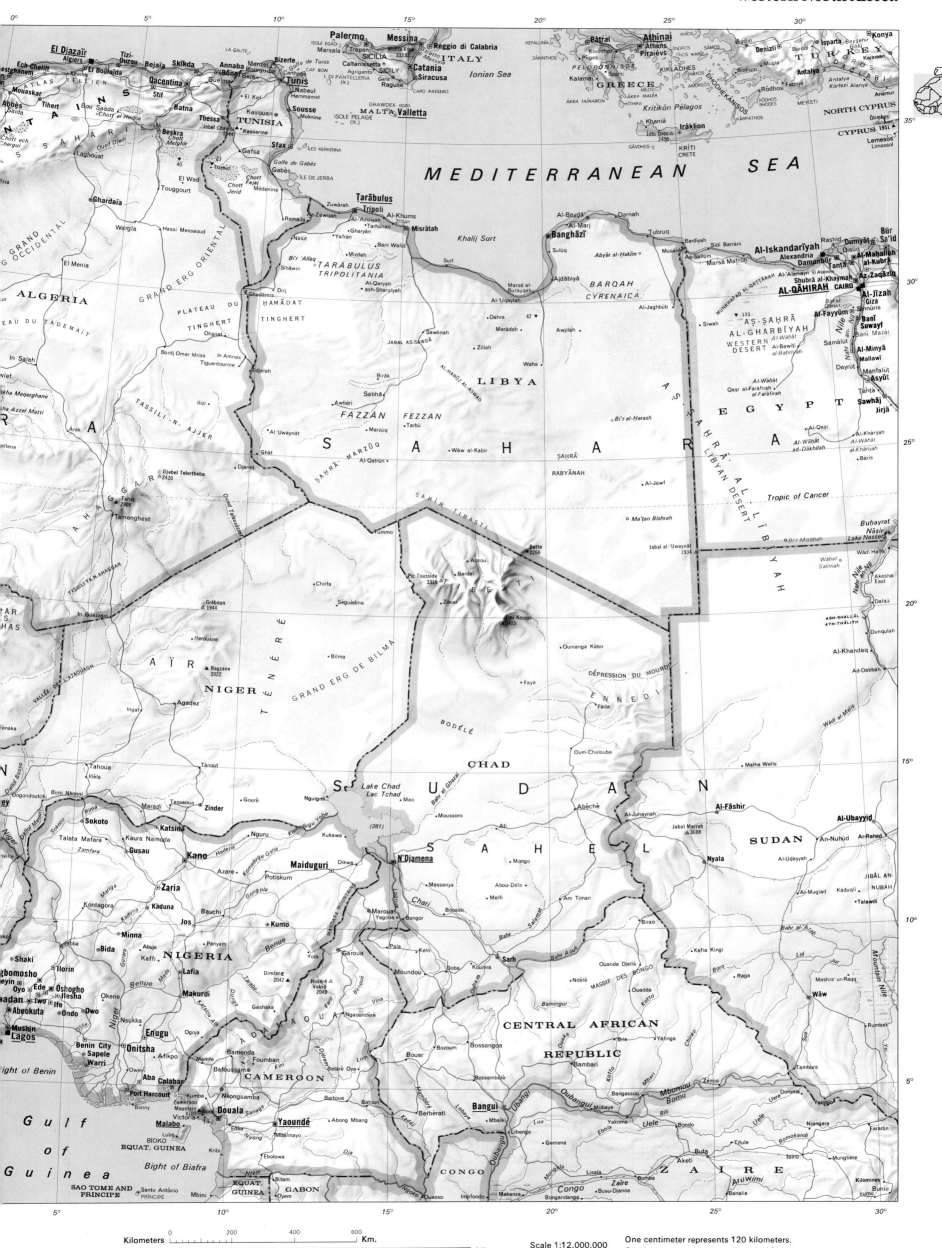

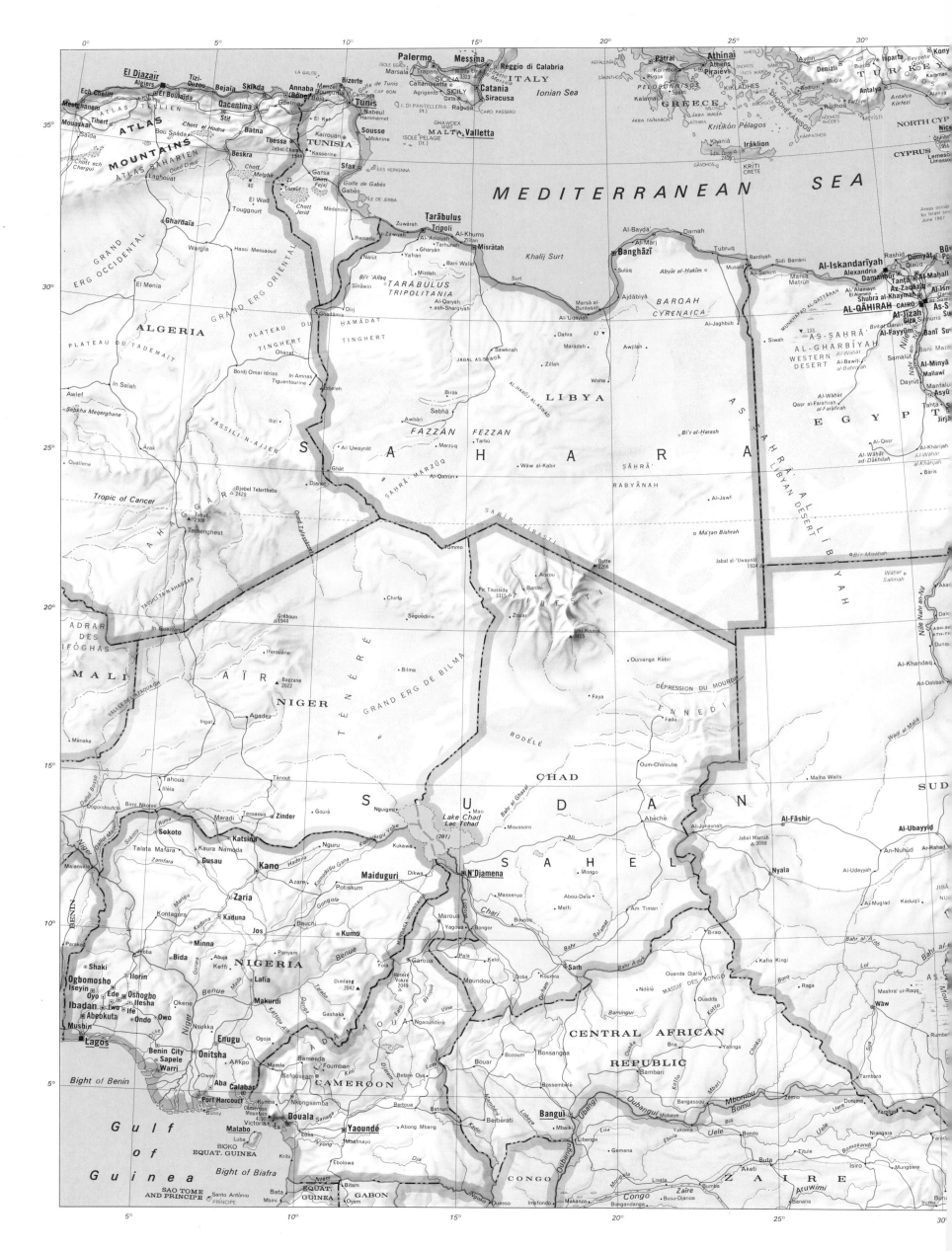

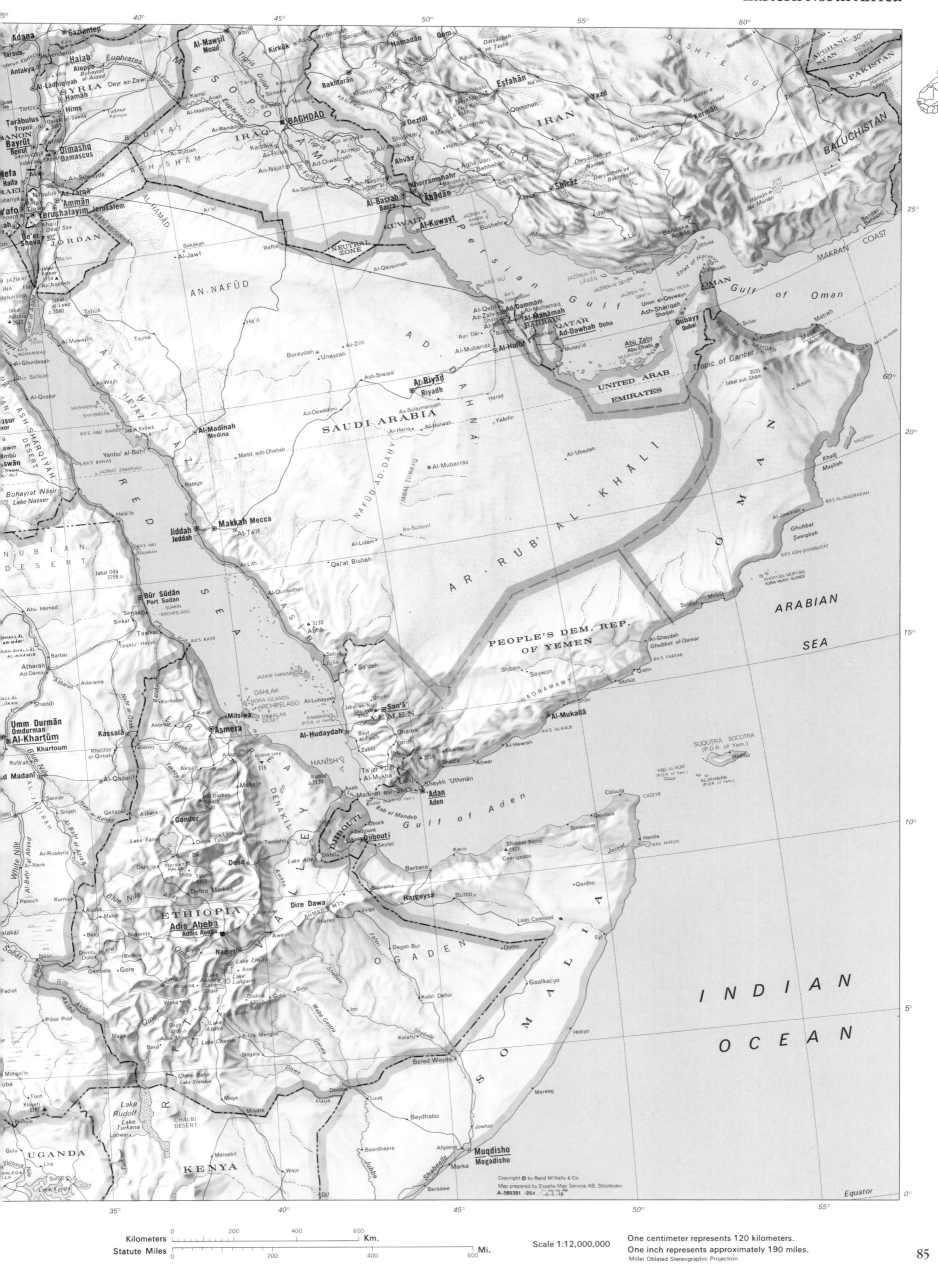

Kilometers 0 200 400 600 Km.

Statute Miles 0 200 400 600 Mi.

Scale 1:12,000,000

One centimeter represents 120 kilometers.
One inch represents approximately 190 miles.
Miller Oblated Stereographic Projection

Copyright © by Rand McNally & Co.
Map prepared by Esselte Map Service AB, Stockholm.
A-589391 -264

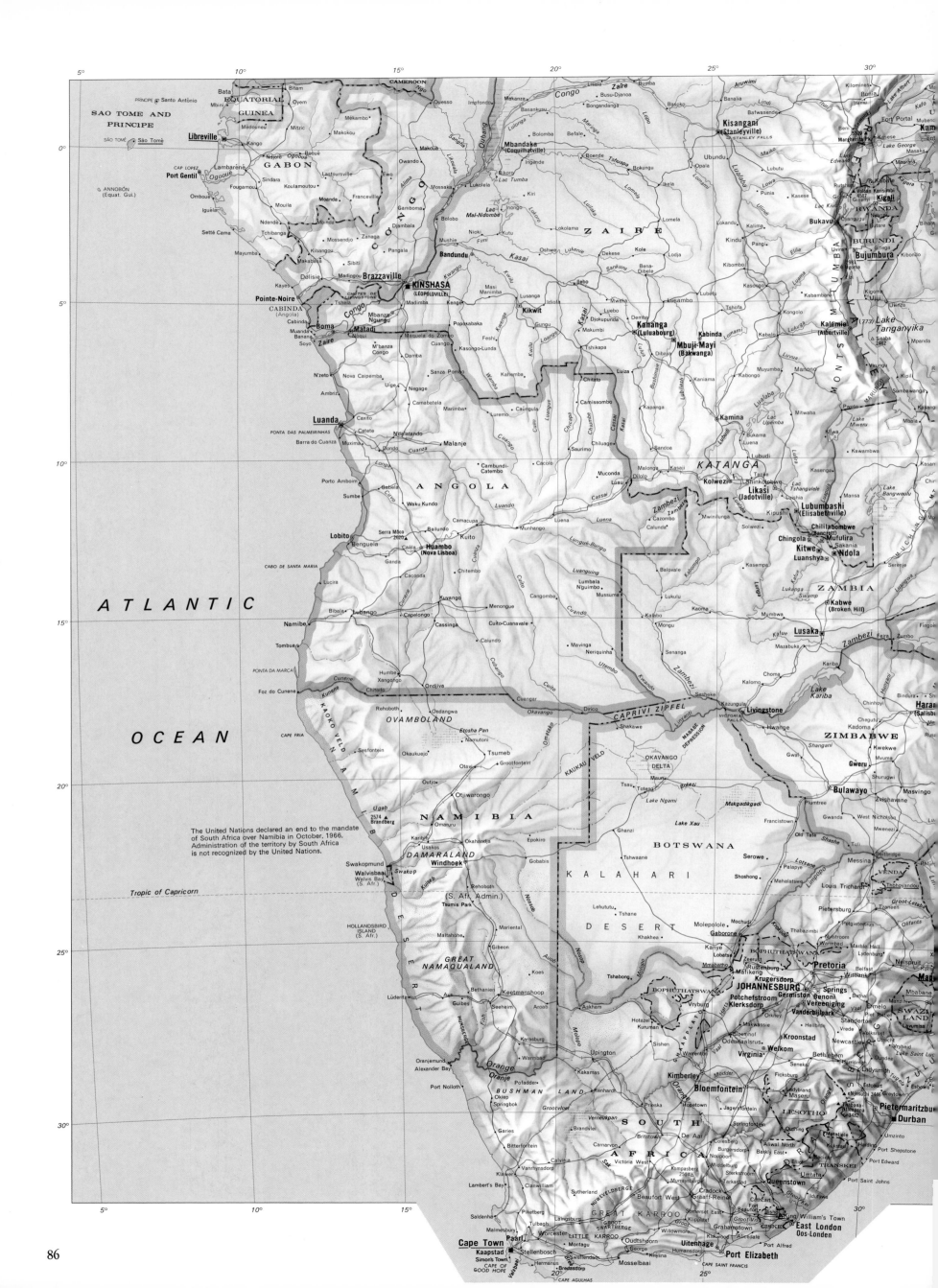

The United Nations declared an end to the mandate
of South Africa over Namibia in October, 1966.
Administration of the territory by South Africa
is not recognized by the United Nations.

INDIAN OCEAN

Equator

SOMALIA

KENYA

Nairobi
Machakos

Mombasa

MASAI
STEPPE

Tanga

Zanzibar

Dar es Salaam

TANZANIA

SEYCHELLES

Victoria

AMIRANTE ISLANDS
(Sey.)   ÎLE DESROCHES
(Sey.)   PLATTE ISLAND (Sey.)

ALPHONSE ISLAND (Sey.)   COETIVY ISLAND
(Sey.)

ALDABRA ISLAND
(Sey.)   PROVIDENCE ISLAND
(Sey.)

COSMOLEDO I.
(Sey.)   SAINT PIERRE ISLAND
(Sey.)   CERF ISLAND
(Sey.)

ASSUMPTION ISLAND
(Sey.)   ASTOVE ISLAND
(Sey.)   FARQUHAR GROUP
(Sey.)

AGALEGA ISLANDS
(Mauritius)

MOZAMBIQUE

Lake
Nyasa
Lake Malawi

MALAWI

Lilongwe

Zomba
Blantyre

Quelimane

Beira

CABO DELGADO

Nacala

Nampula

COMOROS
Moroni
ARCHIPEL DES COMORES
Dzaoudzi
MAYOTTE
(Fr.)

ÎLES GLORIEUSES
(Reunion)

CAP D'AMBRE

Antsiranana

NOSY BE
Hell-Ville

MASSIF DU
TSARATANANA

Sambava

Antalaha

Mahajanga

Marovoay

PRESQU' ÎLE
DE MASOALA

ÎLE TROMELIN
(Reunion)

MADAGASCAR

Antananarivo

Antsirabe

Toamasina

Fianarantsoa

Toliara

Faradofay

CAP SAINTE-MARIE

Port Louis
Curepipe   Mahébourg
MAURITIUS

Le Port   Saint-Denis
Saint-Paul   RÉUNION
Saint-Pierre   (Fr.)

MASCARENE
ISLANDS

Tropic of Capricorn

INDIAN OCEAN

Kilometers   0   200   400   600   Km.
Statute Miles   0   200   400   600   Mi.

Scale 1:12,000,000

One centimeter represents 120 kilometers.
One inch represents approximately 190 miles.

Miller Oblated Stereographic Projection

87

Oceania
Profile

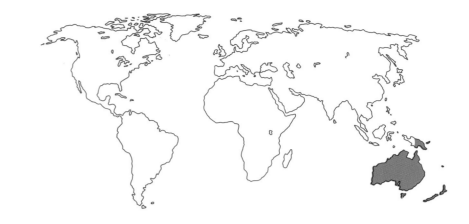

Location and Size

Oceania comprises Australia, New Zealand, Papua New Guinea, and a number of island countries scattered over the southern and central Pacific Ocean. Together, the three countries mentioned above make up nearly 99 percent of the total land area and contain nearly 92 percent of the total population of all Oceania. The continent of Australia alone contains over 90 percent of the total land area and nearly two-thirds of the total population.

The principal Pacific islands and island groups within Oceania may be grouped into three areas: Melanesia, Micronesia, and Polynesia. Occupying the smallest area, Melanesia lies closest to Australia. It extends northwest to southeast, from Papua New Guinea to the Solomon Islands, New Caledonia, Vanuatu, and Fiji. Melanesia means the "black islands."

Micronesia, meaning the "little islands," contains no islands as large as the main ones of Melanesia but is composed of tiny atolls. Polynesia – meaning "many islands" – covers the largest area of the three. Some of these islands are associated politically with the United States, France, or Chile.

Australia extends nearly 2,300 miles (3,700 kilometers) north to south, from Cape York Peninsula in Queensland to South East Cape in Tasmania. Its west-east expanse is similar, stretching from the Western Australia coast near Carnarvon to the Pacific margins of Queensland and New South Wales. Australia is the only continent in the world that is also a country; though it is the world's smallest continent, it is one of its biggest countries. Situated entirely in the Southern Hemisphere, Australia straddles the Tropic of Capricorn.

Landscape

For the most part, Australia is a vast, undulating desert plateau. The great exceptions are: the eastern mountains, or the Great Dividing Range, extending from Cape York Peninsula in the north to Victoria in the south; the lowland area of the central basin, extending from eastern South Australia to the Gulf of Carpentaria; and the plains that are found around most of the coast. Australia has proportionally more desert area than any other continent, and water sources are a great problem in much of the nation.

Australia's rivers fall into two main types. Many comparatively short rivers flow toward the east coast from the divide of the eastern highlands. More major river systems cross parts of the interior, with the Murray and its tributaries the largest. These rivers have a large discharge in their headwaters but lose much as they flow westward across the drier interior lands of the central basin. Parts of this area are drained by rivers that dry up in the hot season or reach lakes whose surface areas vary greatly throughout the year.

A distinctive water feature of Australia is its series of artesian basins. The Great Artesian Basin underlies much of western Queensland, northeastern South Australia, and northwestern New South Wales, extending for 600,000 square miles (1,554,000 square kilometers). In these basins, rainfall in the surrounding areas percolates underground and is stored under such great pressure that it gushes to the land surface through any opening. One needs only dig a hole in the ground to bring the water back to the surface. Artesian water does not, therefore, need to be pumped.

Farther south, the artesian Murray River basin occupies a smaller area. Western Australia has four smaller basins around its coastal margins. In general, the water in these basins is too salty for humans to drink.

The Great Barrier Reef, the world's largest coral reef, extends some 1,200 miles (1,930 kilometers) along Australia's northeastern coast. Although its name implies that it is one giant reef, the Great Barrier Reef is actually a series of more than 2,500 reefs. It is composed of more than three hundred species of corals in a dazzling array of colors and shapes. Its unique beauty and year-round warm waters attract many tourists, snorkelers, and skin divers from around the world.

New Zealand is a long narrow strip of land, divided into two islands by Cook Strait. The land is mostly mountainous and no location is more than 80 miles (130 kilometers) from the sea. The most rugged regions are found in the Southern Alps of South Island; North Island is slightly less mountainous but contains volcanic regions. Fertile, narrow plains

Left: The photogenic skyline of Sydney, Australia, features the Sydney Opera House and the Sydney Harbor Bridge. This metropolis on the southwestern coast is Australia's oldest and most populous.

Right: French Polynesia's reputation as a tropical paradise is well founded and over the years has attracted, among others, the mutinous crew of the *Bounty* and French painter Paul Gauguin. Here, the island of Bora-Bora rises in the distance.

Oceania

Profile continued

lie along some coastal areas.

Most other areas in Oceania are tropical, volcanic islands, filled with a variety of vegetation and animal life. Other islands are simply a series of coral atolls, such as the Gilbert Islands.

Climate

There are three main climates in Australia. Only the temperate humid climate is at all attractive to white settlers who are found only in limited parts of the country. Nowhere in the temperate areas does the average temperature of the coldest winter month, July, fall below freezing, and in summer the averages rise above 64°F (18°C), reaching above 72°F (22°C) in places. The extreme southwest of Western Australia has a Mediterranean type of climate, with summer temperatures reaching the

higher levels and a marked lack of summer rain.

Farther east, in southern South Australia and parts of western Victoria, similar summer temperatures prevail and the rainfall – mainly in the winter – is greater. Still in the temperate group, the east coast climate – from Tasmania to the central Queensland area – shows more even distribution of rainfall in the south. In the south, the highest monthly average temperatures are below 68°F (20°C), but in the north they are well above 72°F (22°C).

The northern coastal areas of the country experience tropical climates, in which even the coolest month has an average temperature 64°F (18°C). Here there is a marked summer maximum in the rainfall, with totals exceeding eighty inches (two thousand millimeters) in places.

The great heartland of Australia – from the Indian Ocean in the west, eastward to the interior slopes of the highlands of the Pacific-bordering states – is an area of marked rainfall deficiency with higher average temperatures than elsewhere in the continent. In the most arid central parts, precipitation rarely exceeds ten inches (250 millimeters). Here, the summer temperature may reach 80°F (27°C) and in the winter drops only to 54°F (12°C). Bordering this region, less extreme climates may be found.

Because Australia is south of the equator, its warmest months are December through March and its coldest are June through September. In other words, the seasons are the reverse of those in the Northern Hemisphere.

As a result of the moderating effects of the ocean, New Zealand experiences

a mild climate with slight seasonal variations. It is subtropical in the north and temperate farther south. The islands of Oceania lie within the tropics, so they experience warm climates.

History, Politics, and Economy

The first humans who lived in the western Pacific around thirty thousand years ago were Aboriginals who established a hunter-gatherer society. Migration from Malaya-Indonesia was helped by the natural land bridges that formed with the shallow sea level of the ice ages. Further migration occurred from Micronesia and Melanesia to Polynesia around 1,000 B.C.

Situated on the opposite side of the globe from Europe, this part of the world was among the last places to be visited by the European explorers. Ferdi-

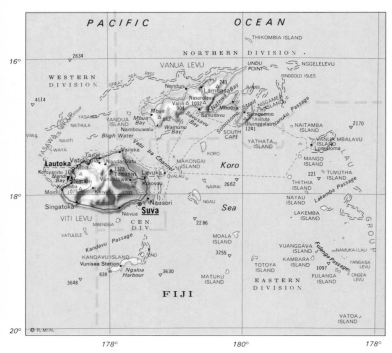

Above, right: These residents of Malakula, Vanuatu (New Hebrides), experience a tropical rain-forest climate year-round.

Right: West of Ayers Rock in the Australian Outback is a group of rocks known as the Olgas. They differ from the Rock in appearance and texture, yet they too display the types of ancient Aboriginal paintings for which the Rock is known.

Opposite: The Isle of Pines, shown here, is one of the several islands that make up New Caledonia. The climate and culture of this French territory attract tourists.

nand Magellan was one of the first to arrive in Oceania when he discovered Guam in 1521.

In 1606, Dutch navigators landed on the northern Australian coast and the Cape York Peninsula. Little impressed by the hot lands, the Dutch took no further interest in this area, which they called New Holland. Some eighty-two years later, the English explorer William Dampier reached the barren wastes of the northwestern coast, and reported unenthusiastically of his finds on his return home. Captain James Cook sailed to Oceania on three voyages – from 1769 to 1779 – and explored Tahiti and New Zealand before reaching Australia. He subsequently laid formal claim to Australia for Great Britain.

Interest in this distant land did not grow, however, until after Great Britain had lost its American penal colonies a few years later. The earliest colony, Port Jackson (now Sydney), in New South Wales, was founded in 1788, and many of the early white residents were British convicts.

For the next thirty years or so, the Blue Mountains presented an impenetrable barrier to westward expansion. Then, beginning in the early 1800s, a squatter movement spread the population to other parts of the island. During subsequent years, many new settlements were established: Tasmania in 1803, Brisbane in 1824, the Swan River colony in the distant southwest in 1829, Melbourne in 1835, and Adelaide in 1836. In turn, settlements became provinces

or colonies: Tasmania (1825), Western Australia (1831), South Australia (1834), Victoria (1851), and Queensland (1859). By 1850 the population had risen to just over 400,000. But it was not until the early 1860s, when the population had risen to over one million, that the first south-north crossing of the country was made.

The first attraction of the new lands was for farming. Merino sheep from Spain soon flourished here and produced the world's finest wool. But with the discovery of gold in 1850, mineral prospecting received a great lift, and many new mining settlements were established.

In 1901, the Commonwealth of Australia claimed independence from the British crown. The nation fought on the side of the British during both world wars.

Today, more attention is being paid to the rights of the indigenous Australian Aboriginals, who number about 160,000. Most are of mixed descent – part Aboriginal, part Anglo – and live on special reserves or on the fringe of white society. To some extent, they maintain their traditional life-style, particularly in art and religion.

The Commonwealth of Australia is a parliamentary state, with a constitution similar to that of the United States. The nation is divided into six states and presides over two territories.

Australia's economy is similar to economies in other developed nations, characterized by a postwar shift from

agriculture to industry and services, and problems of inflation and unemployment. Wool is a major export, and livestock raising takes place on relatively flat, wide grazing lands surrounding an arid central region. Commercial crop raising is concentrated on a fertile southeastern plain. Plentiful mineral resources such as gold, cobalt, copper, manganese, silver, tin, and tungsten provide for a strong mining industry.

New Zealand has a history similar to that of Australia. Captain James Cook first charted the islands in the late 1700s. European settlement was hindered by the fierce Maori, the original settlers, thought to have migrated from Polynesia around A.D. 1000. Nonetheless, European traders and hunters began to arrive, and after an 1840 treaty with the Maori, British rule was established and more settlers were drawn to the islands. Independence came in the 1940s. Today, the population is mainly white, but the number of Maoris, unlike the Aboriginals of Australia, is growing.

Like Australia, New Zealand is a parliamentary state, but it has no written constitution. The nation recognizes Britain's Elizabeth II as queen of New Zealand.

Farming and farm-related industries dominate New Zealand's developed economy. The raising of livestock, particularly sheep, is especially important. The number of livestock on the islands is far larger than the number of people.

After Captain James Cook's exploratory voyages in the late 1700s, the British

and French began to settle on some of the islands of Oceania. Many of the indigenous cultures were altered by European missionaries who came to the region in the nineteenth century. By 1900, the region had mostly come under European dominion.

Japan occupied much of Oceania during World War II, and the South Pacific became a hot battlefield, particularly around New Guinea and the Solomon Islands. After the war, some of the islands were placed under the United Nations trusts until they could achieve self-government. The first nation to realize independence was Western Samoa in 1962; it is now a constitutional monarchy. In 1970, Fiji and Tonga also became independent. Independence soon followed for Papua New Guinea (1975), the Solomon Islands and Tuvalu (1978), Kiribati (1979), and Vanuatu (1980).

For the most part, independence for the island nations of Oceania came peacefully. Recently, however, violence has erupted in New Caledonia's struggle for independence. A group of indigenous Kanaks refuses to discuss limited autonomy with France and will not accept anything less than full independence for New Caledonia.

Today, some of the island nations – such as Fiji, Kiribati, and Nauru – are republics. Some – such as New Caledonia, French Polynesia, and Guam – are administered by Western nations. The islands struggle to make their way in the world economy, and increased tourism in Oceania has helped.

American Samoa

The Samoan Islands are a Polynesian group approximately midway between Australia and Hawaii. The eastern islands have been an unincorporated territory of the United States since 1900. Fishing, especially for tuna, is important, providing the major export item. Other exports include pet foods and native crafts.

Australia

The Land Down Under is the smallest of continents and one of the world's largest countries. Relatively dry (one-third of the land is desert) and thinly populated, this island was originally settled by British convicts, though native Aboriginals have existed on the land for over thirty thousand years. Sheep raising is an important activity, and wool is a major export. Australia fought on the side of the British in both world wars, and postwar years have seen increased attention paid to the rights of the dwindling Aboriginal population.

Cook Islands

Widely scattered throughout the southwest Pacific, these Polynesian islands are mostly of volcanic origin. First discovered in 1773 by Captain James Cook, they were a British protectorate, then a New Zealand territory. Since 1965, however, the Cook Islands have been self-governed.

Fiji

Fiji is a group of nearly 850 islands in the South Pacific. Little is known about Fiji before the arrival of Europeans, though early Melanesians probably migrated there from Indonesia, followed by Polynesian settlers in the second century. Only about one hundred of the islands are inhabited, and traditional sugar cane growing is a principal economic activity. Tourism is growing, and expansion of forestry is planned. The land is characterized by mountains, valleys, and rain forests.

French Polynesia

These South Pacific islands are an overseas French territory and are spread over roughly 1.5 million square miles (3.9 million square kilometers). The territory includes the Marquesas (Marquises) Islands, the Society (Société) Islands, the Tuamotu Archipelago, the Gambier Islands, and the Austral (Australes) Islands. The Marquesas, known for their beauty, form the northernmost group. The Society Islands include Tahiti and Bora-Bora, both popular tourist spots. Pearls, copra, and precision instruments are exported, while coconut, mother-of-pearl, and tourism are also economic contributors. Most inhabitants are Polynesian, with minorities including Chinese and French. The climate is tropical. The French use several of the islands for nuclear testing.

Guam

This largest and most southerly island in the Marianas Archipelago of Micronesia is an unincorporated territory of the United States, ceded from Spain in 1898. It is the United States' most westerly Pacific outpost and is of major strategic importance both as a naval and air base. About a quarter of the present population is United States service personnel and their families. The native population is mainly of Malay origin. Agriculture is a primary activity.

Kiribati

The people of Kiribati, a nation of thirty-three islands in the central Pacific, are mostly Micronesian. Almost all the population lives on the Gilbert Islands in small villages. The official language is English, but Gilbertese is also spoken. With a relatively small land area and few natural resources, Kiribati natives live a subsistence existence. The islands are mostly coral reefs, and the climate is tropical. Kiribati was formerly part of the Gilbert and Ellice Islands; it became independent in 1979. The nation is dependent on economic aid from Australia, New Zealand, and Great Britain.

Nauru

A tiny Micronesian coral island approximately 8.1 square miles (21 square kilometers) in area, Nauru's core contains extensive deposits of high grade phosphates, its sole export. With limited agriculture, nearly all food must be imported. Once governed by Australia, Nauru gained independence in 1968, then gained control of European interests in the phosphate industry in 1970. Most inhabitants are of mixed Polynesian, Melanesian, and Micronesian stock, and the climate is tropical. The government is establishing trust funds to support islanders when the phosphate resources are depleted.

New Caledonia

New Caledonia is a French overseas territory and includes the Isle of Pines and the Loyalty (Loyauté) and Bélep islands. The principal economic activity, the mining and smelting of nickel, has decreased over the years. Copra and coffee are exported, and tourism is important. New Caledonia, the main island, is mountainous, and all the islands are tropical in climate. Most inhabitants are Melanesians, or Kanaks, but there are some French, Asian, and Polynesian inhabitants. Violence erupted in the 1980s, stemming from the desire of the Kanaks for independence.

New Zealand

New Zealand consists of two large islands – North Island and South Island – and many smaller islands scattered throughout the South Pacific. The scenic terrain is greatly varied, ranging from fjords and mountains to a volcanic plateau. Manufacturing, including food-processing and paper industries, is an expanding economic sector, as is tourism. New Zealand supported Britain in both world wars; advancing the rights of the Maori population has become a priority.

Niue

Geographically within the Cook Islands, Niue's area is more than that of all the other islands in that group together, but its population is much smaller. It achieved self-government in 1974 but is economically dependent upon its mother country, New Zealand. Copra, sweet potatoes, and bananas are the main crops.

Norfolk Island

An Australian territory 900 miles (1,400 kilometers) east of the New South Wales coast, this island was originally used as a penal settlement. In 1856, 194 *Bounty* descendants moved from Pitcairn to Norfolk Island. Today, Norfolk's attractive scenery, beaches, and climate have encouraged tourism.

Pacific Islands, Trust Territory of the

Following World War II, the United States was appointed by the United Nations to act as trustee of all formerly Japanese-mandated islands in the Pacific

Right: South Island is the larger, more mountainous, and less populated of the two major islands that make up New Zealand. Shown here is Queenstown, on Lake Wakatipu.

Below: This Aboriginal man is drawing on the Wessel Islands in a manner largely unmodified since the Stone Age.

Below: Some of the geysers and hot springs of New Zealand's North Island have been harnessed to produce electricity. Shown here is Pokutu Geyser.

Bottom: Sheep and cattle farming are all-important to New Zealand. Here cattle graze near Mount Egmont (Taranaki) on North Island.

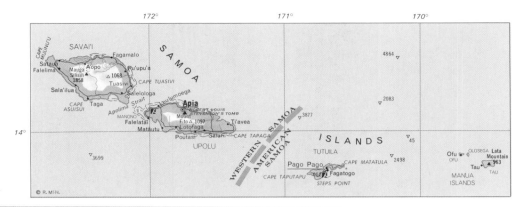

between 1° and 22° north, and 130° and 172° east. These Micronesian islands – over 2,100 atolls and smaller islands – are mainly in the Caroline, Marshall, and Marianas groups and are scattered over three million square miles (eight million square kilometers) of ocean. Each district has its own elected local government.

Papua New Guinea

This nation consists of the eastern half of New Guinea Island, plus New Britain, New Ireland, Bougainville, and six hundred smaller islands. Terrain includes swamps, mountains, broad valleys, volcanoes, and rain forests. It is thought that New Guinea has been inhabited for thousands of years. Almost all inhabitants are Melanesians. More than seven hundred languages are spoken, but most people also speak Motu or a dialect of English. After being occupied by the Japanese in World War II, Papua and New Guinea were united as an Australian territory. The nation became independent in 1975; it has close ties with Australia.

Pitcairn

Lying approximately midway between New Zealand and Panama, Pitcairn is a Polynesian island whose population is declining. Its original inhabitants, who arrived in 1767, were nine mutineers from the *Bounty*, who brought with them eighteen Tahitians. In 1856, the entire population of 194 moved to Norfolk Island, but some returned soon afterward. Pitcairn is a British dependency.

Solomon Islands

Comprising one of the largest island groups in Melanesia in the southwest Pacific, the Solomons are mountainous, forested, and contain low-lying coral atolls. The climate is warm and damp, with heavy annual rainfall. The population is primarily rural, and much of its social structure is patterned on traditional village life. The economy is based on subsistence farming. The area was the site of fierce battles between the Japanese and Allied forces during World War II. In 1978, the islands became a sovereign nation.

Tokelau

Made up of three Polynesian atolls three hundred miles (480 kilometers) north of Western Samoa, Tokelau totals only four square miles (ten square kilometers) in area. An island territory of New Zealand, the country relies heavily on its mother country for economic aid.

Tonga

Due east of Fiji, Tonga consists of about 150 coral and volcanic islands. Most of the islands are coral reefs, but many have fertile soil. Almost all Tongans are Polynesian, and about two-thirds of them live on the main island of Tongatapu. The climate is subtropical. Tonga's economy is dominated by both subsistence and plantation agriculture. This Polynesian nation was a British protectorate until it became independent in 1970.

Tuvalu

Tuvalu consists of nine islands, most of them atolls surrounding lagoons. There is little cultivable soil, and fishing is a major activity. Tuvalu has minimal manufacturing and no mining. The climate is tropical, and most people are Polynesian. Tuvaluans weave mats and baskets for export, and they speak Tuvaluan, derived from Polynesian. The island group became independent from Great Britain in 1978.

Vanuatu

Formerly a joint territory of Britain and France known as the New Hebrides, Vanuatu became independent in 1980. The economy is based on agriculture, and copra is the primary export crop. Fishing is also important, as is the growing tourist industry. Most residents are of Melanesian descent, but there are minorities of Asians, Europeans, and Polynesians. Languages include English and French, the languages of former rulers; and Bislama, a mixture of English and Melanesian.

Wallis and Futuna

The Wallis Islands, Futuna, and Alofi are grouped 380 miles (600 kilometers) northwest of Fiji within Polynesia. Formerly a French protectorate, they are now an overseas territory of France and are mandated by their own internal government. Farming is important, as is fishing.

Western Samoa

Four inhabited Polynesian islands and a number of smaller ones northeast of Fiji and west of American Samoa make up Western Samoa. Bananas, coconuts, and tropical fruits are the most important crops grown and exported. Formerly administered by New Zealand, Western Samoa gained independence and self-government in 1962. Most Western Samoans are of Polynesian descent, and a significant minority is of mixed Samoan and European heritage.

Above: The scattered islands of Oceania contain several distinct indigenous groups. Micronesians generally have dark brown skin and straight black hair. Polynesians are tall, with light brown skin and black hair. Melanesians have dark brown skin and very curly hair, evidenced by these natives of Fiji.

Right: Most New Zealanders are native-born descendants of British immigrants, like this schoolboy. Maoris, of Polynesian descent, were the original settlers, but today they make up less than ten percent of the population.

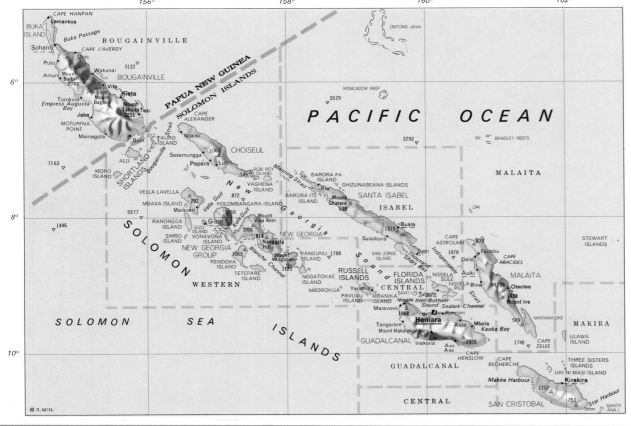

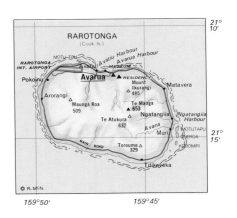

Below: Some of the islands of Oceania are coral atolls built on volcanic bases, and some are formed from the tips of volcanoes on the ocean floor. The volcanic Austral Seamounts are part of French Polynesia. Shown here is the opening from a collapsed volcano, or a caldera, on Rapa.

PACIFIC OCEAN

130° 135° 140° 145° 150°

0° Equator

PULAU WAIGEO
Selat Dampier
SALAWATI
SORONG
JAZIRAH DOBERAI
PULAU MISOL
Teluk Berau
SERAM
Bula
KEPULAUAN BANGA
KEPULAUAN KAI
KAI KECIL
PULAU ADI
Kaimana
KEPULAUAN ARU
Dobo
PULAU WOKAM
PULAU KOBROOR
PULAU TRANGAN
PULAU YAMDENA
KEPULAUAN TANIMBAR
PULAU SELARU

PULAU YAPEN
TANJUNG D'URVILLE
NINIGO GROUP
HERMIT ISLANDS
ADMIRALTY ISLANDS
MANUS ISLAND
NEW HANOVER
KAVIENG
NEW IRELAND
Namatanai
Rabaul
Kokopo
WITU ISLANDS

KEPULAUAN SCHOUTEN
BIAK
PULAU NUMFOOR
Manokwari
PEGUNUNGAN VAN REES
Aitape
Wewak
Sepik
Madang
KARKAR ISLAND
UMBOI ISLAND
Talasea
BISMARCK ARCHIPELAGO
EMIRAU ISLAND
MUSSAU ISLAND
NEW HANOVER

INDONESIA
Jayapura (Sukarnapura)
PEGUNUNGAN MAOKE
Puncak Jaya 5030m
Puncak Trikora 4750m
Digul
Strickland
Fly
Meraukei

NEW GUINEA
Mt.Giluwe 4368m
Mt.Wilhelm 4509m
Ramu
PAPUA NEW GUINEA
Lae
Huon Gulf
Morobe
Gulf of Papua
Popondetta
Port Moresby
OWEN STANLEY RANGE
Samarai

NEW BRITAIN
KIRIWINA ISLANDS
D'ENTRECASTEAUX ISLANDS

Arafura Sea
Torres Strait
TANJUNG VALS
Gulf of Carpentaria

MELVILLE ISLAND
COBOURG PEN.
CROKER ISLAND
WESSEL ISLANDS
Van Diemen Gulf
BATHURST ISLAND
Darwin

AUSTRALIA
CAPE YORK
MOA ISLAND
CAPE YORK PEN.
GREAT BARRIER REEF

Coral Sea

5°

10°

15°

0 100 200 300 Km.
0 100 200 Mi.

A-592200-264-1-1-2   ©1979 R.M&N.

125° 130°

Laut Sawu
Savu Sea
TIMOR
Soe
PULAU ROTI
Kupang

Timor Sea

ASHMORE ISLANDS
HIBERNIA REEF
CARTIER ISLANDS (Austl.)
BROWSE ISLAND
ADÈLE ISLAND
BEAGLE REEF
BONAPARTE ARCHIPELAGO

MELVILLE ISLAND
BATHURST ISLAND
Van Diemen Gulf
CAPE CROKER
GOUL
ARNHEM LA
Humpty Doo
Jabiru
Darwin
Pine Creek
Katherine

CAPE LONDONDERRY
ADMIRALTY Gulf
CAPE LEVEQUE
BUCCANEER ARCHIPELAGO
KING SOUND
Derby
Broome

Joseph Bonaparte Gulf
POINT BLAZE
Rum Jungle
Daly
Victoria
Wyndham
Kununurra
Lake Argyle
Victoria River Downs
Daly Waters

KIMBERLEY PLATEAU
KING LEOPOLD RANGES
DURACK RANGE
Mount Ord 937
Fitzroy
Fitzroy Crossing
Halls Creek

NORTHER
TANAMI
Wave Hill
Newcastle Waters
Lake Woods

Ara

A r

Sea

5°

10°

15°

INDIAN

OCEAN

110° 115° 120° 125° 130°

ROWLEY SHOALS

CAPE LATOUCHE TREVILLE
La Grange
EIGHTY MILE BEACH
Broome

Port Hedland
Goldsworthy
Shay Gap
De Grey
Roebourne
Marble Bar
Nullagine

GREAT SANDY DESERT

TANAMI DESERT

NORTHER
TERRITOR

Dampier
Karratha
MONTE BELLO ISLANDS
DAMPIER ARCHIPELAGO
BARROW ISLAND
MUIRON ISLANDS
NORTH WEST CAPE
Exmouth
Exmouth Gulf
Onslow
Pannawonica
HAMERSLEY RANGE
Mount Brockman 1132
Tom Price 1105
Mount Bruce 1235
Mount Meharry 1251
Paraburdoo
Ashburton
Newman

Gregory Lake
Lake White
Lake Wills
Lake Mackay
Lake Dora
Lake Auld

Lake Disappointment

Savory

Mount Leisler 901
Mount Liebig 1524
Mount Zeil 1511
MACDONNELL RANGES
Lake Neale
Lake Amadeus
Mount Olga 1069
Ayers Rock 867
Mount Aloysius 1085
Mount Cockburn 1138
Mount Woodruffe 1440

Lake Macdonald

20°

Tropic of Capricorn

POINT CLOATES
CAPE CUVIER
Lake Macleod
Mount Augustus 1105
Mount Essendon 906

WESTERN

GIBSON DESERT

AUST
R

25°

Geographe Channel
Carnarvon
BERNIER ISLAND
DORRE ISLAND
DIRK HARTOG ISLAND
Shark Bay
Denham
Gascoyne
Wooramel
ROBINSON RANGE
Peak Hill
Murchison
Meekatharra
Nannine
Wiluna
Cue
Lake Austin
Sandstone
Agnew
Mount Redcliffe 576

Lake Carnegie
Lake Gillen
Lake Wells

Lake Maurice

Maralinga
Ooldea

AUSTRALIA

GREAT VICTORIA DESERT

SOUT

Naturaliste Channel
STEEP POINT
Kalbarri
Northampton
Mullewa
HOUTMAN ABROLHOS
Geraldton
Pindar
Yalgoo
Mount Magnet
Three Springs
Dongara
Lake Moore
GREEN HEAD
Moora
Dalwallinu

Leonora
Laverton
Malcolm
Lake Carey
Lake Ballard
Lake Raeside
Menzies
Lake Barlee
Bonnie Rock
Bencubbin
Bullfinch
Southern Cross
Kalgoorlie
Boulder
Coolgardie
Zanthus
Rawlinna
Haig
Forrest
Deakin

Lake Minigwal

NULLARBOR PLAIN

CAPE ADIEU
SAINT PETER ISLAND
INVESTI

30°

WANNEROO
PERTH
FREMANTLE
DARLING RANGE
Pinjarra
Northam
York
Beverley
Brookton
Hyden
Narrogin
Wagin
Newdegate
BUNBURY
Collie
Busselton
Bridgetown
GEOGRAPHE BAY
CAPE NATURALISTE
Manjimup
Augusta
Pemberton
CAPE LEEUWIN
POINT D'ENTRECASTEAUX
WEST CAPE HOWE
Nyabing
Katanning
Gnowangerup
Bluff Knoll 1096
Mount Barker
Albany
KING GEORGE SOUND
CAPE VANCOUVER

Merredin
Kellerberrin
Lake Johnston
Lake Cowan
Norseman
Lake Dundas
Ravensthorpe
Hopetoun
Esperance
CAPE ARID
ARCHIPELAGO OF THE RECHERCHE
Esperance Bay
HOOD POINT
Eucla
POINT CULVER
Eyre
Point Culver

Great Australian Bight

35°

40°

SOUTHERN   OCE

Copyright © by Rand McNally & Co.
Map prepared by Esselte Map Service AB, Stockholm
A-590200-264-

0 200 400 600
Kilometers   Km.
Statute Miles
0 200 400 600 Mi.

Scale 1:12,000,000

One centimeter represents 120 kilometers.
One inch represents approximately 190 miles.
Miller Oblated Stereographic Projection

96

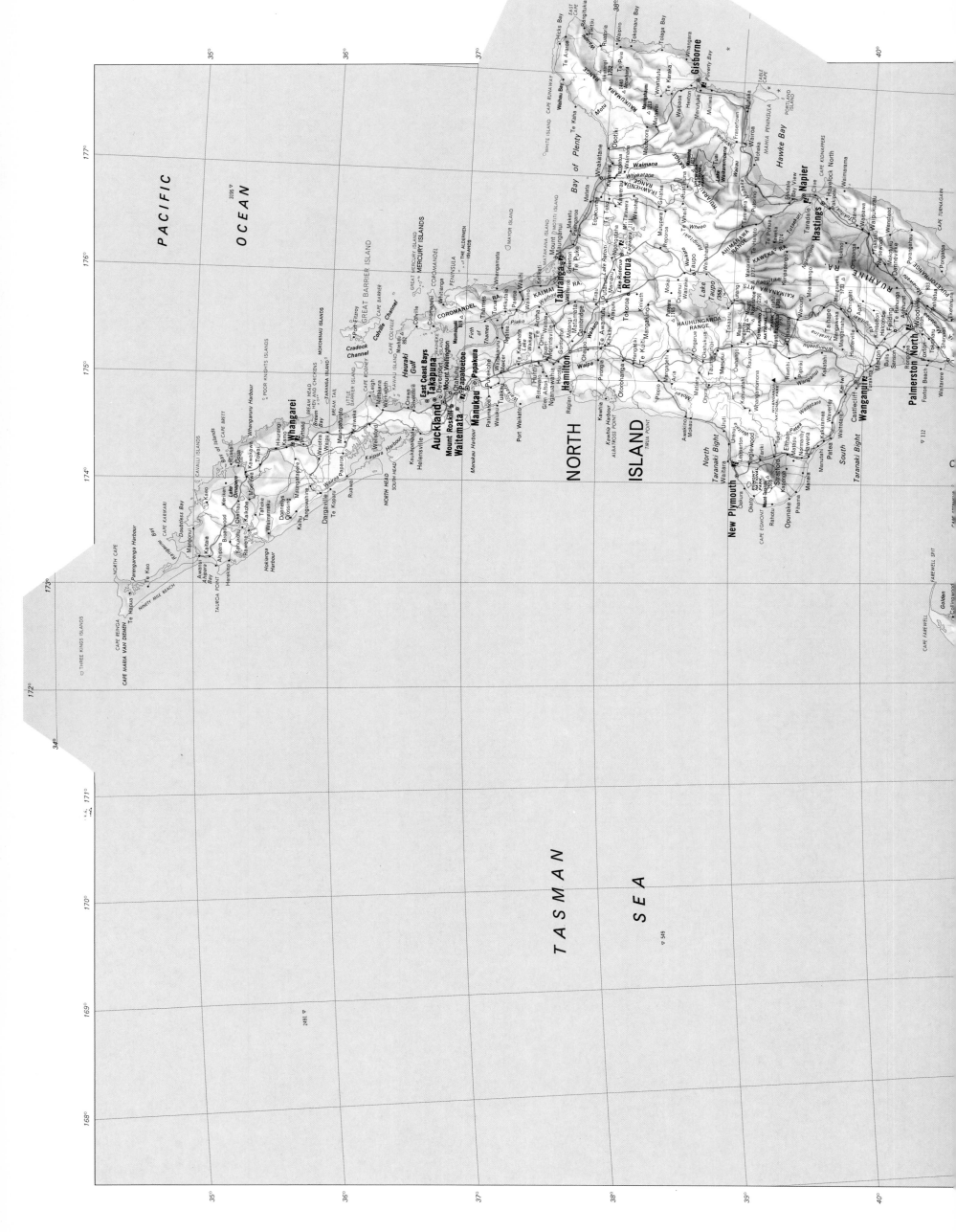

PACIFIC

OCEAN

NORTH

ISLAND

TASMAN

SEA

Whangarei

Auckland
Waitemata **Takapuna**
Mount Roskill **East Coast Bays**
Manukau **Mount Wellington**
Papakura

Hamilton

Rotorua

Tauranga

Bay of Plenty

Gisborne

Napier
Hastings

Hawke Bay

New Plymouth

Wanganui
Palmerston North

98

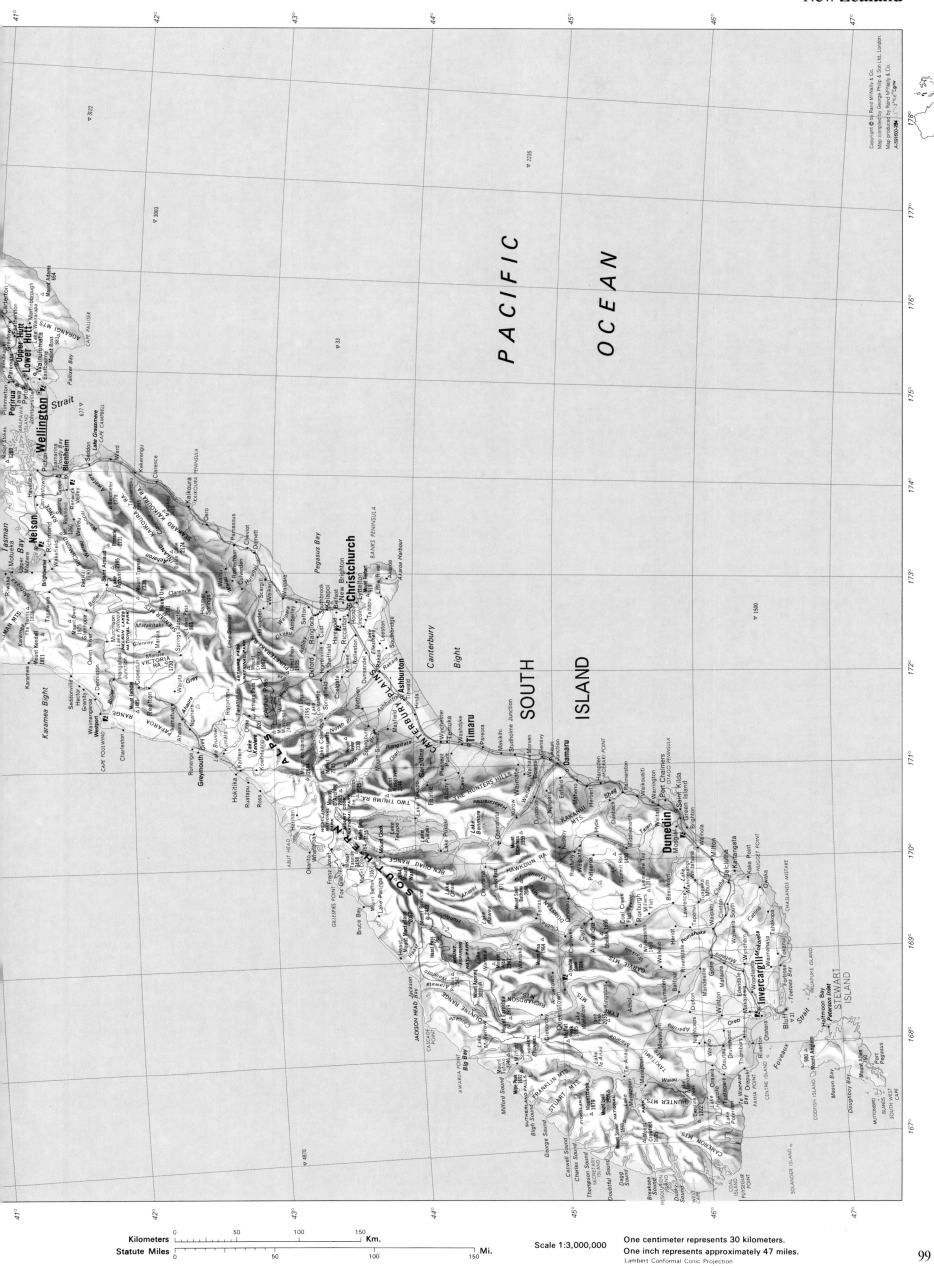

PACIFIC

OCEAN

Wellington

Christchurch

Timaru

Dunedin

Invercargill

SOUTH ISLAND

STEWART ISLAND

SOUTHERN ALPS

CANTERBURY PLAINS

| Kilometers | 0 | 50 | 100 | 150 | Km. |

| Statute Miles | 0 | 50 | 100 | 150 | Mi. |

Scale 1:3,000,000

One centimeter represents 30 kilometers.
One inch represents approximately 47 miles.

Lambert Conformal Conic Projection

99

Middle America
Profile

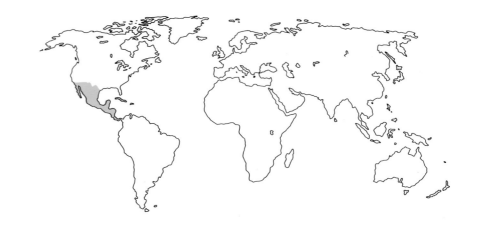

Location and Size

The term *Middle America* refers to Mexico, Central America, and the Caribbean and Atlantic island countries south of the continental United States. *Middle America* therefore includes much more territory than *Central America*. The northwest-to-southeast extent of the mainland is some 3,000 miles (4,800 kilometers). Yet this region is never more than 750 miles (1,200 kilometers) in west-east extent in Mexico and is often far narrower.

Middle America includes the islands of the Bahamas, the Greater and Lesser Antilles, and others lying in the seas between the mainland of the two Americas. These islands, which number about one thousand, are sometimes collectively called the West Indies, and they range in size from Cuba – at more than forty-two thousand square miles (more than 110 thousand square kilometers) – to Saba – at five square miles (thirteen square kilometers).

Landscape

Middle America may be divided into three main physical areas. In the north – in much of Mexico as far south as the Isthmus of Tehuantepec – the great mountain system of western North America continues. The Sierra Madre Occidental runs parallel to the Pacific coast and rises to a maximum of 13,994 feet (4,265 meters). The Sierra Madre Oriental runs parallel to the Gulf of Mexico and rises to greater heights in some of the volcanic peaks, such as Popocatépetl at 17,887 feet (5,452 meters). Between these two ranges, a complex plateau lies at heights of between four thousand feet (1,200 meters) and eight thousand feet (2,400 meters).

To the west of these lies the great depression occupied by the Gulf of California and the elongated Baja California peninsula, an extension of the coastal ranges of the United States.

The southern mainland section of Middle America is physically far more complex. In its northern province, between Tehuantepec and Nicaragua, a series of mainly west-to-east mountain ridges lies across the isthmus from a high volcanic plateau on the Pacific fringe. Each line of mountains is highest in the west. There are limited coastal lowlands in this area, except in the great Yucatan Peninsula, which is an extensive low limestone plain. The mountains of southern Nicaragua, Costa Rica, and Panama are separated from the others by the depression containing Lakes Nicaragua and Managua. These mountains present a formidable barrier to movement across the isthmus, running northwest to southeast, then west to east.

The third physical province is that of the islands, which can be subdivided. To the north lies the line of coral reefs that make up the Bahamas. Then the often-large islands of the Greater Antilles are an eastern continuation of the mountains of southern Mexico, Guatemala, and Honduras. Finally, the Lesser Antilles are mainly a volcanic arc. They are a northeastern extension of the South American Andes. There are also a number of coral islands in this vast area. Thus, the West Indian islands show a great variety of physical features: active volcanoes, extinct volcanoes, coral islands, and mountainous islands.

Climate

Virtually all of Middle America lies within the tropics. The close proximity to the seas and the range of altitudes account for the variety of climates.

Mexico, north of the Tropic of Cancer, experiences dry climates. In the northwest and north-central parts lies a subtropical desert area where the monthly average temperature never drops below 32°F (0°C), but where rainfall is below ten inches (250 millimeters). Central and northeastern Mexico has a subtropical steppe climate in which similar temperatures are accompanied by higher rainfalls, up to twenty-four inches (six

Left: Leaping from heights of 140 feet (40 meters), the cliff divers of Acapulco, Mexico, are but one of the attractions of this seaport on the Pacific Ocean. Acapulco's climate, atmosphere, deep-sea fishing, and beautiful beaches also contribute to its stature as a leading vacation destination.

Right: Belize, the most sparsely populated nation of Central America, lies on the Caribbean Sea next to Mexico and Guatemala. Its mostly low-lying terrain was once heavily forested; timber production, however, has depleted this resource. Here, a remaining wooded area lies below a conical karst hill, formed by erosion of water-soluble rock.

Middle America

hundred millimeters).

Except in the high mountain areas, the remainder of the mainland experiences tropical rainy climates and is wetter on the east coast – except in the Yucatan Peninsula – than on the west. Here is the rain forest area where average monthly temperatures may be around 77°F (25°C) for much of the year, and rainfall exceeds 100 inches (2,500 millimeters). In the drier savanna areas of the west, rainfall is only around one-third of this amount.

Many of the islands experience a similar tropical savanna type of climate, though parts, such as the northern coastal strip of Hispaniola and Puerto Rico, have far higher rainfalls. Hurricanes are an occasional menace.

History, Politics, and Economy

The history of Middle America dates back to the early settlements of Indians who migrated from north to south through the Americas about 10,000 B.C. Developing rich civilizations, their descendants included the Maya of Central America and Mexico; the Aztecs and Toltecs of Mexico; and the Arawak, Lucayo, and Carib peoples of the Caribbean.

In 1492, Christopher Columbus discovered Middle America when he landed on a small island in the Caribbean Sea. Spanish settlement of the New World began in the Caribbean in the same year, when one of Columbus's ships was wrecked and several men were left on

Haiti. Like many early settlements, this one ended unsuccessfully for Europeans when all of the men perished.

In 1513, Vasco de Balboa crossed the Isthmus of Panama and discovered the Pacific Ocean. Soon after, Hernán Cortés launched an expedition to conquer the Aztec Empire, and he succeeded in the early 1520s. Mexico and much of Central America soon became a viceroyalty of Spain. In 1525, Spanish conquistadors established the city of San Salvador in El Salvador. But wars, enslavement, and disease were all factors that thinned the Indian population, and Central America became a relatively impoverished place.

European influence in Middle America from 1500 onward was essentially by two groups. The mainland was part of

an area allocated to Spain under the 1493 agreements between Spain, Portugal, and the Pope; the Caribbean islands were part of the area largely left to the Dutch, French, and British.

Independence movements developed early in the nineteenth century. Mexico was the first mainland country to experience revolution, gaining independence from Spain in 1821. In that same year, five Central American nations gained independence from Spain and later became part of the Federation of Central American States, which lasted for only fourteen years. In 1838, Nicaragua, El Salvador, Honduras, Costa Rica, and Guatemala became autonomous nations. Panama remained part of Colombia until 1903, and in 1981, Belize finally achieved

Opposite, top left: Carnival is a pre-Lenten celebration that includes parades and feasting, held in many Catholic countries. Its festivities appeal to both tourists and residents, as these revelers on St. Vincent demonstrate.

Opposite, top right: Mexico City (Ciudad de México) is the capital and fastest-growing city of the nation. It is among the top five most populous cities in the world. In 1985, the city suffered a major earthquake, which caused much damage and killed thousands.

Opposite, bottom left: The destruction of a 1976 earthquake is still evident in Antigua, Guatemala – a city situated in a valley surrounded by several volcanoes.

Opposite, bottom right: The sugar industry is the heart of the Cuban economy. It employs nearly 500 thousand workers, including these men, and sugar accounts for almost 90 percent of all export income. The industry has been nationalized since 1959.

Left: On the San Blas Islands off the northeastern coast of Panama live the Cuna, an Indian people. They moved to the islands from the mainland in the nineteenth century. Until the 1960s, they prohibited strangers from spending the night on their land.

independence from Great Britain.

Since independence, Mexico has experienced periods of difficulty. It lost considerable territory, including Texas, to the United States during the Mexican War. Subsequent years saw power change hands frequently as liberals demanding social and economic reforms battled conservatives. A brief span of French rule in the mid 1860s interrupted the struggle. Following a revolution that started in 1910, a new constitution was adopted in 1917, and progress toward reform began, culminating in the separation of church and state and the redistribution of land.

The road to prosperity and stability has been rocky for many Central American nations. Resentment about the growing United States influence and control in Central America started to rise in the early nineteenth century. It was fueled by the construction of the Panama Canal in 1914 and the growth of the United States-controlled banana industry.

Military dictators ruled the Central American region until the mid 1940s, when a revolution in Guatemala temporarily halted this trend. The rest of the region made steps toward democracy throughout the 1950s but returned toward a trend of military rule in the 1960s.

For many years, large landowners and political leaders monopolized the valuable land that produced the thriving export crops of Central America. As the economy grew, pressures mounted for democratic reform and economic equality. Tensions between government and its citizens increased and were exacerbated by numerous controlled elections. Many began to support radical, left-wing groups that championed violence as a means to social and political change. In 1979, the Sandinista guerrillas overthrew the Samoza dictatorship in Nicaragua. Then, violence in El Salvador and Guatemala broke out virtually ending tourism and foreign investments.

In 1983, Manual Antonio Noriega became head of the National Guard in Panama, overthrew the government, and installed a figurehead as president. In the meantime, the Panamanian people suffer from the effects of a depressed economy and the loss of democratic rule to a military junta. Corruption in government and a growing drug trade are threatening Panama's current steps toward prosperity and democracy. In Nicaragua, international efforts to end the Sandinista-contra war have been fruitless.

Most Caribbean nations remained under foreign rule until after World War II, and some of them are still administered by other countries. Major exceptions include Cuba, Haiti, and the Dominican Republic.

Cuba became independent from Spain in 1902. In 1952, Sergeant Fulgencio Batista seized power in a coup that established an unpopular and oppressive regime. A group opposed to Batista gained support, and in 1959, he fled the country, leaving its leadership to Fidel Castro and the Communist party.

By 1804, Haiti had achieved independence from France. In 1957, François Duvalier came to power and later declared himself president-for-life. His rule was marked by repression, corruption, and human-rights abuses. His son succeeded him but fled the country in 1986. A new constitution was approved in 1987, but instability continues.

In 1844, the Dominican Republic broke away from Haiti and became independent. The nation has experienced periods of instability and United States intervention, and various presidents have been installed.

Jamaica, at one time the most important sugar and slave center in the New World, became independent from the United Kingdom in 1962. Since then, the nation has faced problems of unemployment, inflation, poverty, and periodic social unrest.

Puerto Rico is affiliated with the United States as a commonwealth. For many years, the island has been allowed to determine its own status. In referenda and public opinion polls, residents have voted to maintain the status quo. There are, however, strong political movements for both statehood and independence.

As politics have changed, so have the economies of Middle America. Mining and subsistence farming have been the traditional activities of most Mexicans. The extraction of petroleum, natural gas, and other minerals has to a large extent replaced silver as a leading mining endeavor. World recessions and fluctuating oil prices have taken their toll on Mexico, and in the early 1980s, the nation was close to bankruptcy. Austerity plans and foreign aid are expected to revitalize the economy.

Cotton, sugar, meat, coffee, and bananas have been major exports in the agricultural economies of Central America. In Nicaragua, years of political instability, a large foreign debt, and a civil war have hindered prosperity. Honduras, Guatemala, and Belize remain underdeveloped. Political instability, a low literacy rate, high population density, and high unemployment have hindered El Salvador. Panama has benefited economically from the strategic Panama Canal, but the nation remains troubled.

Many West Indian economies are also steeped in agriculture, with tropical fruits, spices, sugar, coffee, and cacao major crops. There is considerable mining activity on some islands, and some industry as well. Income stemming from tourism is crucial to many Caribbean economies.

Below: The Bahamas are coral islands, and their thin soils are not well suited for agriculture. A few crops are grown, however, including the bananas being harvested here. Climate is the islands' most important resource, and tourism is the economic mainstay.

Above: Coral reefs and submarine volcanoes have formed the islands of the Caribbean. Many of the coral islands tend to be flat and low-lying; those of primarily volcanic origin tend to be rugged. Shown here is volcanic Saba, in the Leeward Islands.

Anguilla

Anguilla was associated with St. Christopher and Nevis until 1976. The smallest of the Leeward Islands – thirty-five square miles (ninety-one square kilometers) – it is a dependent territory of the United Kingdom. While it enjoys internal self-government, the United Kingdom is responsible for defense and foreign affairs. It is a low coral island with poor soils. Sea salt and fruits are the main products.

Antigua and Barbuda

Tourism is the principal economic contributor of this Caribbean nation composed of the islands of Antigua, Barbuda, and uninhabited Redondo. It gained independence from the United Kingdom in 1981. The climate is tropical. Most Antiguans are descendants of black African slaves brought by the British to work sugar-cane plantations. Formed by volcanoes, the low-lying islands are flat and ringed with white-sand beaches.

Aruba

This self-governing possession of the Netherlands is a beautiful Caribbean island that is home to white sands and a booming tourist industry.

Bahamas

The Bahamas comprise some seven hundred coral islands and cays north of Cuba and east of Florida. Only about twenty-nine of the islands are inhabited, and most of the people live on Grand Bahama and New Providence. Blacks are the majority, mainly descendants of slaves routed through the area or brought by British Loyalists fleeing the American colonies during the revolutionary war. With its semitropical climate, tourism is predominant in the Bahamas. Because it is a tax haven, the country is also an international finance center. The Bahamas achieved independence from Great Britain in 1973.

Barbados

The Caribbean island of Barbados became independent from the British in 1966. Barbados's pleasant tropical climate and its land have determined its economic mainstays: tourism and sugar. Sunshine and year-round warmth attract thousands of visitors and provide an excellent environment for sugar cane cultivation. The coral island's terrain is mostly flat. It is one of the world's most densely populated countries, and most citizens are black descendants of African slaves.

Belize

Central American Belize has a mixed populace, including descendants of black Africans, Spanish-Indians, and Indians. Population is centered in six urban areas along the coast. Sugar is the major crop and export. Formerly known as British Honduras, its name changed to Belize in 1973. In 1981, it gained independence from Great Britain. The hot, humid climate is offset by sea breezes.

Bermuda

Bermuda is made up of North Atlantic islands, 650 miles (1,046 kilometers)

Below and bottom: To many, the Caribbean means sandy beaches, such as this one on St. Thomas. Snorkeling and windsurfing are popular. Cruises have gained momentum as a way to enjoy leisure travel.

east of North Carolina. This dependent territory of the United Kingdom features beautiful beaches and scenic, hilly countryside, which invite a thriving tourist industry. The population is mainly black descendants of African slaves but also includes Portuguese, British, Canadian, Caribbean peoples, and some United States military staff. The archipelago consists of many small islands and islets. About twenty are inhabited, several of which are connected by bridges and collectively known as the island of Bermuda.

Cayman Islands

Grand Cayman is the most important of the three coral islands that compose this British dependency some 200 miles (320 kilometers) northwest of Jamaica. Tourism is important to the islands, as is international banking.

Costa Rica

Costa Rica has one of the most prosperous economies of all Central American countries. Agriculture remains important, producing coffee and bananas. Much of the area is forested, and the mountainous central region is bordered by coastal plains on the east and west. The climate is semitropical to tropical. In the 1980s the country has worked to promote peaceful solutions to armed conflicts in the region.

Cuba

The Republic of Cuba is ruled by its Communist party. It is economically dependent on sugar, but the island also possesses mineral deposits, including oil and nickel. Mountains, plains, and scenic coastlines make Cuba one of the most beautiful islands in the West Indies; it is also the largest island in the Caribbean. The climate is tropical. Most Cubans are descendants of Spanish colonists, African slaves, or a blend of the two.

Dominica

This Caribbean island is volcanic in origin, though the soil is suitable for farming. Mountains and dense forests, however, limit cultivatable land. Hurricanes also hinder production. Its tropical climate and scenic landscape create a basis for tourism. Dominica gained independence from Great Britain in 1978. A small indigenous Carib Indian population is concentrated in the northeastern part of the island and maintains its own customs and life-style.

Dominican Republic

The Dominican Republic forms the eastern two-thirds of the Caribbean island of Hispaniola. The mixed population includes minorities of Haitians, other blacks, Spaniards, and European Jews. Agriculture remains important, with sugar the main crop. The mountainous terrain, however, limits arable area. Aided by a warm, tropical climate, tourism is growing.

El Salvador

Right-wing death squads, poverty, political unrest, and human-rights abuses plague this war-torn country in Central America. With high population density and high unemployment, economic conditions remain very bad in El Salvador. The United States has played a major role in furnishing military and economic aid to the government. The climate is tropical.

Grenada

Rich volcanic soils and heavy rainfall have made agriculture the chief economic activity. Also known as the Isle of Spice, Grenada is one of the world's leading producers of nutmeg and mace. Many tropical fruits are also raised, and the small plots of peasant farmers dot the hilly terrain. Tourism is another economic contributor, with visitors who are drawn by the beaches and tropical climate of this Caribbean island. After the United States led an invasion that deposed a Marxist regime, a new government was installed in 1984.

Guadeloupe

One of the four overseas departments of France, Guadeloupe is a group of two main and five smaller islands. The main western island is dominated by an active volcano; the eastern island is much flatter. They are all situated between the British Leeward Islands and Dominica in the Caribbean. Bananas, sugar, rum, and pineapples are the principal products and export items.

Guatemala

This mountainous Central American country sits below Mexico between the Pacific Ocean and the Caribbean Sea. Largely undeveloped, Guatemala consists of northern rain forests and grasslands. A 1976 earthquake resulted in heavy loss of life and property. Since a 1983 coup, military rule has been established, although some reforms are being made.

Haiti

Occupying the western third of Hispaniola in the central Caribbean, Haiti has an overall mountainous terrain and a tropical climate. Haiti's economy remains underdeveloped and its politics unstable. Most people are poor and rely on subsistence farming, though productivity is hampered by high population density in productive regions. Coffee is a main commercial crop and export. Voodooism, which blends Christian and African beliefs, is still practiced.

Honduras

Central American Honduras has an underdeveloped economy based on banana cultivation. Mostly mountainous with lowlands along some coastal regions, Honduras has a temperate to tropical climate. Since the 1950s, civilian

Below: As is the case with many other Caribbean islands, most of the residents of Antigua are the descendants of black African slaves brought here by Europeans to work sugarcane plantations. Today, the island depends upon tourism.

governments have alternated with military coups and rule. Controversies focus on issues of poverty, land distribution, and a border dispute with El Salvador. The country has been an important base for United States activities in Central America, evidenced by ongoing United States military maneuvers in the area.

Jamaica

Despite periodic unrest, this Caribbean island is a popular tourist spot. Its mountainous inland region is surrounded by coastal plains and beaches, and its tropical climate is tempered by ocean breezes. Most Jamaicans are of African or Afro-European descent. Sugar cane and bananas are principal crops, and more than a third of the population is engaged in farming. A 1988 hurricane damaged much of the island.

Martinique

Situated near Dominica, the Caribbean island of Martinique is an overseas territory of France. The north is dominated by a volcano that is responsible for one of the worst natural disasters of modern times; on May 8, 1902, its eruption killed forty thousand people. Bananas, sugar, and rum are its main exports.

Mexico

By far the largest Middle American country, Mexico is also among the most northerly. Mexico's terrain and climate are greatly varied, ranging from tropical jungles along the coast to desert plains in the north. Most Mexicans are mestizos, descended from Indians and the Spaniards who conquered Mexico. The nation is a leading producer of petroleum and silver; a growing manufacturer of iron, steel, and chemicals; and an exporter of coffee and cotton. Drawn by archaeological sites and warm, sunny weather, foreign visitors often tour Mexico. Mexico has been troubled by inflation, declining oil prices, and rising unemployment.

Montserrat

This scenically attractive island is a British colony situated southwest of Antigua and northwest of Guadeloupe. The economy is heavily dependent on British aid.

Netherlands Antilles

The Netherlands Antilles are composed of two groups: the three islands of Aruba, Curaçao, and Bonaire; and St. Martin, St. Eustatius, and Saba. The islands are self-governing territories of the Netherlands, and the two groups are separated by many miles of sea. Over 92 percent of the population lives on Aruba and Curaçao. Tourism is important.

Nicaragua

Nicaragua is Middle America's second largest country and is situated between Honduras and Costa Rica. The terrain includes a low-lying Pacific region, central highlands, and a flat Caribbean area. The climate is tropical. Nicaragua is chiefly an agricultural nation, and it relies on the production of textiles, coffee, and sugar. Political unrest and poverty plague the country.

Panama

Linking North America and South America, Panama has been a strategic center for trade and transportation. The 1914 opening of the Panama Canal, connecting the Atlantic and Pacific oceans, has provided additional revenue and jobs; the canal area is now Panama's most economically developed region. Panama has a mountainous interior and a tropical climate. A military government rules in Panama. In 1988, civilian-military clashes arose.

Puerto Rico

This Caribbean island is marked by mountains, lowlands, and valleys. A rising population has caused poverty, housing shortages, and unemployment. Puerto Rico is a commonwealth of the United States, and many Puerto Ricans live in the United States, mostly in New York and other large cities. Most of the population is descended from Spaniards and black African slaves. Once dependent on such plantation crops as sugar and coffee, Puerto Rico is now reliant upon manufacturing.

St. Christopher and Nevis

The Caribbean islands of St. Christopher, often called St. Kitts, and Nevis became independent from British control in 1983. The rural, black population is concentrated along the coasts. Agriculture is a mainstay, with sugar cane the main crop, and tourism is enhanced by the tropical climate, beaches, and scenic mountainous terrain.

St. Lucia

This Caribbean island gained independence from Great Britain in 1979 and has remained politically stable since. Banana and cocoa growing are important activities. Tourism is becoming increasingly important, with visitors drawn by the tropical climate, scenic mountainous

terrain, and beaches. During the colonial period, the island frequently shifted from British to French control, and its culture reflects both British and French elements.

St. Vincent and the Grenadines

These Caribbean islands were once possessions of Great Britain but have been independent since 1979. St. Vincent is the largest island, and about one hundred smaller islands make up the Grenadines. The population is mainly descended from black African slaves. The terrain is mountainous, with coastlines marked by sandy beaches. The climate is tropical.

Trinidad and Tobago

Situated very near the coast of Venezuela, the two Caribbean islands of Trinidad and Tobago form a single nation. Trinidad has nearly all the land mass and population. About 80 percent of all Trinidadians are either black African or East Indian, and about 20 percent are European, Chinese, and of mixed descent. Although tourism and agriculture are important, the economy is based on oil. The nation became independent from British control in 1962.

Turks and Caicos Islands

These two groups of islands are a British dependent territory lying southeast of the Bahamas. Only six are inhabited. Until 1976, they were associated with

Above: The remains of Spanish colonists' fortifications against English, French, and Dutch attack can still be seen on Puerto Rico. Shown here is El Morro in San Juan.

the Cayman Islands. Fishing is the most important activity, but tourism has been increasing.

Virgin Islands, British

This dependent territory of Great Britain lies in the Caribbean Sea and is made up of many islands, islets, rocks, and cays. Most are of volcanic origin. The two major islands, Tortola and Virgin Gorda, along with Anegada and Jost Van Dyke, contain most of the population. Standards for education and health are among the highest in the Caribbean. Tourism is the economic mainstay, but a variety of tropical crops are grown.

Virgin Islands, United States

Constitutionally an unincorporated territory of the United States, this group of Caribbean islands is made up of St. Thomas, St. Croix, St. John, and about fifty other smaller islands. Tourism is now the base of the economy, although agriculture is also important. Additionally, St. Croix has mineral-processing plants, and St. Thomas is an important commercial center. Standards for health and education are quite high, and the climate is very pleasant.

ATLANTIC OCEAN

Tropic of Cancer

WEST INDIES

GREATER ANTILLES

CARIBBEAN SEA

LESSER ANTILLES

One centimeter represents 120 kilometers.
One inch represents approximately 190 miles.

Scale 1:12,000,000

Kilometers

Statute Miles

Oblique Conic Conformal Projection

South America
Profile

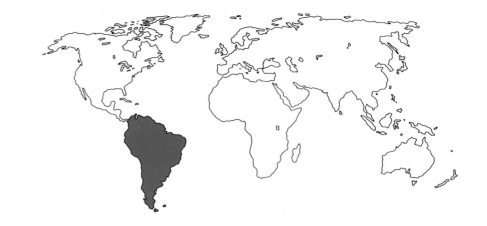

Location and Size

The dividing line between Middle and South America lies at the Colombian-Panamanian border, the narrowest land bridge dividing the Pacific Ocean from the Caribbean Sea. The north-south extent of the continent is 4,600 miles (7,450 kilometers). The west-to-east extent varies greatly, but in the central equatorial regions – from northern Peru to eastern Brazil – it extends some 3,200 miles (5,150 kilometers).

South America is essentially triangular in shape. The north and east coasts are comparatively straight, but the west coast has a straight southern part and then a convex northern part.

Although the coastline of South America is largely uncomplicated, the continent includes a number of offshore islands. The Falkland (Malvinas) Islands are to the southeast, off the shore of southern Argentina. The Galapagos Islands (Archipiélago de Colón) – home of a variety of unusual wildlife – are to the west, off Ecuador. The Chonos Archipelago is to the southwest, off the rugged coast of Chile. And finally, the remote Tierra del Fuego lies at the southernmost tip of Argentina.

Landscape

South America can be divided into eight distinct physical regions, four of which are essentially lowlands and the rest uplands. Within each of these two groups is a dominant member: the Amazon (Amazonas) Basin is by far the most extensive lowland area and the Andes Mountains the most extensive upland area. Three of the lowland regions are river basins, and one is coastal plain. The upland areas are, for the most part, rugged and mountainous.

The Amazon Basin is an extremely low-lying area dominated by dense tropical rain forest. It covers a part of central and eastern South America that is almost as big as the entire United States. The main rivers discharge more water than any other single system in the world. The Amazon itself is some 3,900 miles (6,275 kilometers) long.

The continent's second largest river system is dominated by the Paraná, Paraguay (Paraguai), and Uruguay (Uruguai) rivers. These reach the sea via the Río de la Plata, which is really an inlet of the Atlantic Ocean that extends some 205 miles (330 kilometers) inland at the border of Uruguay and Argentina.

The third, but far smaller, river basin is that of the Orinoco in the north. This river drains a smaller area than the Amazon, from which it is divided by an extremely low watershed. The rivers in this region drain the eastern and northern flanks of the Andes as well as the Guiana Highlands. Most of this region is known as the llanos and is dominated by vast swamplands.

The last area of lowland, along the Pacific coastal fringes, is the most fragmented. The coastal plains are widest in the extreme north and parts of Chile, where they may reach fifty miles (eighty kilometers) at their maximum. The humid regions of these lowlands are crossed by a number of short rivers that plunge steeply westward from the Andes.

The magnificent Andes run parallel to the Pacific coast. They are second only to the Himalayas in their towering heights, and they form the longest chain of peaks in the world. In the south, there is one main ridge; in the north, however, there are several ridges, with large valleys and the flat altiplano of Bolivia and Peru between them. At its widest, the whole range stretches for about 310 miles (500 kilometers) from west to east. The Andes chain contains a number of active and extinct volcanoes and is still an active region of earthquakes – it is part of the Ring of Fire, a narrow zone of frequent geologic activity that encircles the Pacific Ocean. Mount Aconcagua in Argentina rises to 22,831 feet (6,959 meters), the highest point in the Western Hemisphere.

South and east of the Amazon lies the second largest upland area, the triangularly shaped Brazilian Highlands. These rise quite steeply from the Atlantic coast and then slope gently into the interior. These highlands are far older than the Andes; thus they are lower.

The smaller Guiana Highlands to the north, between the Orinoco and Amazon basins, rise steeply from the former and then slope gently toward the north.

The plateau that is Patagonia lies in southern Argentina. It is a lower, irregular, windswept tableland that rises to a variety of heights.

Climate

Extending from the world's largest equatorial basin to the most southerly point in the Southern Hemisphere outside Antarctica, South America exhibits a wide range of climates. East of the Andes

Right: The Sierra of Peru is a high-altitude region of gentle slopes surrounded by the towering peaks of the Andes. Land suitable for farming is found between the mountains, and this is where about half of the population lives. Shown here is a farming community near the Urubamba, a river that is used extensively for irrigation.

Opposite: Brazil's natural resources make it a leading producer of hydroelectric power, with potential for further development. Forming part of the border between Brazil and Argentina, the spectacular Iguassu (Iguaçu) Falls would provide great power if harnessed.

South America

Profile continued

and north of 20°S is a large area that experiences equatorial and tropical climates. These make for dense rain forests near the equator and the savanna of Venezuela, Guyana, Suriname, French Guiana, and the Brazilian interior. This region of rain forest is the largest in the world, but it is threatened by encroaching civilization, especially in Brazil. Average monthly temperatures never fall below 64°F (18°C). Rainfall at its maximum exceeds 100 inches (2,500 millimeters). Similar humid tropical climates are also found on some of the Brazilian coastal fringes and some of the Colombian coast.

Hot or warm climates are found along some of the Pacific coastal lowlands south of the equator and in a small area of about the same latitude on the other side of the Andes. Here, rainfall is mainly below five inches (125 millimeters) per year, and average monthly temperatures reach the low

80°sF (high 20°sC) in the north and the mid 70°sF (mid 20°sC) in the south. Patagonia is an area of midlatitude desert, where rainfall rarely reaches ten inches (250 millimeters) and average temperatures range between 66°F (19°C) and 32°F (0°C). Steppe climates are found in a north-south belt east of the Andes near the Tropic of Capricorn, in northeastern Brazil, and in a small coastal area of Venezuela.

Warm and cool temperature climates dominate the Pacific coastlines south of the Tropic of Capricorn and the southern parts of Brazil and Uruguay. Along the Pacific, the north of this region experiences a Mediterranean climate while farther south it becomes cooler and much wetter. The climate in the larger Atlantic-facing area has higher temperatures, with greater temperature ranges and rainfall totals of between 22 inches (550 millimeters) and 40 inches (1,000 millimeters).

History, Politics, and Economy

Nomadic hunter-gatherers roamed the Americas at least ten thousand years ago. They probably came to South America from the north, and their ancient tools have been found in Venezuela, Ecuador, and Argentina. It is estimated that humans first reached the southern tip of South America about 7000 B.C.

Before the arrival of Europeans, various Indian peoples inhabited South America. Among these were the Incas, whose sophisticated civilization flourished in the areas of present-day Ecuador, Peru, and Bolivia.

The discovery of an American continent by a European was accomplished in 1498, when Christopher Columbus landed at the Peninsula of Paria, Venezuela. Ferdinand Magellan was the first to realize the immensity of South America when he sailed down its coast and rounded its southern tip in 1520. Fran-

cisco Pizarro conquered the mighty Inca Empire in the early 1530s.

The first major wave of Europeans came in the wake of the conquistadors, with Spanish and Portuguese settlements. The resistance offered by most Indian groups was ineffectual, and for the most part, Indian lands fell quickly to the invaders. Lima, Peru, was founded in 1535; Santiago, Chile, in 1541; and Rio de Janeiro, Brazil, in 1565.

Many of the early settlers were drawn to South America by the promise of wealth. As word of the continent's natural riches spread back to Europe, fortune-seeking colonists flocked to the region. Oftentimes the promise of gold and silver remained unfulfilled, but most settlers stayed on, establishing large plantations that laid the basis for much of South America's present economy. The colonists took the conquered Indians as slaves to work their farmlands, and soon a thriving agriculture was established.

Top : The second largest city in Brazil and one of the most populous in the world, Rio de Janeiro is a popular tourist destination.

Right: These Indians are descendants of the Incas, rulers of the largest native empire in the Americas. The Inca realm included twelve million people in Peru, Ecuador, Chile, Bolivia, and Argentina.

Far right: La Paz is Bolivia's most populous city and its commercial center. Situated at the edge of the altiplano, its elevation is 12,001 feet (3,658 meters) above sea level.

Below: Rugged Mount Fitzroy towers above the surrounding Andean peaks in Patagonia, at the border of Chile and Argentina. Fitzroy is known for its shark-fin-like spires and the remarkable climbs they have inspired.

Much of the indigenous population disappeared during the colonial period. Wars with the settlers, labor-intensive plantations, and exposure to European diseases claimed thousands of Indian lives. In addition, many Indians who managed to survive intermarried with the Europeans. Modern South America's large mestizo population, of mixed Spanish and Indian blood, is a result of these liaisons.

As the Indians died out, blacks were brought from Africa to continue slave labor on the plantations. Development increased, and the descendants of the early settlers soon established a uniquely South American culture, combining influences of both their Spanish ancestors and the indigenous peoples into a life-style evolved from the plantation economy. Many of the Indians continued their traditional ways of life, however, and remained far from the centers of development, unaffected by the waves of change.

Prosperity continued, and in time the large-estate holders, many of them mestizos, found themselves wielding economic influence by enjoying few of the benefits of their profits. Native-born South Americans of Spanish descent were equally dissatisfied with colonial status. Political power remained in the hands of the mother country, whose people and government now had little in common with South American life. Resentment toward the ruling powers grew, along with the colonies' demands for a voice in a government that did not always consider their welfare.

The struggle for independence began in the late eighteenth century. Two prominent men emerged as leaders of the fight for freedom in the Spanish colonies: the Venezuelan Simón Bolívar and the Argentine José de San Martín. Bolívar helped liberate Venezuela (1821), Colombia (1813), Ecuador (1822), and Peru (1821); San Martín had a hand in Peru's independence and helped Chile to freedom in 1818. Brazil, Portugal's South American stronghold, became an independent country in 1822.

Politically, South America remained unstable after independence. For instance, following a military coup in 1889, Brazil became a republic. Economic problems resulted in a 1930 military coup and a dictatorship lasting until 1945, plus military takeovers in 1954 and 1964.

The nineteenth century saw political instability and revolutionary fervor in Venezuela, followed by a succession of dictatorships in the twentieth century. In

Top: Some of the Indians of the Brazilian Amazon Basin still exist by the slash-and-burn method of agriculture, in which patches of jungle are cut down, farmed and lived upon for a few years, and then allowed to return to forest. Groups of these people, who make up a fraction of the population, have been uprooted as the rain forest has been cleared.

Right: The altiplano of Peru and Bolivia is a flat area between two ranges of the Andes. The plateau is rich in minerals, but, because of poor soil and low precipitation, supports little vegetation. Some agriculture takes place, however, evidenced by these chilies drying in the sun.

Colombia, Conservative-Liberal conflict led to civil war (1899-1902) and to La Violencia, a civil disorder that continued from the 1940s to the 1960s and resulted in about 200,000 deaths. From 1925 to 1948, no Ecuadoran leader was able to complete a full term in office.

Economically, however, the newly independent nations continued to develop, concentrating the wealth more solidly in the hands of the few. In many cases, this unevenly distributed prosperity led to more unrest. For example, by the 1920s, dissent arising from unequal power and land distribution in Chile united the middle and working classes, and eventually led to military intervention and a new constitution. Resultant social-welfare, education, and economic programs, however, were unable to eliminate inequalities rooted in the past.

Continued unrest has led to military control for several South American nations. In Paraguay, after years of turmoil, General Alfredo Stroessner came to power in 1954 and ruled continuously until 1989, when he was ousted by another military faction. Political unrest, caused in part by economic depression, resurfaced in Uruguay in the 1970s and led to military intervention in the government.

While some of the giant countries of South America struggled independently, the small nations of northeastern South America long remained under foreign rule. Guyana, for example, became British Guiana in 1831 and remained under British control until 1966. Suriname changed hands among the British, Dutch, and French until 1815, when the Netherlands gained control; independence did not come until 1975. And French Guiana, famous for its penal colonies, remains an overseas department of France, which has controlled the region since the 1600s.

Today, agriculture continues its important role in South America's economy, with large commercial plantations producing crops for export and domestic consumption. Mining is a major contributor in some countries, and manufacturing is growing. Yet many South Americans are isolated from twentieth-century development, living much as their ancestors did and practicing subsistence agriculture according to ancient methods.

The destruction of South America's rain forest, one of the continent's most urgent issues, has economic considerations. In Amazonia, land is being cleared and burned for farms, cattle ranches, dams, and roads. In Brazil alone, fifty-one million acres were burned in 1987, leaving bare areas that, added together, just about equal the size of Kansas. This destruction not only threatens the millions of species that live in the jungle, but it also may contribute to global warming. Conservation efforts require cash, however, and recession-stricken Brazil's international debt is already among the world's highest. Unless Brazil experiences some economic relief, environmentalists fear the rain forest will continue to burn.

South America
Countries

Argentina

The second largest nation in South America, Argentina stretches from the Tropic of Capricorn to the southern tip of the continent. The nation has a varied terrain, with northern lowlands, the east-central pampas, the Andes in the west, and the southern Patagonian steppe. The climate likewise varies. An indigenous Indian population, Spanish settlement, and a turn-of-the-century influx of immigrants have made Argentina an ethnically diverse nation. Today, most Argentines are descendants of Spanish and Italian immigrants. Political difficulties beginning in the 1930s have resulted in economic problems and have kept this one-time economic giant from realizing its potential. High inflation rates have exacerbated the situation in the 1980s. Elections in 1983 resulted in a new government that is trying to resolve continued economic problems, deal with human-rights transgressions, and institute other reforms.

Bolivia

This is a landlocked nation in central South America. The terrain includes the western altiplano, or high plain; the eastern llano, or low plain; and the central yungas, formed from hills and valleys. The climate varies with altitude. Indians compose the majority of Bolivia's population. Minorities include mestizos of Spanish-Indian descent and Europeans. Bolivia is underdeveloped and among South America's poorest nations. Farming is the main activity, although mining makes the largest contribution to the gross national product. Instability and social unrest have continued since a 1964 coup, but the nation is now controlled by its elected congress. Cocaine trafficking is a current problem.

Brazil

The largest South American nation, Brazil is also the most populous. It takes up a huge region in east-central South America and faces the Atlantic Ocean. Forests cover about half the country; the other regions range from plains to mountains. The climate is semitropical to tropical. The mixed population was shaped by indigenous Indians, Portuguese colonists, black African slaves, and European and Japanese immigrants. Brazil is the only Portuguese-speaking nation in the Americas. The economy is a diversified mix of agriculture, mining, and industry. In 1985, an election ended twenty-one years of military rule. Severe economic recession grips the nation, and its foreign debt is among the largest in the world.

Chile

Chile is a long, narrow nation on South America's southwestern Pacific coast. Chile's land barriers – the eastern Andes, western coastal range, and northern desert – have resulted in a mostly urban population concentrated in a central valley. The climate varies but is generally mild. Chile's land provides the natural resources necessary for a successful economy, but longtime instability has taken its toll. A repressive military junta seized power from an elected Socialist government in 1973 and has remained in control ever since.

Colombia

This nation sits at the extreme northwestern corner of South America and links the continent to Central America. The terrain is characterized by a flat coastal region, central highlands, and wide eastern llanos, or plains. The climate is tropical except in the highlands. Colombia's mixed population traces its roots to indigenous Indians, Spanish colonists, and black African slaves. Industry now keeps pace with traditional agriculture in economic contributions, and mining is also important. Coffee is a traditional crop, and emeralds are an important mineral. Although Colombia has the strongest tradition of democracy in South America, political unrest exists. As cocaine has become the nation's most profitable agricultural product, the government has had problems with corruption of its officials and with controlling drug traffic in and out of the country.

Ecuador

The equator runs through this smallish nation in northwestern South America. The nation is largely mountainous, and climate varies with altitude. Ecuador's ethnicity was established by an indigenous Indian population and Spanish colonists. Despite an oil boom in the 1970s, Ecuador remains underdeveloped. The nation is a member of the Organization of Petroleum Exporting Countries (OPEC), but agriculture remains important for much of the population. Following military rule, a new constitution was established in 1978. Declining oil exports have caused economic recession in the 1980s, a situation that was worsened by a 1987 earthquake that left twenty thousand homeless and destroyed part of a key pipeline.

Right: Machu Picchu, an ancient Inca town, is situated 7,875 feet (2,400 meters) above sea level in the Andes, about fifty miles (eighty kilometers) northwest of Cuzco, Peru. The story behind the once-fortified city is not clear, but certain structures and artifacts suggest religious significance. Machu Picchu was never found by Spanish conquistadors and remained unknown until its discovery in 1911.

Falkland Islands

These South Atlantic islands east of Argentina are a dependent territory of the United Kingdom. The population is mainly of British descent. Sheep raising is the main activity, supplemented by fishing. Although the islands have been under British rule since the 1800s, continued Argentine claims resulted in a 1982 Argentine invasion and occupation. The British won the subsequent battle and continue to govern the Falklands.

French Guiana

Sitting on the Atlantic Ocean in northeastern South America, French Guiana is an overseas department of France. Fertile coastal plains in the north give way to hills and mountains along the Brazilian border. Rain forests cover much of the landscape. The majority population is of African and mixed African-European descent. Shrimp production and a growing timber industry are French Guiana's economic mainstays. The land remains largely undeveloped, however, and reliance on French aid continues. The region has been administered by France since the 1600s.

Guyana

Just north of the equator in northeastern South America lies Guyana. Inland forests give way to savanna and a coastal plain. The climate is tropical. The population includes descendants of black African slaves and East Indian, Chinese, and Portuguese laborers brought to work sugar plantations. Agriculture and mining compose the backbone of the Guyanese economy. Guyana became a republic in 1970 and has pursued Socialist policies. The mostly nationalized economy remains severely depressed.

Paraguay

The Tropic of Capricorn passes through Paraguay, a landlocked nation in south-central South America. There are semi-arid plains in the west; the east is fertile and more temperate. Paraguay's population displays a homogeneity unusual in South America: most people are a mix of Spanish and Guarani Indian ancestry. Agriculture forms the keystone of the economy. The lack of direct access to the sea, unskilled labor, and a history of war and instability have resulted in an underdeveloped economy; manufacturing in particular has suffered. A repressive military regime was in power from 1954 to 1989, when it was overthrown in a military coup. It is doubtful that reforms will be made.

Peru

Peru lies just south of the equator on South America's Pacific coast. Climate varies from arid and mild in the coastal desert to temperate but cool in the Andean highlands and hot and humid in the eastern jungles and plains. The Indian population constitutes the nation's largest ethnic group and the largest Indian concentration in North or South America. Considerable natural resources have made Peru a leader in the production of minerals and in fishing. Productivity has been slowed, however, by a mountainous terrain that impedes transport and communication, earthquakes and other natural disasters, a largely unskilled work force, and years of stringent military rule. Peru had been under military rule before 1980, when it returned to democratic leadership. Police and labor strikes, a border dispute with Ecuador, and terrorist activities by Maoist groups have recently plagued the nation.

Suriname

A small nation in northeastern South America, Suriname borders on the Atlantic Ocean. The terrain is marked by a narrow coastal swamp, central forests and savanna, and southern jungle-covered hills. The climate is tropical. Suriname contains a portion of the vast Amazonian rain forest that is currently being cleared despite international protests and environmental ramifications. Suriname's diverse ethnicity was shaped by the importation of black African slaves and contract laborers from the East. The economy is based on mining and metal processing, but agriculture plays an important role as well. In 1980, the military seized power, and a joint military-civilian government was subsequently established. Instability has continued, with coup attempts.

Uruguay

Uruguay is situated on the Atlantic Ocean in southeastern South America. Most Uruguayans are white descendants of nineteenth- and twentieth-century immigrants from Spain, Italy, and other European countries. Uruguay's soil, plains, and climate provide the basis for agriculture and are especially conducive to livestock raising. Previously under military control, civilian government was restored in 1985. Uruguay's standard of living was once one of the highest in South America. In the 1980s, however, economic deterioration, including inflation, has forced Uruguay to incur a significant international debt.

Venezuela

Venezuela sits at the top of South America on the Caribbean Sea. The varied Venezuelan landscape is dominated by the Andes, a coastal zone, high plateaus, and plains. Temperatures vary with altitude. Spanish colonial rule of the nation is reflected in its predominantly mestizo population. Since the expansion of the petroleum industry in the 1920s, Venezuela has experienced rapid economic growth, but the economy has been hampered by unevenly distributed wealth, a high birthrate, and fluctuations in the price of oil. Venezuela was a founding member of the Organization of Petroleum Exporting Countries (OPEC). Since 1958, Venezuela has tried to achieve a representational form of government and has held a number of democratic elections. Thought to contain the world's largest oil reserves, the Orinoco tar belt is under development.

Below: One of the most famous festivals in the world, Carnival is held annually before and on Shrove Tuesday in Rio de Janeiro, Brazil. Among other sights, Carnival features all-night parades in which the local samba clubs compete for prizes for the best costumes and music.

Top: Montevideo, Uruguay, lies on the *Río de la Plata* in the southern part of the nation. The port city is the capital as well as the financial, industrial, and cultural center of Uruguay and contains nearly half of the nation's total population.

Right: Inhabited before the eleventh century, Quito, Ecuador, is situated in the Andes, only fifteen miles (twenty-four kilometers) south of the equator. The city is the capital and second largest city in Ecuador, after the more populous Guayaquil.

ATLANTIC OCEAN

Scale 1:12,000,000

One centimeter represents 120 kilometers.
One inch represents approximately 190 miles.

Oblique Conic Conformal Projection

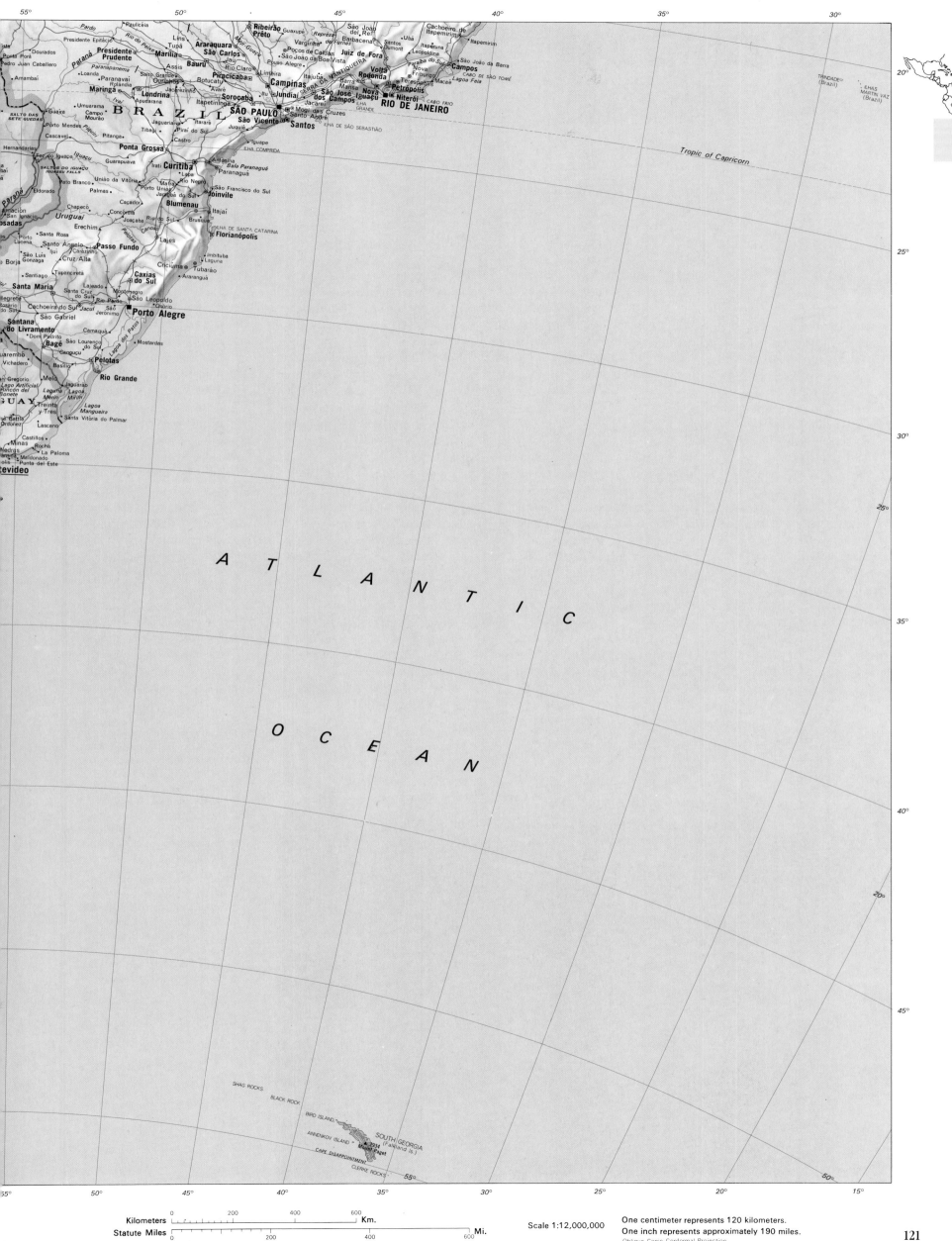

55° 50° 45° 40° 35° 30°

20°

Pardo
Presidente Epitácio · Raulicéia
Guaxupé
São João del Rei
Barbacena
Cachoeiro de Itapemirim
Itapemirim
Ponta Porã · Dourados
Presidente Prudente
Lins
Tupã
Araraquara
São Carlos
Represa
Varginha
Furnas
Ubá
Leopoldina
São João da Barra
Pedro Juan Caballero · Paranapanema
Marília
Bauru
Pocos de Caldas
Juiz de Fora
Itaperuna
Nova
Friburgo
Campos
· Amambaí
Loanda
Rolândia
Piracicaba
São João da Boa Vista
Pouso Alegre
Itajubá
Volta Redonda
Barra Mansa
Paraíba do Sul
Macaé
Lagoa Feia
CABO DE SÃO TOMÉ

Maringá
Londrina
Apucarana
Jacarezinho
Rio Claro
Limeira
Campinas
Jundiaí
São José dos Campos
Petrópolis
Teresópolis

BRAZIL
Sorocaba
Itapetininga
SÃO PAULO
Mogi das Cruzes
Jacareí
Niterói
RIO DE JANEIRO
CABO FRIO

· Güaíra
Campo Mourão
Itararé
São André
São Vicente
Santos

SALTO DAS SETE QUEDAS
Ponta Grossa
Castro

20°

Pitanga

Iguape
ILHA COMPRIDA

Cascavel · Hernandarias
Iguaçu
Curitiba
Lapa
Antonina
Baía Paranaguá
Paranaguá

Tropic of Capricorn

San Ignacio · Eldorado
União da Vitória
Rio Negro
Mafra
São Francisco do Sul

Uruguai
Chapecó
Cações
Jaraguá do Sul
Joinvile

Erechim
Concórdia
Rio do Sul
Brusque
Itajaí

Santo Ângelo
Carazinho
Joaçaba
Canoas

25°

Santa Rosa · Ijuí
Passo Fundo
Lajes
ILHA DE SANTA CATARINA

Cruz Alta
Florianópolis

São Luís Gonzaga
Santa Cruz
Lajeado
Imbituba

Santiago
Tupanciretã
Criciúma
Tubarão
Laguna

Santa Maria
Cachoeira do Sul
Jacuí
São Jerônimo
São Leopoldo
Montenegro
Caxias do Sul
Araranguá

São Gabriel
Camaquã
Porto Alegre

Santana do Livramento
São Lourenço do Sul
Osório

URUGUAY
Bagé
Canguçu
Pelotas

30°

Vichadero
Basílio
Rio Grande

San Gregorio
Jaguarão
Lagoa dos Patos

Melo
Laguna Merín
Mirim
Lagoa Mangueira

Treinta y Tres
Santa Vitória do Palmar

Lascano
Castillos
Rochas

Minas
La Paloma
Maldonado
Punta del Este

Montevideo

25°

A T L A N T I C

O C E A N

35°

40°

20°

45°

SHAG ROCKS
BLACK ROCK

BIRD ISLAND
ANNENKOV ISLAND
SOUTH GEORGIA
Falkland Is.
CAPE DISAPPOINTMENT
CLERKE ROCKS

50°

55° 50° 45° 40° 35° 30° 25° 20° 15°

Kilometers 0 200 400 600 Km.
Statute Miles 0 200 400 600 Mi.
Scale 1:12,000,000
One centimeter represents 120 kilometers.
One inch represents approximately 190 miles.
Oblique Conic Conformal Projection
121

North America
Profile

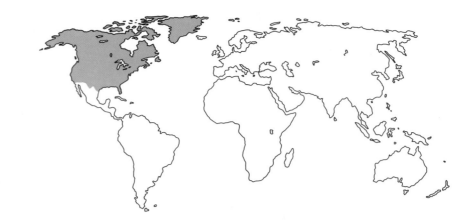

Location and Size

The Americas stretch from well north of the islands of Canada and Greenland to Cape Horn. For the purposes of this atlas, we have departed from the more traditional divisions of South and North America. What we define here as North America extends from the northern tips of the Canadian islands to the Florida Keys – a distance of some 3,900 miles (6,250 kilometers). The most westerly point on the mainland of the continent is the farthest reaches of Alaska. On the Atlantic coast, Newfoundland and Greenland extend farthest to the east.

Mainland North America is compact and essentially rectangular, with appendages in the northwest and southeast. Beyond the mainland lie many islands, especially in the north. Within the main rectangle are hundreds of lakes, with the open sea of Hudson Bay in the north.

The North American coastline shows a number of contrasting features. Some regions, such as British Columbia and Maine, have a complex, fretted outline with a number of offshore islands. Elsewhere, the outline is far more simple, as in Oregon and California. In places such as Texas and Louisiana, the coast is one of bars and lagoons.

Landscape

North America can be broadly divided into four major physical regions. In the north, surrounding Hudson Bay in a great crescent-shaped area, lies the Canadian Shield. It has been stripped of most of its soil during recent glaciations, has hundreds of lakes dotted on its surface, and has little agricultural potential. The main interest lies in the mineral resources of the old rocks and in forestry.

Along the east side of the continent lie ranges of mountains with a maximum height of 6,684 feet (2,037 meters) in the Blue Ridge region of the Appala-chians. Extending from Alabama in the south to the Canadian border in the north, the Appalachians continue into the mainland Maritime Provinces and Newfoundland.

The mountains of the west are far more complex and extensive. The Rocky Mountains are the most easterly of these, while farther west lie the Sierra Nevada, the Cascades, the Coast Ranges, and the Alaska Range. Between and within these lie a number of plateaus; desert basins, including the notorious Death Valley; and such fertile areas as the Central Valley of California and the Willamette Valley-Puget Sound lowlands farther north. These mountains today form the highest areas of the continent, rising 20,320 feet (6,194 meters) at Mount McKinley, Alaska. In this most unstable region of the continent lie the famous geysers of Yellowstone National Park and the much-feared San Andreas Fault, which threatens many of the urban areas of California.

A wide lowland area stretches from the Arctic Ocean in the north to the Gulf of Mexico in the south. Parts of this region are very low, especially the floors of the Mississippi and Mackenzie valleys, but the high plains reach to some 5,000 feet (1,600 meters) above sea level at the front ranges of the Rocky Mountains.

North America is a land of great rivers and river basins, most of which drain toward the Atlantic and Arctic oceans, Hudson Bay, and the Gulf of Mexico. The central lowlands are drained southward by the Mississippi-Missouri river system and northward by the Mackenzie River and the Saskatch-ewan-Nelson system. Rivers flowing to the Pacific are mainly shorter, though a few – especially the Colorado and Snake – have developed impressive scenic courses through the mountains to the coast. The Great Lakes compose another distinctive water feature of the continent, with Lake Superior the largest lake in the Western Hemisphere.

The largest island in the world, Greenland is composed of an inland

Left: The Rocky Mountains form the most extensive mountain system in North America. They are part of the great cordillera that runs down the western regions of North, Middle, and South America. The Teton Range, shown here, is one of the attractions of Grand Teton National Park, Wyoming.

Right: Ancestors of modern Pueblos, a Native American group, inhabited what is now Canyon de Chelly National Monument, Arizona, between the years 350 and 1300. They built villages here and left behind many ruins and artifacts.

plateau, coastal mountains and fjords, and offshore islands.

Climate

Climatically, the North American continent extends from the tropics to the polar reaches and has a full west-east range from one ocean to the other. Parts of mainland Canada, Greenland, and other islands lie well inside the Arctic Circle. In the west of the continent lies the great mountain region, which acts as a major barrier to the movement of air from west to east. In the east, the Appalachians have a similar effect to air movements. Thus the interior of the continent is effectively sealed from oceanic influences, though the unimpeded passage for air moving northward and southward from the Gulf or the Arctic does mean that, at times, warm air may penetrate well north or cold air well south.

In the extreme west, limited areas experience warm and cool temperate climates of an oceanic type. In parts, California enjoys a climate akin to that of some Mediterranean areas, but the Coast Ranges ensure that the Central Valley, for example, has great temperature extremes and, in the south, an acute water shortage. Farther north, in the coastal strip of Oregon, Washington, and British Colombia, the average temperature of the coldest month stays above freezing level, but the summer average monthly temperatures never exceed 72°F (22°C).

East of this coastal area, the climates of the mountain ranges are largely inhospitable. Those of the basins and ranges and into the western Great Plains can be classified as dry; annual precipitation is below ten inches (250 millimeters) and, with the heat of most areas, this moisture has little useful effect. Temperatures are more extreme here than on the coasts, with the monthly average below freezing for parts of the year. Although these regions are largely semiarid, in Arizona, Utah, and New Mexico the more extreme conditions of hot deserts prevail, with July temperatures of 91°F (33°C) and 55°F (13°C) in January.

Except for the tropical tip of Florida, the eastern United States south of Kansas, Kentucky, and Virginia enjoys a subtropical climate with rainfall throughout the year and distinctly warm summers. North of this area are progressively cooler and mainly drier zones. Thus the southern parts of the prairie provinces and the Great Lakes region experience a cool temperate climate, with rainfall increasing in the east.

Still farther north, the climates become less and less inviting. Here there is a broad belt of subarctic climates, which lies between the arctic north and the temperate south. In the tundra margins of northern Canada, an arctic climate prevails, and no month has an average temperature in excess of 50°F (10°C).

More than 80 percent of Greenland is covered by permanent ice. The climate is cold, with warmer temperatures and more precipitation in the southwest. Much of Greenland lies within the Arctic Circle and is considered a polar region.

Below: Hawaii became the fiftieth state of the United States in 1959. The Pacific islands are now among the world's most popular vacation destinations – a position they have earned with their tropical climate and sandy beaches. Shown here is Hanauma Bay, Oahu.

Left: British Columbia is the westernmost province of Canada. It remained isolated from the rest of the nation in its early provincial years because of its largely mountainous terrain. Today it is the site of several national parks, including Yoho National Park, shown here.

Middle, left: The Calgary Stampede, held annually in Calgary, Alberta, is one of the most prestigious rodeos.

Middle, right: Niagara Falls, on the waterway between Lakes Ontario and Erie at the United States-Canada border, attracts thousands of tourists who don waterproof gear to view the torrent up close.

Bottom: Kodiak Island, Alaska, is home to the Kodiak brown bear, which inhabits the wildlife refuge to which three-quarters of the island is dedicated. Also situated on the island off Alaska's southern coast is the city of Kodiak.

North America

Profile continued

Below: On the Utah-Arizona border is a scenic region known as Monument Valley. Here are found sandstone buttes, mesas, and arches, some of them rising up to one thousand feet (three hundred meters) above the sandy plain below.

Right: Luring immigrants from around the world, many of the large cities of the United States have ethnic enclaves such as New York's Chinatown.

Below: The United States leads the world in heavy industry. Shown here is an automotive plant in Detroit, Michigan.

History, Politics, and Economy

There is some evidence that humans first entered North America more than twenty thousand years ago. A land bridge at the site of the Bering Strait was probably their access route. While more sophisticated Indian civilizations flourished farther south, with a few exceptions, the Native Americans of North America remained largely hunter-gatherers.

Although the Norse and most likely the Irish knew of North America long before, the flood of European settlement began after Christopher Columbus's discovery in 1492. England established a colony at Jamestown, Virginia, in 1607; subsequent rivalries for power in the northern New World saw Britain eventually gain control of much territory. In the 1763 Treaty of Paris, for example, France lost Canada and other North American territory to Britain.

The United States of America gained its independence when thirteen British colonies won a war waged from 1775 to 1783. Expansion continued westward throughout the nineteenth century. The issues of black slavery and states' rights led to the American Civil War from 1861 to 1865, a struggle that pitted the North against the South and resulted in the end of slavery. Opportunities for prosperity accompanied the industrial revolution in the late nineteenth century and led to a large influx of immigrants. From 1917 to 1918, the country joined the Allies in World War I. A severe economic depression began in 1929, and the United States did not really recover until military spending during World War II stimulated industry and the economy in general. Allied victory came in 1945. Postwar conflicts included the Korean War of the early fifties and the Vietnam War, which involved the United States from the late 1950s to 1973.

To aid in resolving the continued conflict between French and English residents of Canada, the British North America Act of 1867 united the colonies into the Dominion of Canada. In 1926, Canada declared itself an independent member of the British Commonwealth, and in 1931, Britain recognized the declaration. Post World War II years saw an improved economy and the domination of two parties: Liberal and Progressive Conservative.

The United States and Canada – two giants in the world economy – are so bound together economically and agriculturally that they tend to share the same economic problems. When the United States is in an economic downturn, so is Canada, since about half of Canada's manufacturing industry is owned by American firms. When Canada has a bumper crop of wheat and finds it difficult to locate a buyer, it is generally because the United States has harvested a bumper crop the same year. Being neighbors has created both tensions and opportunities for the two countries.

It is estimated that humans migrated from the east to Greenland as early as 4000 B.C. Norwegian Vikings sighted Greenland in the ninth century, and in the tenth century, Erik the Red brought the first settlers from Iceland. Greenland united with Norway in the 1200s, and the two regions came under Danish rule in the 1300s. Denmark retained control of Greenland when Norway left the union in 1814. In 1953, the island became a province of Denmark and in 1979 gained home rule. Although Greenland determines its own fate in international affairs, Denmark continues to handle some international matters.

Below: Sapphire blue Crater Lake, in Crater Lake National Park, Oregon, was formed by the explosion of an ancient volcano. The lake has no outlet or inlet; thus it is maintained solely by precipitation.

Canada

Canada is a huge nation situated north of the United States. It is second in size only to the Soviet Union. Canada was greatly influenced by French and British rule, and its culture reflects this dual nature. Descendants of British and French settlers compose the two main population groups, and languages include both English and French. Minorities include descendants of various European groups, indigenous Native Americans, and Inuit. French-speaking inhabitants, called Québecois, are concentrated in the Province of Québec, where they constitute over 80 percent of the population. These Québecois have strongly resented the anglicization

imposed on all of Canada, including Québec, by Canadians of British descent. Historically, that resentment has shown itself in several ways: Québec's insistence that French be the official language of Canada along with English; that the old Canadian flag be replaced by the Maple Leaf flag; and the demand that Québec be allowed to form its own independent republic. Because of the rugged terrain and harsh climate of northern Canada, population is concentrated near the United States border. Rich natural resources – including mineral deposits, fertile land, forests, and lakes – helped shape Canada's economy, which ranks among the world's most prosperous. The economy has shifted from one that is based on pro-

duction and export of raw agricultural items and natural resources to one that is based on manufacturing those raw materials. Economic problems are those common to most modern industrial nations. Agriculture, mining, and industry are highly developed. Canada is a major wheat producer; mineral output includes asbestos, zinc, silver, and nickel; and crude petroleum in an important export. The service sector is also active. Canada is a self-governing parliamentary state within the Commonwealth of Nations. Canadians recognize Queen Elizabeth II of England as the head of state. The last legislative control Britain had over Canada was severed in 1982 when Canada gained the right to amend its own constitution. In recent years, the

New Democratic party has challenged the domination of the Liberal and Progressive Conservative parties in politics. In 1987, Canadian leaders agreed on an amendment to the constitution that recognizes Québec as a distinct society within the Canadian Federation.

Greenland

Situated almost entirely within the Arctic Circle, northeast of mainland Canada, is huge Greenland, the largest island in the world. Certain areas of Greenland have twenty-four consecutive hours of daylight in summer and darkness in winter. Most Greenlanders are native-born descendants of mixed Inuit-Danish ancestry. Lutheranism, the predominant religion, reflects Danish ties. Descended from an indigenous Arctic people, pure Inuit are a minority and usually follow traditional life-styles. Because of the harsh northern climate, the population is concentrated along the southern coast. Fishing is Greenland's economic backbone. Despite a difficult arctic environment, mining of zinc and lead continues; but iron, coal, uranium, and molybdenum deposits remain undeveloped. Greenland is a self-governing territory under Danish protection.

St. Pierre and Miquelon

This group of eight islands to the immediate south of Newfoundland is a territorial collectivity of France and the only French-held territory in North America. The islands lie in two distinct sections; the far smaller St. Pierre group contains 90 percent of the total population. The once-plentiful forests have been cut; the islands are now largely bare rock or scrub and do not support much agriculture. Cod fishing is the main occupation, and fish-processing industries are important. Tourism has been increasing.

United States

The United States of America consists of fifty states and extends from the Atlantic to Pacific coasts of North America, directly south of Canada. Two of the states – Alaska and Hawaii – are non-contiguous, and the nation administers several outlying territories. The diverse population of the United States is mostly composed of whites, many descended from eighteenth- and nineteenth-century immigrants; blacks, mainly descended from African slaves; peoples of Spanish and Asian origin; and indigenous Native Americans, Inuit, and Hawaiians. Nearly three-quarters of the population lives in urban areas. Great regional variations in population density exist, with the greatest density in New Jersey and the lowest in Alaska. Religions encompass the world's major faiths; predominating are Protestantism, Roman Catholicism, and Judaism. English is the official language, though Spanish is spoken by many, and other languages are often found in ethnic enclaves. The United States is an international economic power, and all sectors of the economy are highly developed. Fertile soils produce high crop yields, with considerable land under cultivation. Mineral output includes petroleum and natural gas, coal, copper, lead, and zinc, but high consumption makes the United States dependent on foreign oil. The country is a leading manufacturer, and about one-quarter of the work force is engaged in manufacturing. As is the case with other highly developed nations, the service sector employs most of the work force and accounts for the largest percentage of the gross national product. Tourism is also important. The gross national product of the United States is the highest in the world, and the per capita income is among the highest.

The United States is a republic, with the Democratic and Republican parties dominating elections. The more conservative Republican party has held the presidency since the beginning of the 1980s, first with Ronald Reagan and then with George Bush, who took office in 1989. The overwhelming social problem in the United States has historically been racial, particularly the status of blacks, and, more recently, Third World immigrants. Internationally, the United States has begun to reevaluate its foreign policy and its position in the worldwide economic picture. Primary concerns are how to handle the federal budget deficit, increasing military spending, foreign debt, the threat of inflation, and the loss of jobs in manufacturing. Additionally, long-term defense planning is under scrutiny, particularly the development of the Strategic Defense Initiative (SDI) or Star Wars program. By most measures, the United States remains the world's dominant power. Nations in the rest of the world, especially countries in Asia and the Pacific, are becoming increasingly productive, however, and may threaten the United States' stature as world leader.

Canada

Baffin Bay

Davis Strait

**GREENLAND
KALAALLIT
NUNAAT
(Denmark)**

**Labrador
Sea**

**ATLANTIC
OCEAN**

**Hudson
Bay**

LABRADOR

**James
Bay**

QUEBEC

All islands within Hudson Bay, James Bay,
and Ungava Bay lie within Northwest Territories

ONTARIO

NEWFOUNDLAND

**Ungava
Bay**

**PENINSULE
D'UNGAVA**

**PRINCE EDWARD
ISLAND**

NOVA SCOTIA

**NEW
BRUNSWICK**

**ST. PIERRE
AND MIQUELON**

MONTREAL

TORONTO

DETROIT

CHICAGO

BOSTON

NEW YORK

PHILADELPHIA

**ATLANTIC
OCEAN**

MICHIGAN

WISCONSIN

APPALACHIAN MTS.

Copyright © by Rand McNally & Co.
Map prepared by Rand McNally & Co.
A-520000-264

Kilometers   0   200   400   600   Km.
Statute Miles   0   200   400   600   Mi.

Scale 1:12,000,000

One centimeter represents 120 kilometers.
One inch represents approximately 190 miles.

Lambert Conformal Conic Projection

131

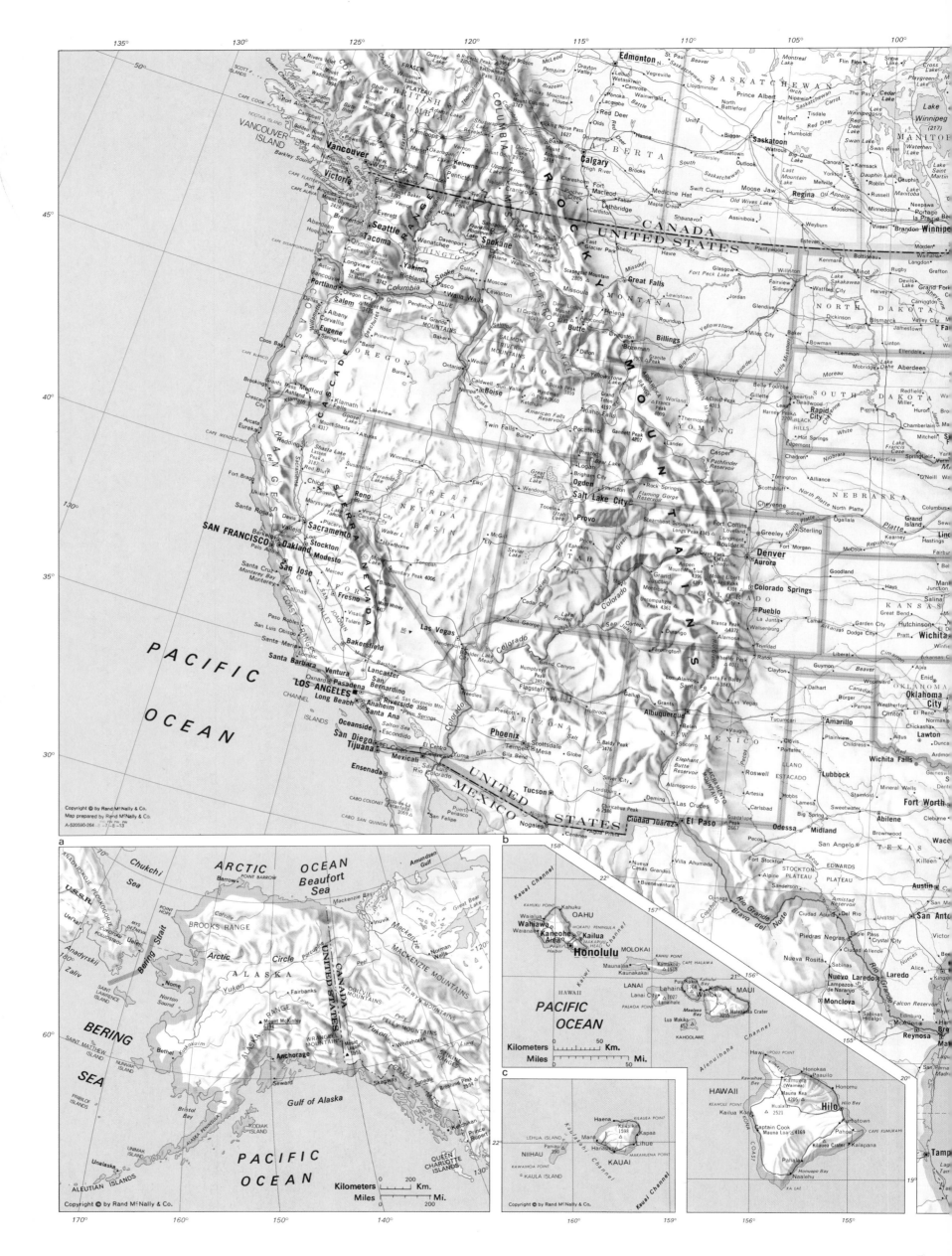

Kilometers
Statute Miles

Scale 1:12,000,000

One centimeter represents 120 kilometers.
One inch represents approximately 190 miles.

Albers Conical Equal-Area Projection

133

United States
Northeast

The great natural ports of North America's Atlantic coast have welcomed world travelers since 1620, when the pilgrims anchored at Plymouth, Massachusetts. From Boston, Massachusetts, to Baltimore, Maryland, whalers, traders, and other seafarers sailed into the harbors that became thriving cities during the nation's first decades of independence. You can now trace more than two hundred years of history in the great cities of the Northeast. Boston, Philadelphia, New York, and Washington, D.C., have all played major roles in United States history, and in all, you can visit historic sites.

Beyond the Northeast's major cities, you'll find the calm beauty of fishing towns, farms, and mountain resorts. Additionally, the Northeast offers extensive coastline – from the rocky shores of Maine's Acadia National Park, the only national park in New England, to the sandy shores of Cape Cod National Seashore in Massachusetts to the casinos and boardwalk of Atlantic City, New Jersey.

Right: Washington, D.C., the capital of the United States, is surrounded on three sides by Maryland, with the other side formed by the banks of the Potomac River. The city's many cultural, memorial, and federal buildings include the Capitol, shown here, which houses the legislative branch of the government.

Below: The international metropolis known as New York City is the United States' leading cultural and commercial center as well as its largest city. The Big Apple is central to the eastern megalopolis that extends from New Hampshire to northern Virginia.

Below: The United States Military Academy at West Point, New York, trains officers of the army.

Right: Long a maritime center, New London, Connecticut, has one of the finest deep-water ports on the Atlantic coast.

Bottom, left: Vermont's picturesque towns and mountainous terrain make it a popular tourist destination.

Bottom, right : These lobster pots contribute to Maine's position as the nation's leading lobster producer.

Kilometers 0 50 100 150 Km.

Statute Miles 0 50 100 150 Mi.

Scale 1:3,000,000

One centimeter represents 30 kilometers.
One inch represents approximately 47 miles.

Albers Conical Equal-Area Projection

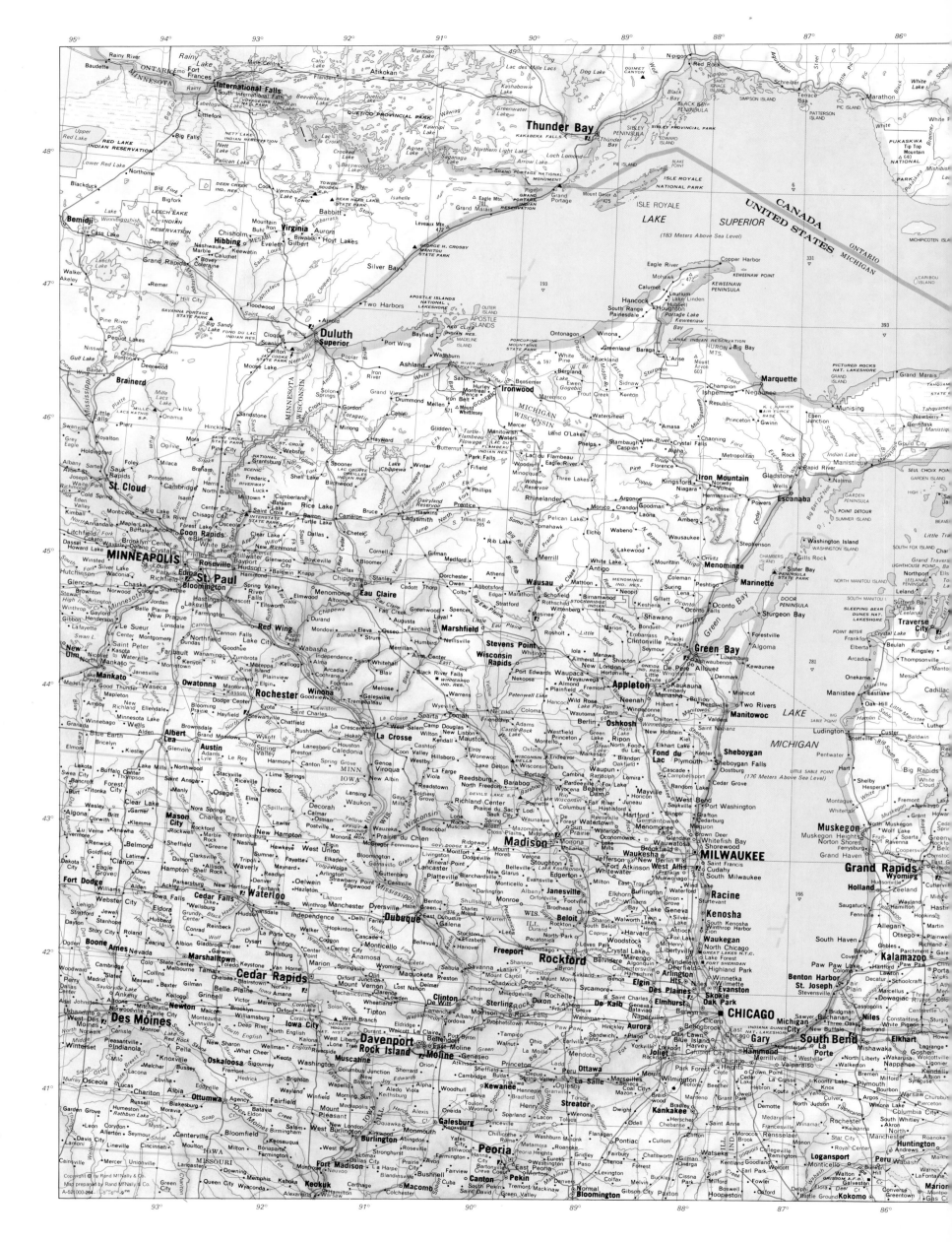

Kilometers | 0 | 50 | 100 | 150 | Km.

Statute Miles | 0 | 50 | 100 | 150 | Mi.

Scale 1:3,000,000

One centimeter represents 30 kilometers.
One inch represents approximately 47 miles.

Albers Conical Equal-Area Projection

United States
Great Lakes Region

The five Great Lakes formed a natural, navigable route for Native Americans and early American explorers long before trains sped across the continent. But once the railroads were built, great cities grew up along the shores of the lakes, each one a connecting point for ship and railroad cargoes. During the nineteenth century, grain and beef from the plains, iron ore from Minnesota, cotton from the South, and manufactured goods from the East all met in Chicago, Illinois. As technology advanced, the raw materials were turned into steel, refined oil, and automobiles and shipped from the mills and factories of Detroit, Michigan; Gary, Indiana; and Cleveland, Ohio. People from around the world found work in the Great Lakes cities.

In addition to their commercial worth, the Great Lakes are a valuable recreation resource. Chicagoans enjoy fine city beaches only blocks away from some of the world's tallest skyscrapers. Nature enthusiasts of all types retreat in all seasons to the wilderness regions of Minnesota, Wisconsin, and Michigan.

The arts, too, have flourished in the Great Lakes region. Chicago's long musical tradition today boasts the world's most highly acclaimed symphony orchestra as well as fine ensembles that specialize in more contemporary genres.

Above: The plains of the southern Great Lakes region form part of the American Midwest. Sophisticated farming techniques and fertile soils help make this region one of the world's most productive.

Right: Much of the northern Great Lakes region consists of forests and small lakes, both of which attract visitors with a variety of recreational interests. Shown is here the Upper Peninsula of Michigan.

Below: Situated on the southwestern shore of Lake Michigan, Chicago, Illinois, has long been a center for transportation, industry, and culture. The Windy City is the nation's third largest.

Sunshine and palm trees, antebellum mansions and Spanish moss, and Southern cooking and hospitality are the traditional hallmarks that draw visitors to the Southeast. Add to these the bustling cities of Atlanta, Georgia, and Miami, Florida, and the picture of today's Southeast begins to take shape.

This region offers a contrast of old and new. Founded by Spanish settlers in 1565, St. Augustine, Florida, is the oldest city in the United States. The restoration at Williamsburg, Virginia, offers tourists a rare opportunity to experience the life-style of colonial Virginians. Savannah's historical seaport and Charleston's lovely gardens recall the serene dignity of another era. Those who enjoy modern playgrounds, however, might head for Florida's Gold Coast or Orlando area, South Carolina's Hilton Head, or North Carolina's Pinehurst.

The Southeast's natural landmarks are varied. They range from Florida's swampy Everglades to the glorious elevations of the Blue Ridge to the spectacular dunes of the Outer Banks.

Left: Cypress trees such as these in Florida thrive in the many swampy regions of the Southeast. Home to a wide variety of wildlife, some of the major swamplands – such as Okefenokee Swamp and the Everglades – have become federally protected.

Bottom, left: The American South was once supported by a thriving plantation economy, which was largely destroyed in the wake of the Civil War. Some of the plantations remain, however, and have been turned into tourist attractions. Shown here is Orton Plantation, near Wilmington, North Carolina.

Below: Among Florida's many vacation destinations are its theme and amusement parks. Shown here is a castle at Walt Disney World, near Orlando.

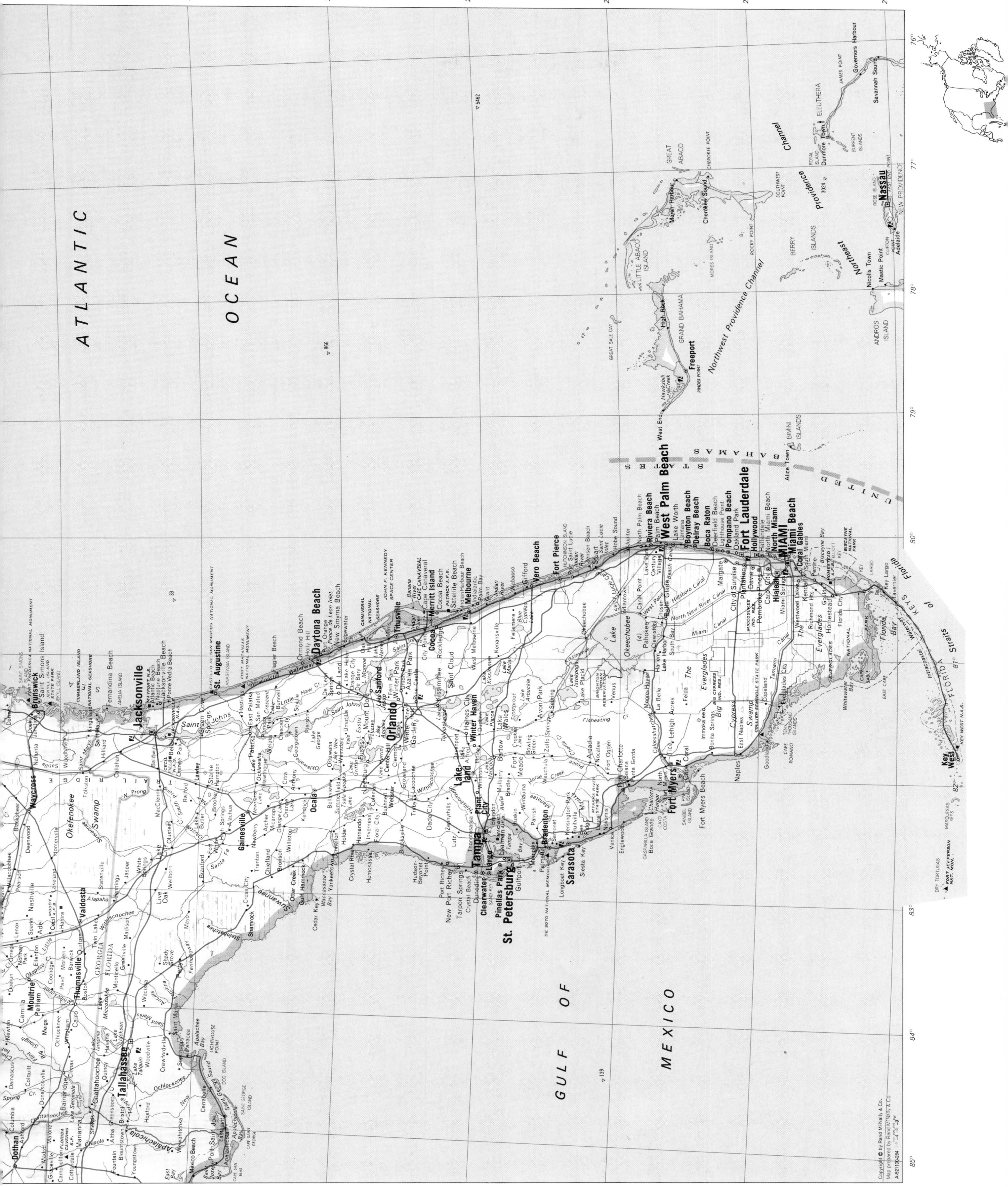

ATLANTIC

OCEAN

GULF OF MEXICO

GEORGIA

FLORIDA

Tallahassee

Jacksonville

St. Augustine

Daytona Beach

Orlando

Cocoa

Titusville

Melbourne

Vero Beach

Fort Pierce

West Palm Beach

Riviera Beach

Boynton Beach

Delray Beach

Boca Raton

Pompano Beach

Fort Lauderdale

Hollywood

MIAMI

Miami Beach

Coral Gables

Hialeah

Tampa

St. Petersburg

Clearwater

Pinellas Park

Sarasota

Bradenton

Plant City

Winter Haven

Lakeland

Ocala

Gainesville

Brunswick

Waycross

Valdosta

Moultrie

Thomasville

Dothan

Fort Myers

Key West

Okefenokee Swamp

Lake Okeechobee

Everglades National Park

BAHAMAS

UNITED STATES

GRAND BAHAMA

Freeport

LITTLE ABACO ISLAND

GREAT ABACO

BERRY ISLANDS

BIMINI ISLANDS

NEW PROVIDENCE

Nassau

ANDROS ISLAND

ELEUTHERA

Northwest Providence Channel

Providence Channel

FLORIDA KEYS

DRY TORTUGAS

Kilometers 0 50 100 150 Km.

Statute Miles 0 50 100 150 Mi.

Scale 1:3,000,000

One centimeter represents 30 kilometers.

One inch represents approximately 47 miles.

Albers Conical Equal-Area Projection

143

Copyright by Rand McNally & Co.

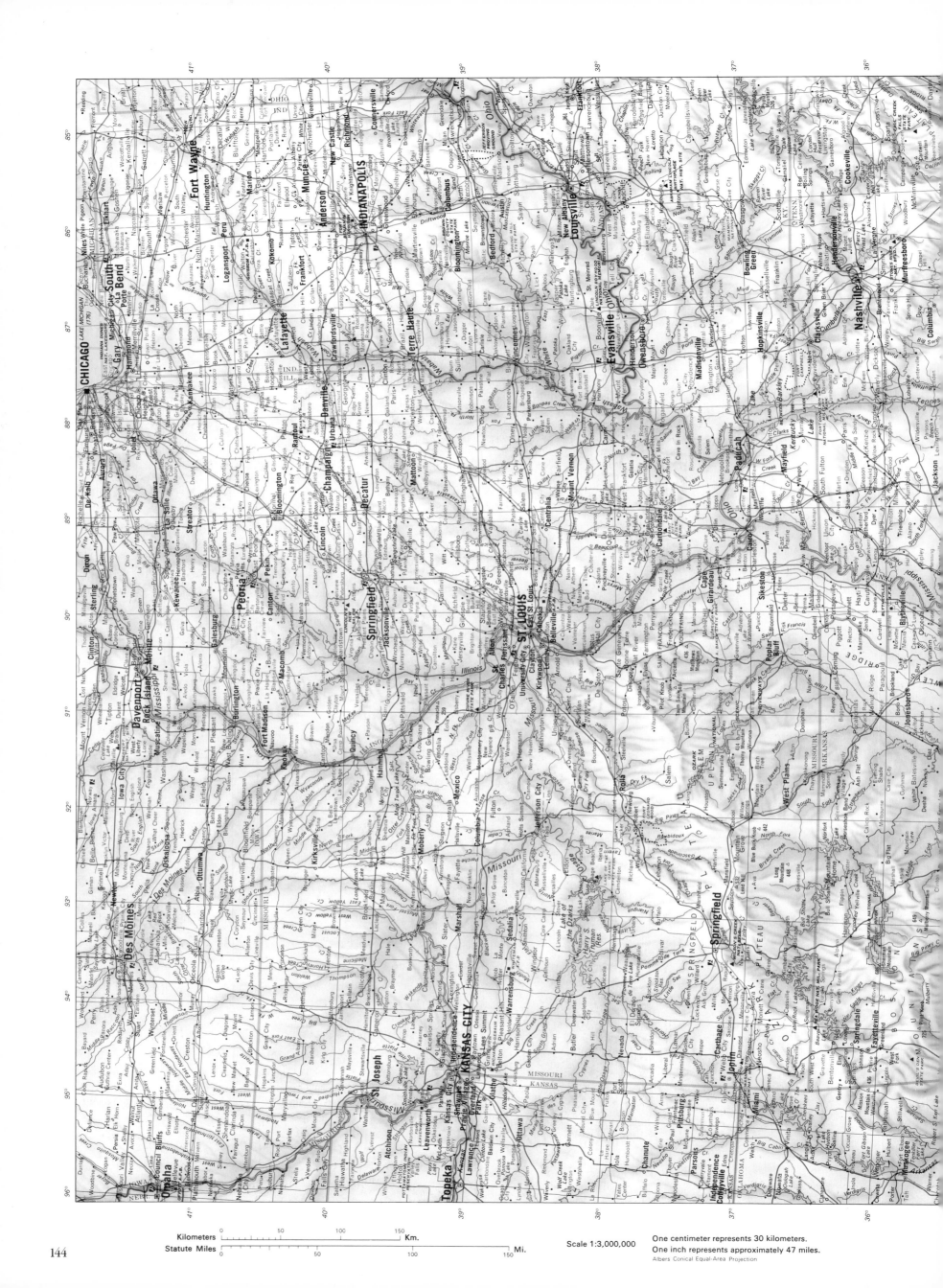

Kilometers

Statute Miles

Scale 1:3,000,000

One centimeter represents 30 kilometers.
One inch represents approximately 47 miles.

Albers Conical Equal-Area Projection

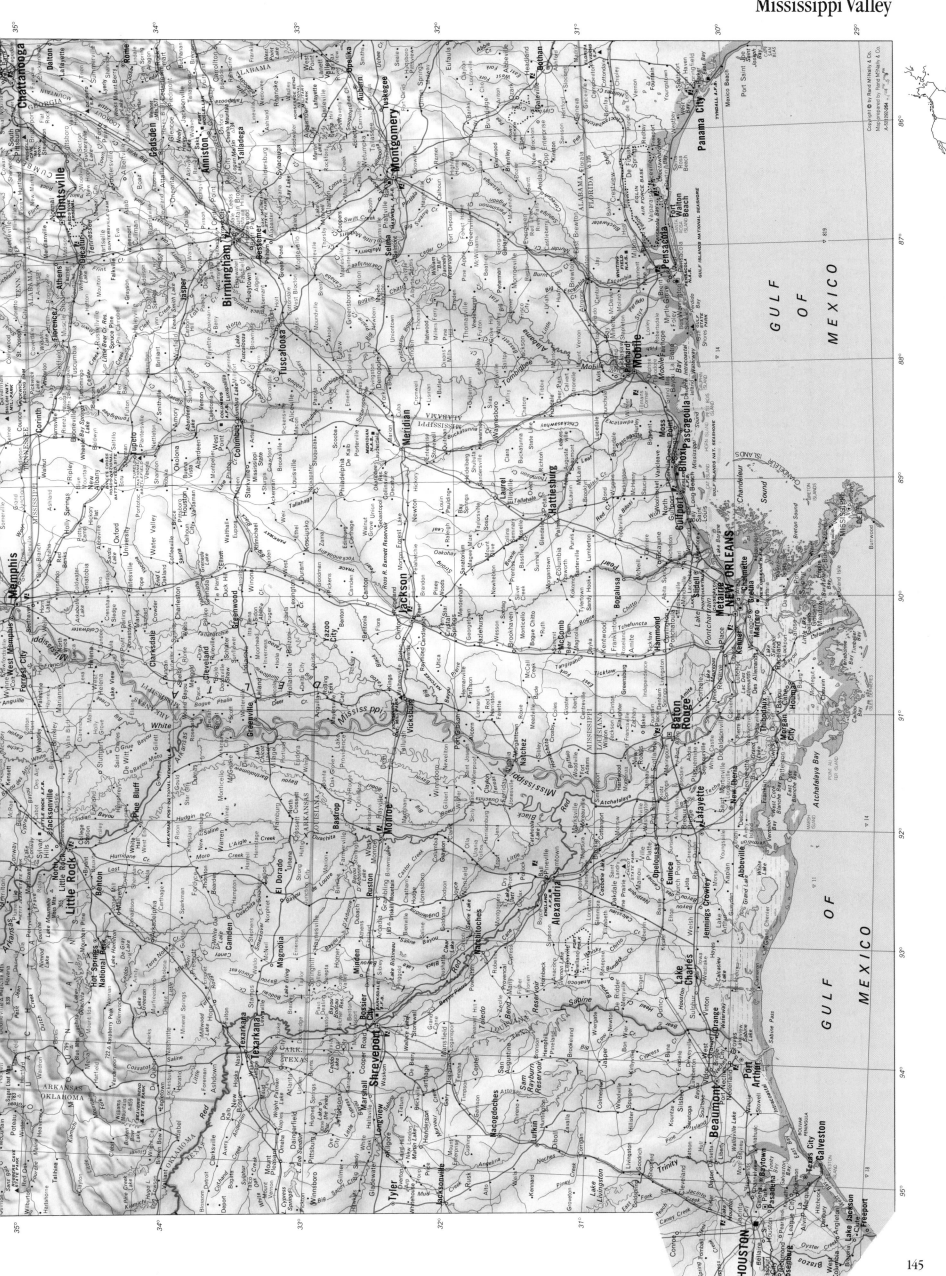

United States
Mississippi Valley

The rousing strains of Dixieland jazz, the foot-stomping twang of bluegrass, and the soulful ballads of country music are as much a part of the Mississippi Valley as the stockyards of Kansas City, Missouri, and the breweries of St. Louis, Missouri. On the farms, in the hills, and in the back quarters of rowdy river towns, some of the United States' native music was born and nurtured. Today, the sounds still beckon listeners to concert halls and nightclubs in cities such as Nashville and New Orleans.

The Mississippi's most famous character is Huckleberry Finn, the raft-roving runaway who has charmed children and provoked literary adults since Mark Twain created him in 1876. If you visit the author's family home in Hannibal, Missouri, you'll find that it remains true to the famous humorist's writings.

But what would Mark Twain make of modern St. Louis, with its towering Gateway Arch? He would undoubtedly recognize the old mansions of Natchez and the thriving commerce of Memphis. And who knows what he would think of the cuisine of today's New Orleans and Louisiana's bayous.

Top: The Mississippi River and its tributaries form the most significant river system in the United States. The mighty Mississippi has played a major role in the settlement of the nation, and many cities have flourished along its banks. The river rises in Minnesota and flows south for more than 2,300 miles (3,700 kilometers) to Louisiana, forming borders for ten states along the way.

Above: Visitors to some cities along the Mississippi can relive the region's past by taking steamboat rides.

Right: One of the United States' greatest contributions to world culture has been jazz, which originated in New Orleans, Louisiana. Visitors and residents alike are still drawn to the city's incomparable jazz bands.

Southern Rocky Mountains

Vistas rise to the heights of Pikes Peak, Colorado, and fall to the depths of the Grand Canyon in Arizona in the breathtakingly beautiful southern Rockies region. Outdoors enthusiasts cherish the ski slopes of Colorado and Utah, the extraordinary rock formations in a variety of national parks and monuments, the open skies of the ranches, and the crystalline splendor of the mountain lakes.

The list of national parks and monuments found in the southern Rockies is impressive. Among them are Colorado's Rocky Mountain and Mesa Verde national parks and Dinosaur National Monument; Utah's Bryce Canyon, Zion, Arches, Canyonlands, and Capitol Reef national parks and six national monuments; Arizona's Grand Canyon and Petrified Forest national parks and six national monuments; and New Mexico's Carlsbad Caverns National Park and ten national monuments.

The human-made attractions of the region span the ages. There are ancient Native American ruins in New Mexico and Arizona, which contrast with the metropolises of the southern Rockies. People come to Salt Lake City, Utah, to gaze on the sparkling white buildings as well as the Great Salt Lake and its surrounding desert. Visitors to Denver, Colorado, enjoy the offerings of a big city along with those of the nearby mountains. Phoenix, Arizona, has become the region's largest city, and travelers are drawn by its sun-drenched climate and unique culture.

Some of North America's oldest settlements – those of the Hopi, Navajo, and Pueblo – flourished beneath the southern Rockies. Sophisticated, agricultural Native American societies were centered mainly south of the Rio Grande, but these were the exceptions. Descendants of these ancient peoples still live in the region and remain culturally active.

Right: Tourists come to Canyonlands National Park, near Moab, Utah, to view spectacular rock formations, canyons, arches, spires, Native American ruins, and desert vegetation.

Above: About 1.5 million Native Americans live in the United States, many of them in the southern Rocky Mountain region. Arizona has more Native Americans than almost any other state.

Left: Havasu Creek flows into the Colorado River in Grand Canyon National Park, Arizona, tumbling over four major falls along the way. The Grand Canyon is one of the most spectacular sights in North America.

148

Kilometers

Km.

Statute Miles

Mi.

Scale 1:3,000,000

One centimeter represents 30 kilometers.
One inch represents approximately 47 miles.

Albers Conical Equal-Area Projection

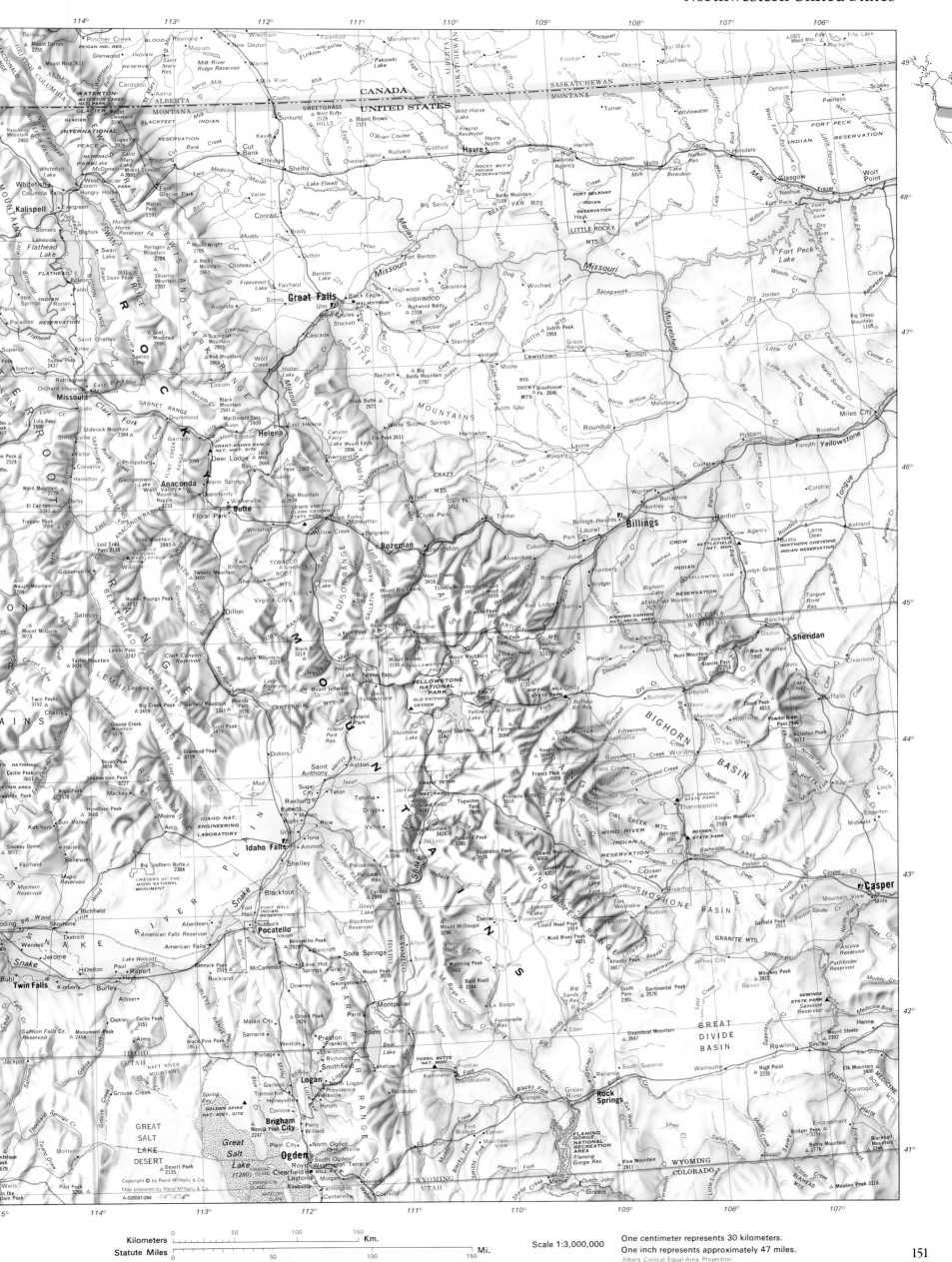

Kilometers 0 50 100 150 Km.

Statute Miles 0 50 100 150 Mi.

Scale 1:3,000,000

One centimeter represents 30 kilometers.
One inch represents approximately 47 miles.

Albers Conical Equal-Area Projection

United States
Northwest

The Lewis and Clark Expedition that began in 1804 was the turning point for this corner of the United States. Soon after word of the region returned to the East, the previously unexplored Northwest was crisscrossed by numerous fur traders, missionaries, salmon fishermen, and, finally, settlers.

Today's residents of the Northwest often boast that their region has everything. There's much truth to this claim, for Washington's timberlands, the Willamette valley farms and orchards, the inland cattle ranges, and the coastal fishing industry contribute to a diverse bounty. The cities of Portland, Oregon, and Seattle, Washington, are known for their peaceful prosperity and cultural sophistication.

This is also the land of the Snake River, with its spectacular Hells Canyon at the border of Idaho and Oregon; the geysers, grizzly bears, and jagged Teton Range of Wyoming; the Big Sky country of Montana; the glaciers of North Cascades National Park in Washington; and the marine life and rugged Pacific shoreline of Washington and Oregon.

Top, left: Shown here is Sunshine Peak, one of the more than one thousand mountains in Colorado that rise to 10,000 feet (3,048 meters) or more. Visitors are attracted not only to the peaks themselves but, in the fall, also to the foliage of aspens and other trees.

Above: Seattle's Space Needle dominates the skyline of the city on Washington's Puget Sound. Seattle is now the largest city in the northwestern United States.

Left: Cattle ranching, which is possible between the mountain peaks, is an important economic activity in the Northwest.

Top, left: Livestock that graze on Montana's eastern plains contribute to the state's income, two-thirds of which is agriculturally based.

Above: Abandoned dwellings such as this mill on Colorado's Crystal River speak of the region's past: the gold rush brought waves of settlers, who abandoned some settlements as the rush subsided.

Left: Tourists are drawn to Idaho's mountainous terrain and now contribute substantially to the state's income.

153

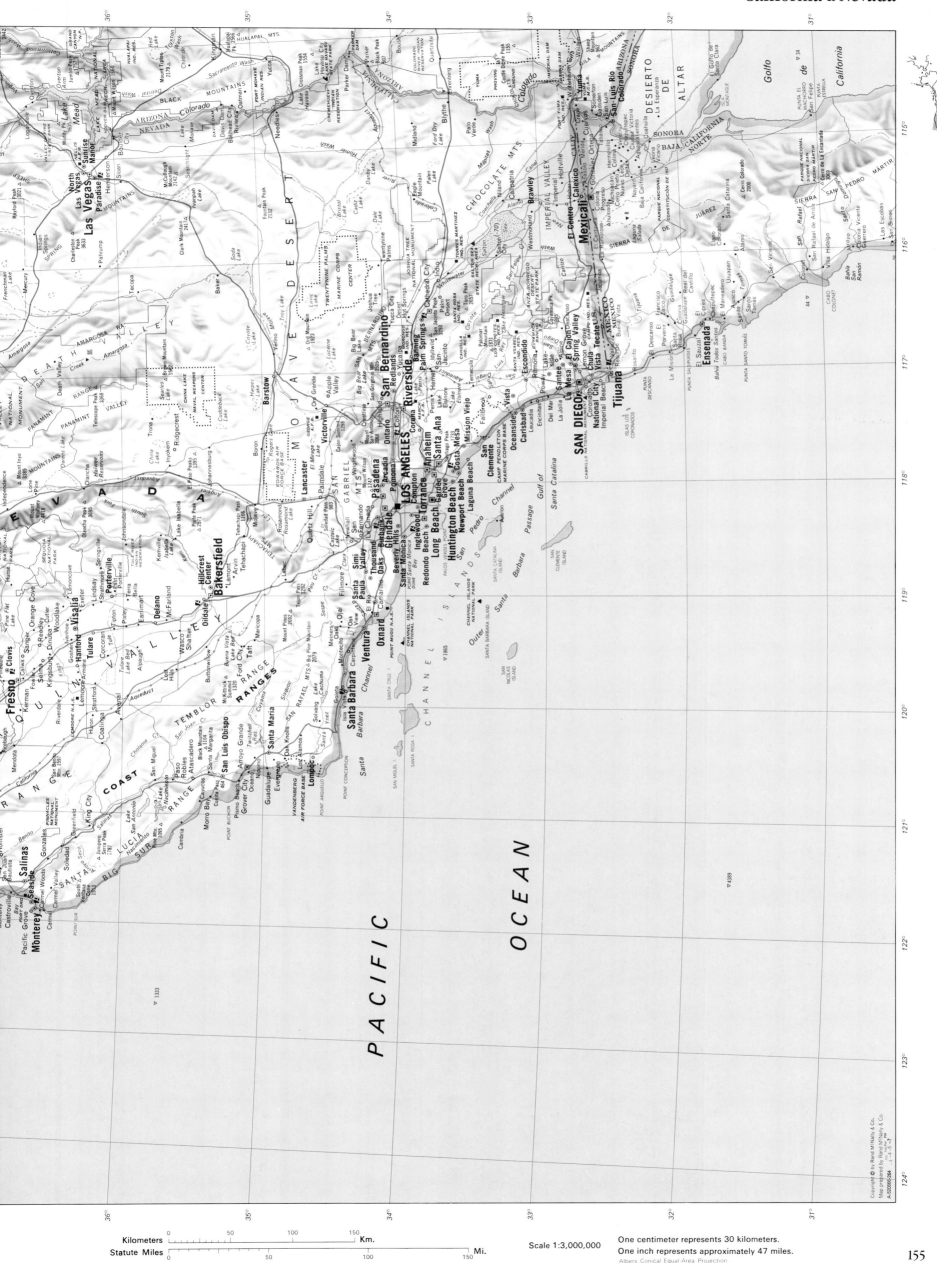

PACIFIC OCEAN

DEATH VALLEY

MOJAVE DESERT

Las Vegas

NEVADA

Fresno

Bakersfield

LOS ANGELES

San Bernardino
Riverside

Santa Barbara

Ventura
Oxnard

Long Beach
Huntington Beach
Santa Ana
Anaheim

San Diego

Tijuana

Mexicali
Calexico
El Centro

Ensenada

Kilometers
Statute Miles

Scale 1:3,000,000

One centimeter represents 30 kilometers.
One inch represents approximately 47 miles.

Albers Conical Equal-Area Projection

Copyright © by Rand McNally & Co.
Map prepared by Rand McNally & Co.

United States
California & Nevada

Dreams of wealth and glamour have lured travelers to California and Nevada ever since miners saw the glint of gold and silver here. After Mormons founded Nevada's first permanent settlement, major lodes of gold and silver were struck in the state, and the population boom was on. Nevada's population increased sixfold in one decade in the late 1800s. California's story is similar, with its gold rush of 1849 and its own population subsequently tripling.

Today, flocks of people still seek to strike gold in the region: aspiring entertainers move to Los Angeles with their sights set on breaking into show business; tourists visit Hollywood and Beverly Hills, hoping to catch a glimpse of movie, television, and rock stars; and gamblers eye the roulette wheels of Las Vegas, Reno, and Lake Tahoe.

But the most fabulous riches of the region are to be found in its near-perfect climate and stunning scenery. The winding road that hugs California's Pacific coastline reveals a treasury of citrus groves, truck farms, and vineyards. The redwood forests, the stark desert, and the Sierra Nevada compete in the grandeur. The sparkling waters of Lake Mead invite boaters and water-skiers; the glacier-cut cliffs of Yosemite thrill hikers and campers; and the breathtaking scenes of Lake Tahoe appeal to almost everyone.

The cities along the West Coast offer their own treasures. From San Francisco in the north, through Monterey, Santa Barbara, Los Angeles, and finally San Diego in the south, these cities share coastline on the Pacific, yet each retains a unique atmosphere.

Opposite, top: Hollywood, home of the entertainment industry, is part of Los Angeles, the largest city in California and the second largest in the United States.

Opposite, bottom: Many factors have drawn enough people to California to make it the most populous state in the nation. Scenic beauty is but one of these factors. Yet many wild regions still exist, often within close proximity to urban areas. Shown here is the stunning Santa Ynez valley, near Santa Barbara.

Above: California has more than 800 miles (1,300 kilometers) of coastline along the Pacific. Southern California features sand beaches, but most of the coast is rocky. Shown here are sandstone forms at Salt Point State Park.

Middle, left: Las Vegas is the largest city in Nevada. Approximately fifteen million tourists annually flock to its hotels, casinos, and nightclubs.

Middle, right: The ancient sequoias, or redwoods, that grow in the Sierra Nevada are among the world's tallest trees. Shown here are redwoods in Yosemite National Park, California.

Right: The lowest elevation in the Western Hemisphere – 282 feet (86 meters) below sea level – is in Death Valley National Monument, in California and Nevada. The desert basin was once a valuable mining region.

157

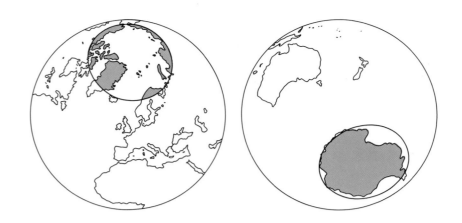

Polar Regions
Profile

Location and Size

The Arctic is an area of extreme cold surrounding the geographic North Pole. It is usually demarcated by the Arctic Circle, an imaginary line north of which there are periods of twenty-four-hour daylight in summer and darkness in winter. The Arctic comprises the Arctic Ocean, which has an area of roughly 5.4 million square miles (14 million square kilometers), and the northern reaches of the Soviet Union, Alaska, Canada, Iceland, Norway, Sweden, Finland, most of Greenland, and a number of islands.

Antarctica surrounds the South Pole and lies almost entirely within the Antarctic Circle. Larger than either Europe or Australia, Antarctica covers some 5.1 million square miles (13.2 million square kilometers).

At the North Pole, the sun rises above the horizon at the spring equinox, about March 21. It does not set until the autumnal equinox, about September 22, after which it does not rise again until the spring equinox. At the South Pole, the same phenomenon occurs, but in opposite seasons.

Landscape

The Arctic Ocean is covered with ice for much of the year, but it melts in summer months. The region's only permanent ice sheet is in Greenland. Continental Arctic land is mostly low-lying, while the islands are somewhat rugged and mountainous. Four of the world's major rivers flow into the Arctic Ocean.

If all of Antarctica's permanent ice cap were removed, a very rugged landscape would be revealed. Relieved of the weight of ice, the land would rise, and the highest peaks would probably match those of the Himalayas.

Climate

Monthly average temperatures in the Arctic range from –40°F (–40°C) in winter to as high as 59°F (15°C) in summer. Precipitation is low; the region is a cold desert.

The climate of Antarctica is far more severe than that of the Arctic. From the center of this mass representing about 90 percent of the world's permanent ice

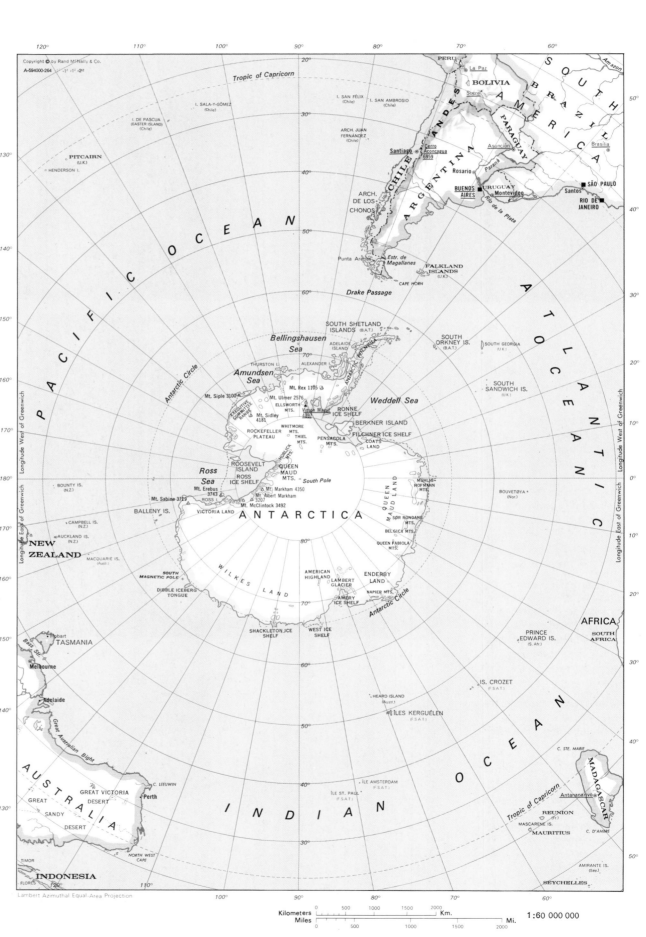

Opposite: **The Antarctic Peninsula, shown here, is one of the few points on the continent to extend north of the Antarctic Circle. The tip of the peninsula is only 600 miles (960 kilometers) from South America.**

Name	Page	Lat.	Long.
Pforzheim	30	48.54 N	8.42 E
Pfronten	30	47.34 N	10.33 E
Pfunds	30	46.58 N	10.33 E
Pfungstadt	30	49.48 N	8.36 E
Phangan, Ko I	68	9.45 N	100.04 E
Phanom Dongrak, Thiu Khao ⚒	68	14.25 N	103.30 E
Phan-rang	68	11.34 N	108.59 E
Phan-thiet	68	10.56 N	108.06 E
Pheba	144	33.35 N	88.56 W
Phelps, N.Y., U.S.	136	42.57 N	77.03 W
Phelps, Wi., U.S.	138	46.03 N	89.05 W
Phenix City	142	32.28 N	85.00 W
Phetchabun, Thiu Khao ⚒	68	16.20 N	100.55 E
Philadelphia, Ms., U.S.	144	32.46 N	89.07 W
Philadelphia, N.Y., U.S.	136	44.09 N	75.42 W
Philadelphia, Pa., U.S.	136	39.57 N	75.09 W
Phil Campbell	144	34.21 N	87.42 W
Philippeville → Skikda	82	36.50 N	6.58 E
Philippi	136	39.09 N	80.02 W
Philippines (Pilipinas) □[1]	68	13.00 N	122.00 E
Philippine Sea ⊤[2]	8	20.00 N	135.00 E
Philipsburg	136	40.53 N	78.13 W
Phillips	138	45.41 N	90.24 W
Phillipsburg, Ga., U.S.	142	31.34 N	83.31 W
Phillipsburg, N.J., U.S.	136	40.41 N	75.11 W
Philo, Il., U.S.	144	40.01 N	88.09 W
Philo, Oh., U.S.	136	39.51 N	81.54 W
Phimai	68	15.13 N	102.30 E
Phitsanulok	68	16.50 N	100.15 E
Phnom Penh → Phnum Pénh	68	11.33 N	104.55 E
Phnum Pénh	68	11.33 N	104.55 E
Phoenix, Az., U.S.	148	33.26 N	112.04 W
Phoenix, N.Y., U.S.	136	43.13 N	76.18 W
Phoenix Islands II	8	4.00 S	172.00 W
Phoenixville	136	40.07 N	75.30 W
Phrae	68	18.09 N	100.08 E
Phra Nakhon Si Ayutthaya	68	14.21 N	100.33 E
Phuket	68	7.53 N	98.24 E
Phuket, Ko I	68	8.00 N	98.22 E
Phu-ly	68	20.32 N	105.56 E
Phu-quoc, Dao I	68	10.12 N	104.00 E
Piacenza	40	45.01 N	9.40 E
Pianella	40	42.24 N	14.02 E
Pianosa, Isola I	40	42.35 N	10.04 E
Piaseczno	30	52.05 N	21.01 E
Piatra-Neamț	48	46.56 N	26.22 E
Piatra Olt	48	44.24 N	24.16 E
Piave ≃	40	45.32 N	12.44 E
Piazza Armerina	40	37.23 N	14.22 E
Pibor ≃	84	8.26 N	33.13 E
Pibor Post	84	6.48 N	33.08 E
Picardie □[9]	36	49.45 N	2.50 E
Picayune	144	30.31 N	89.40 W
Pichanal	120	23.19 S	64.13 W
Picher	144	36.59 N	94.49 W
Pickens	142	34.53 N	82.42 W
Pickle Crow	130	51.30 N	90.04 W
Pickwick Lake ⊜[1]	144	34.55 N	88.10 W
Picton	98	41.18 S	174.01 E
Picton, Isla I	120	55.02 S	66.57 W
Pictou	130	45.41 N	62.43 W
Pictured Rocks National Lakeshore ♦	138	46.35 N	86.20 W
Pidurutalagala ∧	70	7.00 N	80.46 E
Piedmont, Al., U.S.	144	33.55 N	85.36 W
Piedmont, Mo., U.S.	144	37.09 N	90.41 W
Piedras Negras	108	28.42 N	100.31 W
Pieksämäki	22	62.18 N	27.08 E
Pielinen ⊜	22	63.15 N	29.40 E
Pierre	132	44.22 N	100.21 W
Pierre Part	144	29.57 N	91.12 W
Pierson	142	29.14 N	81.27 W
Pierz	138	45.58 N	94.06 W
Piešt'any	30	48.36 N	17.50 E
Pietermaritzburg	86	29.37 S	30.16 E
Pietersburg	86	23.54 S	29.25 E
Pietrasanta	40	43.57 N	10.14 E
Pietrosu, Vîrful ∧, Rom.	48	47.08 N	25.11 E
Pietrosu, Vîrful ∧, Rom.	48	47.36 N	24.38 E
Pieve di Cadore	40	46.26 N	12.22 E
Pigeon	138	43.49 N	83.16 W
Pigeon Forge	142	35.47 N	83.33 W
Piggott	144	36.22 N	90.11 W
Pihlava	22	61.33 N	21.36 E
Pikes Peak ∧	148	38.51 N	105.03 W
Pikesville	136	39.22 N	76.43 W
Piketon	136	39.04 N	83.00 W
Pikeville	142	37.28 N	82.31 W
Piła (Schneidemühl)	30	53.10 N	16.44 E
Pilcomayo ≃	120	25.21 S	57.42 W
Pīlībhīt	70	28.38 N	79.48 E
Pilica ≃	30	51.52 N	21.17 E
Pilot Knob	144	37.37 N	90.38 W
Pilot Mountain	142	36.23 N	80.28 W
Pilot Peak ∧	150	44.58 N	109.53 W
Pilsen → Plzeň	30	49.45 N	13.23 E
Pinang → George Town	68	5.25 N	100.20 E
Pinang, Pulau I	68	5.23 N	100.15 E
Pinar del Río	108	22.25 N	83.42 W
Pinardville	136	42.59 N	71.30 W
Pinckney	138	42.27 N	83.56 W
Pinckneyville	144	38.04 N	89.22 W
Pińczów	30	50.32 N	20.35 E
Píndhos Óros ⚒	48	39.49 N	21.14 E
Pindus Mountains → Píndhos Óros ⚒	48	39.49 N	21.14 E
Pine Barrens ◆[1]	136	39.48 N	74.35 W
Pine Bluff	144	34.13 N	92.00 W
Pine Castle	142	28.28 N	81.22 W
Pine City	138	45.49 N	92.58 W
Pine Creek	96	13.49 S	131.49 E
Pine Creek ≃	136	41.10 N	77.16 W
Pine Creek Lake ⊜[1]	144	34.05 N	95.05 W
Pinedale	154	36.50 N	119.48 W
Pinega ≃	54	64.08 N	41.54 E
Pine Grove	136	40.32 N	76.23 W
Pine Hills	142	28.33 N	81.27 W
Pinehouse Lake ⊜	130	55.32 N	106.35 W
Pinehurst	150	45.15 N	116.20 W
Pine Island I	142	26.35 N	82.06 W
Pinellas Park	142	27.50 N	82.41 W
Pine Mountain ∧	142	32.51 N	84.47 W
Pine Point	130	61.01 N	114.15 W
Pinerolo	40	44.53 N	7.21 E
Pinetops	142	35.47 N	77.38 W
Pineville, Ky., U.S.	142	36.45 N	83.41 W
Pineville, La., U.S.	144	31.19 N	92.26 W
Pineville, N.C., U.S.	142	35.04 N	80.53 W
Ping ≃	68	15.42 N	100.09 E
Pingdingshan	66	33.45 N	113.17 E
Pingliang	66	35.32 N	106.41 E
P'ingtung	66	22.40 N	120.29 E
Pingxiang	66	22.09 N	106.43 E
Pingyao	66	37.16 N	112.09 E
Piniós ≃	48	39.54 N	22.45 E
Pinjarra	96	32.37 S	115.53 E
Pinnacle ∧	98	41.49 S	173.17 E
Pinnacle Buttes ∧	150	43.44 N	109.57 W
Pinneberg	30	53.40 N	9.47 E
Pinos, Mount ∧	154	34.50 N	119.09 W
Pinrang	68	3.48 S	119.38 E
Pins, Île des I	92	22.37 S	167.30 E
Pinsk	54	52.07 N	26.04 E
Piombino	40	42.55 N	10.32 E
Pionki	30	51.30 N	21.27 E
Piotrków Trybunalski	30	51.25 N	19.42 E
Pipestone ≃	130	52.53 N	89.23 W
Pipmuacan, Réservoir ⊜[1]	130	49.35 N	70.30 W
Piqua	136	40.08 N	84.14 W
Piracicaba	118	22.43 S	47.38 W
Piraeus → Piraiévs	48	37.57 N	23.38 E
Piraiévs (Piraeus)	48	37.57 N	23.38 E
Pirapora	118	17.21 S	44.56 W
Pirdop	48	42.42 N	24.11 E
Pires do Rio	118	17.18 S	48.17 W
Pírgos	48	37.41 N	21.28 E
Pirin ⚒	48	41.40 N	23.30 E
Pirmasens	30	49.12 N	7.36 E
Pirna	30	50.58 N	13.56 E
Pirón ≃	44	41.23 N	4.31 W
Pirot	48	43.09 N	22.35 E
Pīr Panjāl Range ⚒	70	33.37 N	74.32 E
Pisa	40	43.43 N	10.23 E
Pisa ≃	30	53.15 N	21.52 E
Pisco	118	13.42 S	76.13 W
Pișcolt	48	47.35 N	22.18 E
Písek	30	49.19 N	14.10 E
Pismo Beach	154	35.08 N	120.38 W
Pisticci	40	40.23 N	16.34 E
Pistoia	40	43.55 N	10.54 E
Pisz	30	53.38 N	21.49 E
Pit ≃	154	40.45 N	122.22 W
Pitcairn □[2]	8	25.04 S	130.05 W
Piteå	22	65.20 N	21.30 E
Piteälven ≃	20	65.14 N	21.32 E
Pitești	48	44.52 N	24.52 E
Pitigliano	40	42.38 N	11.40 E
Pitt, Mount ∧	93	29.01 S	167.56 E
Pittsboro, Ms., U.S.	144	33.56 N	89.20 W
Pittsboro, N.C., U.S.	142	35.43 N	79.10 W
Pittsburg, Ks., U.S.	144	37.24 N	94.42 W
Pittsburg, Tx., U.S.	144	32.59 N	94.57 W
Pittsburgh	136	40.26 N	79.59 W
Pittsfield, Il., U.S.	144	39.36 N	90.48 W
Pittsfield, Me., U.S.	136	44.46 N	69.23 W
Pittsfield, Ma., U.S.	136	42.27 N	73.14 W
Pittsfield, N.H., U.S.	136	43.18 N	71.19 W
Pittston	136	41.19 N	75.47 W
Piura	118	5.12 S	80.38 W
Piute Peak ∧	154	35.27 N	118.24 W
Piva ≃	48	43.21 N	18.51 E
Piwniczna	30	49.27 N	20.42 E
Placentia Bay ⊂	130	47.15 N	54.30 W
Placerville	154	38.43 N	120.47 W
Placetas	108	22.19 N	79.40 W
Plačkovica ⚒	48	41.45 N	22.35 E
Plainfield, Ct., U.S.	136	41.40 N	71.54 W
Plainfield, In., U.S.	144	39.42 N	86.23 W
Plainfield, N.J., U.S.	136	40.37 N	74.26 W
Plains	142	32.02 N	84.23 W
Plainview, Mn., U.S.	138	44.09 N	92.10 W
Plainview, Tx., U.S.	132	34.11 N	101.42 W
Plainwell	138	42.26 N	85.38 W
Plaistow	136	42.50 N	71.05 W
Planeta Rica	118	8.25 N	75.36 W
Plano	138	41.39 N	88.32 W
Plantation	142	26.07 N	80.14 W
Plant City	142	28.01 N	82.06 W
Plantersville	144	32.39 N	86.55 W
Plaquemine	144	30.17 N	91.14 W
Plasencia	44	40.02 N	6.05 W
Plasy	30	49.56 N	13.24 E
Plata, Río de la ⊂[1]	120	35.00 S	57.00 W
Platani ≃	40	37.24 N	13.16 E
Platte ≃, U.S.	144	39.16 N	94.50 W
Platte ≃, Ne., U.S.	132	41.04 N	95.53 W
Platte City	144	39.22 N	94.46 W
Platteville	138	42.44 N	90.28 W
Plattsburg	144	39.33 N	94.26 W
Plattsburgh	136	44.41 N	73.27 W
Plattsmouth	144	41.00 N	95.52 W
Plauen	30	50.30 N	12.08 E
Pleasant, Mount ∧	142	37.44 N	79.10 W
Pleasant Gap	136	40.52 N	77.44 W
Pleasant Grove	148	40.21 N	111.44 W
Pleasant Hill	144	38.47 N	94.16 W
Pleasantville	136	39.23 N	74.31 W
Pleiku	68	13.59 N	108.00 E
Plenty, Bay of ⊂	98	37.40 S	177.00 E
Plessisville	130	46.14 N	71.47 W
Pleszew	30	51.54 N	17.48 E
Pleven	48	43.25 N	24.37 E
Plješevica ⚒	40	44.40 N	15.45 E
Pljevlja	48	43.21 N	19.21 E
Ploaghe	40	40.40 N	8.45 E
Ploče	40	43.04 N	17.26 E
Płock	30	52.33 N	19.43 E
Plöckenpass)(	30	46.36 N	12.58 E
Pločno ∧	40	43.23 N	17.57 E
Ploiești	48	44.56 N	26.02 E
Plomb du Cantal ∧	36	45.03 N	2.46 E
Plön	30	54.09 N	10.25 E
Płońsk	30	52.38 N	20.23 E
Płoty	30	53.49 N	15.16 E
Ploudalmézeau	36	48.32 N	4.39 W
Plovdiv	48	42.09 N	24.45 E
Plumtree	86	20.30 S	27.50 E
Plymouth, Monts.	108	16.42 N	62.13 W
Plymouth, Eng., U.K.	26	50.23 N	4.10 W
Plymouth, In., U.S.	144	41.20 N	86.18 W
Plymouth, Ma., U.S.	136	41.57 N	70.40 W
Plymouth, N.H., U.S.	136	43.45 N	71.41 W
Plymouth, N.C., U.S.	142	35.52 N	76.44 W
Plymouth, Oh., U.S.	136	41.00 N	82.40 W
Plymouth, Pa., U.S.	136	41.14 N	75.56 W
Plymouth, Wi., U.S.	138	43.44 N	87.58 W
Plzeň	30	49.45 N	13.23 E
Po ≃	40	44.57 N	12.04 E
Poarta Orientală, Pasul)(	48	45.06 N	22.18 E
Pobeda, gora ∧	56	65.12 N	146.12 E
Pobedy, pik ∧	54	42.02 N	80.05 E
Pocahontas	144	36.15 N	90.58 W
Pocatello	150	42.52 N	112.26 W
Pocola	144	35.13 N	94.28 W
Pocomoke City	136	38.04 N	75.34 W
Pocono Mountains ⚒[2]	136	41.10 N	75.20 W
Pocono Summit	136	41.07 N	75.25 W
Poços de Caldas	118	21.48 S	46.34 W
Poděbrady	30	50.08 N	15.07 E
Podkamennaja Tunguska ≃	54	61.36 N	90.18 E
Podlasie ◆[1]	30	52.30 N	23.00 E
Podol'sk	20	55.26 N	37.33 E
Podravina ◆[1]	48	45.40 N	17.40 E
Podu Turcului	48	46.12 N	27.23 E
Poel I	30	54.00 N	11.26 E
Pogăniș ≃	48	45.41 N	21.22 E
Poggibonsi	40	43.28 N	11.09 E
P'ohang	66	36.03 N	129.20 E
Point Au Fer Island I	144	29.15 N	91.15 W
Pointe-à-Pitre	108	16.14 N	61.32 W
Pointe-Noire	86	4.48 S	11.51 E
Point Imperial ∧	148	36.16 N	111.58 W
Point Pelee National Park ♦	138	41.57 N	82.30 W
Point Pleasant, N.J., U.S.	136	40.04 N	74.04 W
Point Pleasant, W.V., U.S.	136	38.50 N	82.08 W
Point Reyes National Seashore ♦	154	38.00 N	122.58 W
Poissy	36	48.56 N	2.03 E
Poitiers	36	46.35 N	0.20 E
Pola de Laviana	44	43.15 N	5.34 W
Poland (Polska) □[1]	30	52.00 N	19.00 E
Polesje ◆[1]	54	52.00 N	27.00 E
Polgár	30	47.52 N	21.08 E
Policastro, Golfo di ⊂	40	40.00 N	15.30 E
Police	30	53.35 N	14.33 E
Polillo Islands II	68	14.50 N	122.05 E
Polistena	40	38.25 N	16.05 E
Polk	136	41.22 N	79.55 W
Polkton	142	35.00 N	80.12 W
Pollino, Monte ∧	40	39.55 N	16.11 E
Pollock	144	31.31 N	92.24 W
Pollux ∧	98	44.14 S	168.53 E
Polo, Il., U.S.	138	41.59 N	89.34 W
Polo, Mo., U.S.	144	39.33 N	94.02 W
Polock	20	55.31 N	28.46 E
Polson	150	47.41 N	114.09 W
Poltava	54	49.35 N	34.34 E
Polynesia II	8	4.00 S	156.00 W
Pomabamba	118	8.50 S	77.28 W
Pomahaka ≃	98	46.09 S	169.34 E
Pomerania □[9]	30	54.00 N	16.00 E
Pomeranian Bay ⊂	30	54.00 N	14.15 E
Pomeroy	150	46.28 N	117.36 W
Pomme de Terre ≃	144	38.11 N	93.24 W
Pomme de Terre Lake ⊜[1]	144	37.51 N	93.19 W
Pomona	154	34.03 N	117.45 W
Pomona Park	142	29.30 N	81.35 W
Pomorie	48	42.33 N	27.39 E
Pomorskij proliv ʊ	20	68.30 N	50.00 E
Pompano Beach	142	26.14 N	80.07 W
Pompei	40	40.45 N	14.30 E
Pompei ⊥	40	40.45 N	14.30 E
Pompton Lakes	136	41.00 N	74.17 W
Ponca City	132	36.42 N	97.05 W
Ponce	108	18.01 N	66.37 W
Ponce de Leon	144	30.43 N	85.56 W
Ponce de Leon Inlet ⊂	142	29.04 N	80.55 W
Poncha Pass)(	148	38.25 N	106.05 W
Ponchatoula	144	30.26 N	90.26 W
Pondicherry	70	11.56 N	79.53 E
Ponente, Riviera di ≗[2]	40	44.10 N	8.20 E
Ponferrada	44	42.33 N	6.35 W
Pongolo ≃	86	26.57 S	32.17 E
Ponoj ≃	54	66.59 N	41.17 E
Ponoka	130	52.42 N	113.35 W
Ponta Grossa	120	25.05 S	50.09 W
Pontão	44	39.55 N	8.22 W
Pontarlier	36	46.54 N	6.22 E
Pontassieve	40	43.46 N	11.26 E
Pont Canavese	40	45.25 N	7.36 E
Pontchartrain, Lake ⊜	144	30.10 N	90.10 W
Pont-de-Vaux	36	46.26 N	4.56 E
Ponte Caldelas	44	42.23 N	8.30 W
Pontedera	40	43.40 N	10.38 E
Ponte Nova	118	20.24 S	42.54 W
Pontevedra	44	42.26 N	8.38 W
Ponte Vedra Beach	142	30.14 N	81.23 W
Pontiac, Il., U.S.	138	40.52 N	88.37 W
Pontiac, Mi., U.S.	138	42.38 N	83.17 W
Pontianak	68	0.02 S	109.20 E
Pontivy	36	48.04 N	2.59 W
Pontoise	36	49.03 N	2.06 E
Pontotoc	144	34.14 N	88.59 W
Pontremoli	40	44.22 N	9.53 E
Pontresina	36	46.28 N	9.53 E
Pontypridd	26	51.37 N	3.22 W
Pony	150	45.39 N	111.53 W
Ponziane, Isole II	40	40.55 N	12.57 E
Poole	26	50.43 N	1.59 W
Poopó, Lago ⊜	118	18.45 S	67.07 W
Popayán	118	2.27 N	76.36 W
Pope	144	34.12 N	89.56 W
Poperinge	30	50.51 N	2.43 E
Popești-Leordeni	48	44.23 N	26.10 E
Poplar Bluff	144	36.45 N	90.23 W
Poplarville	144	30.50 N	89.32 W
Popocatépetl, Volcán ∧[1]	108	19.02 N	98.38 W
Popovo	48	43.21 N	26.13 E
Poprad	30	49.03 N	20.18 E
Poprad ≃	30	49.38 N	20.42 E
Poquoson	142	37.07 N	76.21 W
Porbandar	70	21.38 N	69.36 E
Porcuna	44	37.52 N	4.11 W
Porcupine ≃	130	66.35 N	145.15 W
Porcupine Mountains State Park ♦	138	46.47 N	89.50 W
Pordenone	40	45.57 N	12.39 E
Poreč	40	45.13 N	13.37 E
Pori	22	61.29 N	21.47 E
Porirua	98	41.08 S	174.51 E
Porkkala	22	59.59 N	24.26 E
Porlamar	118	10.57 N	63.51 W
Porretta Terme	40	44.09 N	10.59 E
Porsangen ⊂[2]	20	70.58 N	27.00 E
Porsangerhalvøya ≻[1]	20	70.50 N	25.00 E
Porsgrunn	22	59.09 N	9.40 E
Portadown	26	54.26 N	6.27 W
Portage, Mi., U.S.	138	42.12 N	85.34 W
Portage, Wi., U.S.	138	43.32 N	89.27 W
Portage-la-Prairie	130	48.59 N	98.18 W
Portageville	144	36.25 N	89.41 W
Port Alberni	130	49.14 N	124.48 W
Portalegre	44	39.17 N	7.26 W
Portales	132	34.11 N	103.20 W
Port Alfred	86	33.36 S	26.55 E
Port Allegany	136	41.48 N	78.16 W
Port Allen	144	30.27 N	91.12 W
Port Angeles	150	48.07 N	123.25 W
Port Antonio	108	18.11 N	76.28 W
Port Arthur, Austl.	96	43.09 S	147.51 E
Port Arthur → Thunder Bay, On., Can.	130	48.23 N	89.15 W
Port Arthur, Tx., U.S.	144	29.53 N	93.55 W
Port Arthur → Lüshun, Zhg.	66	38.48 N	121.16 E
Port Askaig	26	55.51 N	6.07 W
Port Augusta	96	32.30 S	137.46 E
Port-au-Prince	108	18.32 N	72.20 W
Port Barre	144	30.33 N	91.57 W
Port Blair	70	11.40 N	92.45 E
Port Byron	138	41.36 N	90.20 W
Port-Cartier	130	50.01 N	66.52 W
Port Chalmers	98	45.49 S	170.37 E
Port Charlotte	142	26.58 N	82.05 W
Port Chester	136	41.00 N	73.39 W
Port Clinton	136	41.30 N	82.56 W
Port Clyde	136	43.55 N	69.15 W
Port Coquitlam	150	49.16 N	122.46 W
Port Dickson	68	2.31 N	101.48 E
Port Edward	86	31.02 S	30.13 E
Port Edwards	138	44.21 N	89.51 W
Port Elizabeth	86	33.58 S	25.40 E
Porterville	154	36.03 N	119.00 W
Port-Étienne → Nouâdhibou	82	20.54 N	17.04 W
Port Gamble	150	47.51 N	122.34 W
Port Gentil	86	0.43 S	8.47 E
Port Gibson	144	31.57 N	90.59 W
Port Harcourt	82	4.43 N	7.05 E
Port Hedland	96	20.19 S	118.34 E
Port Henry	136	44.02 N	73.27 W
Port Hope	138	43.56 N	82.42 W
Port Huron	138	42.58 N	82.25 W
Portimão	44	37.08 N	8.32 W
Port Jervis	136	41.22 N	74.41 W
Portland, Austl.	96	38.21 S	141.36 E
Portland, In., U.S.	144	40.26 N	84.58 W
Portland, Me., U.S.	136	43.39 N	70.15 W
Portland, Mi., U.S.	138	42.52 N	84.54 W
Portland, Or., U.S.	150	45.31 N	122.40 W
Portland, Tn., U.S.	144	36.34 N	86.30 W
Portland, Bill of ≻	26	50.31 N	2.27 W
Port Laoise	26	53.02 N	7.17 W
Port Leyden	136	43.35 N	75.21 W
Port Lincoln	96	34.44 S	135.52 E
Port Loko	82	8.46 N	12.47 W
Port Louis	86	20.10 S	57.30 E
Port Moresby	96a	9.30 S	147.10 E
Port Neches	144	29.59 N	93.57 W
Port Nolloth	86	29.17 S	16.51 E
Port Norris	136	39.14 N	75.02 W
Porto	44	41.11 N	8.36 W
Porto Alegre	120	30.04 S	51.11 W
Portobelo	108	9.33 N	79.39 W
Pôrto de Mós	44	39.36 N	8.39 W
Porto Empedocle	40	37.17 N	13.32 E
Porto Esperança	118	19.37 S	57.27 W
Porto Esperidião	118	15.51 S	58.28 W
Porto Farina	40	37.10 N	10.12 E
Port of Spain	108	10.39 N	61.31 W
Portogruaro	40	45.47 N	12.50 E
Porto Lucena	120	27.51 S	55.01 W
Portomaggiore	40	44.42 N	11.48 E
Porto Mendes	120	24.30 S	54.20 W
Porto Murtinho	118	21.42 S	57.52 W
Porto-Novo	82	6.29 N	2.37 E
Port Orange	142	29.06 N	80.59 W
Port Orchard	150	47.32 N	122.38 W
Porto San Giorgio	40	43.11 N	13.48 E
Porto Sant'Elpidio	40	43.15 N	13.45 E
Porto Torres	40	40.50 N	8.24 E
Porto-Vecchio	40	41.35 N	9.16 E
Porto Velho	118	8.46 S	63.54 W
Portoviejo	118	1.03 S	80.27 W
Port Patrick	92	20.08 S	169.47 E
Port Phillip Bay ⊂	96	38.07 S	144.48 E
Port Pirie	96	33.11 S	138.01 E
Port Richey	142	28.16 N	82.43 W
Port Royal, Pa., U.S.	136	40.32 N	77.23 W
Port Royal, S.C., U.S.	142	32.22 N	80.41 W
Portrush	26	55.12 N	6.40 W
Port Said → Būr Saʿīd	84	31.16 N	32.18 E
Port Saint Joe	142	29.49 N	85.18 W
Port Saint Johns	86	31.38 S	29.33 E
Port Saint Lucie	142	27.20 N	80.20 W
Port Sanilac	138	43.25 N	82.32 W
Portsmouth, Eng., U.K.	26	50.48 N	1.05 W
Portsmouth, N.H., U.S.	136	43.04 N	70.45 W
Portsmouth, Oh., U.S.	136	38.43 N	82.59 W
Portsmouth, Va., U.S.	142	36.50 N	76.17 W
Port Sudan → Būr Sūdān	84	19.37 N	37.14 E
Port Sulphur	144	29.28 N	89.41 W
Port Talbot	26	51.36 N	3.47 W
Porttipahdan tekojärvi ⊜[1]	20	68.08 N	26.40 E
Port Townsend	150	48.07 N	122.45 W
Portugal □[1]	44	39.30 N	8.00 W
Portugalete	44	43.19 N	3.01 W
Portuguese Guinea → Guinea-Bissau □[1]	82	12.00 N	15.00 W
Port Vila	92	17.44 S	168.19 E
Port Washington	138	43.23 N	87.52 W
Port Wentworth	142	32.08 N	81.09 W
Porvenir	120	53.18 S	70.22 W
Porvoo (Borgå)	22	60.24 N	25.40 E
Porz	30	50.53 N	7.03 E
Porzuna	44	39.09 N	4.09 W
Posada ≃	40	40.39 N	9.45 E
Posadas, Arg.	120	27.23 S	55.53 W
Posadas, Esp.	44	37.48 N	5.06 W
Posavina V	48	45.00 N	19.00 E
Posen → Poznań, Pol.	30	52.25 N	16.55 E
Posen, Mi., U.S.	138	45.15 N	83.41 W
Poso, Danau ⊜	68	1.52 S	120.35 E
Pössneck	30	50.42 N	11.37 E
Poste-de-la-Baleine	130	55.17 N	77.45 W
Post Falls	150	47.43 N	116.57 W
Postojna	40	45.47 N	14.13 E
Potchefstroom	86	26.46 S	27.01 E
Poteau	144	35.03 N	94.37 W
Poteau ≃	144	35.23 N	94.26 W
Potenza	40	40.38 N	15.49 E
Poteriteri, Lake ⊜	98	46.06 S	167.08 E
Potholes Reservoir ⊜[1]	150	47.01 N	119.19 W
Potiskum	82	11.43 N	11.05 E
Potomac	144	40.18 N	87.48 W
Potomac ≃	136	38.00 N	76.18 W
Potomac Heights	136	38.36 N	77.08 W
Potosí, Bol.	118	19.35 S	65.45 W
Potosi, Mo., U.S.	144	37.56 N	90.47 W
Potsdam, D.D.R.	30	52.24 N	13.04 E
Potsdam, N.Y., U.S.	136	44.40 N	74.58 W
Pottstown	136	40.14 N	75.39 W
Pottsville	136	40.41 N	76.11 W
Poughkeepsie	136	41.42 N	73.55 W
Poulan	142	31.30 N	83.47 W
Poulaphouca Reservoir ⊜[1]	26	53.08 N	6.31 W
Poulsbo	150	47.44 N	122.38 W
Poultney	136	43.31 N	73.14 W
Pound	142	37.07 N	82.36 W
Poutasi	93	14.01 S	171.41 W
Pouthīsăt	68	12.32 N	103.55 E
Považská Bystrica	30	49.08 N	18.27 E
Povljen ⚒	48	43.55 N	19.30 E
Póvoa de Varzim	44	41.23 N	8.46 W
Povungnituk	130	60.02 N	77.10 W
Poway	154	32.57 N	117.02 W
Powder ≃, U.S.	132	46.44 N	105.26 W
Powder ≃, Or., U.S.	150	44.45 N	117.03 W
Powderly	144	37.09 N	87.10 W
Powell	150	44.45 N	108.45 W
Powell ≃	142	36.29 N	83.42 W
Powell, Lake ⊜[1]	148	37.25 N	110.45 W
Powell, Mount ∧	148	39.46 N	106.20 W
Powellhurst	150	45.30 N	122.32 W
Powell River	130	49.52 N	124.33 W
Powellton	136	38.05 N	81.19 W
Powers	138	45.41 N	87.31 W
Powhatan, La., U.S.	144	31.52 N	93.12 W
Powhatan, Va., U.S.	142	37.32 N	77.55 W
Powys □[6]	26	52.17 N	3.20 W
Poyang Hu ⊜	66	29.00 N	116.25 E
Poygan, Lake ⊜	138	44.09 N	88.50 W
Poynette	138	43.23 N	89.24 W
Požarevac	48	44.37 N	21.11 E
Poznań	30	52.25 N	16.55 E
Pozoblanco	44	38.22 N	4.51 W
Pozo-Cañada	44	38.48 N	1.45 W
Pozzuoli	40	40.49 N	14.07 E
Prabuty	30	53.46 N	19.10 E
Prachatice	30	49.01 N	14.00 E
Prachin Buri	68	14.03 N	101.22 E
Prades	36	42.37 N	2.26 E
Prague → Praha	30	50.05 N	14.26 E
Praha (Prague)	30	50.05 N	14.26 E
Praha ∧	30	49.40 N	13.49 E
Prahova ≃	48	44.43 N	26.27 E
Praia	82	14.55 N	23.31 W
Prairie City, Il., U.S.	144	40.37 N	90.28 W
Prairie City, Ia., U.S.	138	41.35 N	93.14 W
Prairie du Chien	138	43.03 N	91.08 W
Prairie du Sac	138	43.17 N	89.43 W
Prairie Grove	144	35.58 N	94.19 W
Prairie Village	144	38.59 N	94.38 W
Praslin Island I	86	4.19 S	55.44 E
Prasonísi, Ákra ≻	48	35.42 N	27.46 E
Praszka	30	51.04 N	18.26 E
Pratas Island → Tungsha Tao I	66	20.42 N	116.43 E
Prato	40	43.53 N	11.06 E
Prattsburg	136	42.31 N	77.17 W
Prattville	144	32.27 N	86.27 W
Praya	68	8.42 S	116.17 E
Preetz	30	54.14 N	10.16 E
Přelouč	30	50.02 N	15.34 E
Premnitz	30	52.32 N	12.19 E
Premuda, Otok I	40	44.20 N	14.37 E
Prentice	138	45.32 N	90.17 W
Prentiss	144	31.35 N	89.52 W
Prenzlau	30	53.19 N	13.52 E
Preparis Island I	68	14.52 N	93.41 E
Preparis North Channel ʊ	68	15.27 N	94.05 E
Preparis South Channel ʊ	68	14.40 N	94.00 E
Přerov	30	49.27 N	17.27 E
Prescott, On., Can.	130	44.43 N	75.31 W
Prescott, Az., U.S.	148	34.32 N	112.28 W
Prescott, Ar., U.S.	144	33.48 N	93.22 W
Prescott, Wi., U.S.	138	44.44 N	92.48 W
Presidencia Roque Sáenz Peña	120	26.47 S	60.27 W
Presidente Prudente	118	22.07 S	51.22 W
Prešov	30	49.00 N	21.15 E
Prespa, Lake ⊜	48	40.55 N	21.00 E
Presque Isle	132	46.40 N	68.00 W
Presque Isle ≻[1]	136	42.09 N	80.06 W
Přeštice	30	49.34 N	13.20 E
Preston, Eng., U.K.	26	53.46 N	2.42 W
Preston, Id., U.S.	150	42.05 N	111.52 W
Preston Peak ∧	154	41.50 N	123.37 W
Prestonsburg	142	37.39 N	82.46 W
Prestwick	26	55.29 N	4.37 W
Pretoria	86	25.45 S	28.10 E
Préveza	48	38.57 N	20.44 E
Priboj	48	43.35 N	19.31 E
Příbram	30	49.42 N	14.01 E
Price	148	39.35 N	110.48 W
Price ≃	148	39.10 N	110.06 W
Prichard	144	30.44 N	88.04 W
Priego de Córdoba	44	37.26 N	4.11 W
Prien	30	47.51 N	12.20 E
Prieska	86	29.40 S	22.42 E
Priest Lake ⊜	150	48.34 N	116.52 W
Priest River	150	48.10 N	116.54 W
Prieta, Peña ∧	44	43.01 N	4.44 W
Prievidza	30	48.47 N	18.37 E
Prijedor	40	44.59 N	16.43 E
Prikaspijskaja nizmennost' ≚	54	48.00 N	52.00 E
Prilep	48	41.20 N	21.33 E
Prince Albert	130	53.12 N	105.46 W
Prince Charles Island I	130	67.50 N	76.00 W
Prince Edward Island □[4]	130	46.20 N	63.20 W
Prince Frederick	136	38.32 N	76.35 W
Prince George	130	53.55 N	122.45 W
Prince of Wales Island I, Austl.	96	10.40 S	142.10 E
Prince of Wales Island I, N.T., Can.	130	72.40 N	99.00 W
Prince of Wales Strait ʊ	130	73.00 N	117.00 W
Prince Regent Inlet ⊂	130	73.00 N	90.30 W
Prince Rupert	130	54.19 N	130.19 W
Princess Anne	136	38.12 N	75.41 W
Princeton, Il., U.S.	138	41.22 N	89.27 W
Princeton, In., U.S.	144	38.21 N	87.34 W
Princeton, Ky., U.S.	144	37.06 N	87.52 W
Princeton, Mn., U.S.	138	45.34 N	93.34 W
Princeton, N.J., U.S.	136	40.20 N	74.39 W
Princeton, W.V., U.S.	142	37.21 N	81.06 W
Princeton, Wi., U.S.	138	43.51 N	89.07 W
Príncipe I	86	1.37 N	7.25 E
Prineville	150	44.18 N	120.51 W
Prip'at' ≃	54	51.21 N	30.09 E
Pripet → Prip'at' ≃	54	51.21 N	30.09 E
Pripet Marshes → Polesje ◆[1]	54	52.00 N	27.00 E
Priština	48	42.39 N	21.10 E
Pritzwalk	30	53.09 N	12.10 E
Privolžskaja vozvyšennost' ⚒[1]	54	52.00 N	46.00 E
Prizren	48	42.12 N	20.44 E
Prizzi	40	37.43 N	13.26 E
Probolinggo	68	7.45 S	113.13 E
Prochowice	30	51.17 N	16.22 E
Proctor, Mn., U.S.	138	46.44 N	92.13 W
Proctor, Vt., U.S.	136	43.39 N	73.02 W
Proddatūr	70	14.44 N	78.33 E
Progreso	108	21.17 N	89.40 W
Prokopjevsk	56	53.53 N	86.45 E
Prokopyevsk → Prokopjevsk	56	53.53 N	86.45 E
Prokuplje	48	43.14 N	21.36 E
Prome (Pyè)	68	18.49 N	95.13 E
Prophetstown	138	41.40 N	89.56 W
Prosna ≃	30	52.10 N	17.39 E
Prosser	150	46.12 N	119.46 W
Prostějov	30	49.29 N	17.07 E
Provadija	48	43.11 N	27.26 E
Provencal	144	31.39 N	93.12 W
Provence □[9]	36	44.00 N	6.00 E
Providence, Ky., U.S.	144	37.23 N	87.45 W
Providence, R.I., U.S.	136	41.49 N	71.24 W
Providence, Ut., U.S.	148	41.42 N	111.48 W
Providence Island I	86	9.14 S	51.02 E
Providencia, Isla de I	108	13.21 N	81.22 W
Provincetown	136	42.03 N	70.10 W
Provins	36	48.33 N	3.18 E
Provo	148	40.14 N	111.39 W
Provo ≃	148	40.14 N	111.44 W
Prudnik	30	50.19 N	17.34 E
Pruszków	30	52.11 N	20.48 E
Prut ≃	48	45.30 N	28.12 E
Pryor	144	36.19 N	95.19 W
Przasnysz	30	53.01 N	20.55 E
Przedbórz	30	51.06 N	19.53 E
Przemyśl	30	49.47 N	22.47 E
Pskov	20	57.50 N	28.20 E
Pskovskoje ozero ⊜	22	58.00 N	28.00 E
Pszczyna	30	49.59 N	18.57 E
Ptolemaís	48	40.31 N	21.41 E
Ptuj	40	46.25 N	15.52 E
Pucallpa	118	8.23 S	74.32 W
Pucheng	66	27.55 N	118.31 E
Púchov	30	49.08 N	18.20 E
Pudukkottai	70	10.23 N	78.49 E
Puebla	108	19.03 N	98.12 W
Puebla de Don Fadrique	44	37.58 N	2.26 W
Pueblo	148	38.15 N	104.36 W
Pueblo Mountain ∧	150	42.06 N	118.39 W
Puente-Genil	44	37.23 N	4.47 W
Puente Nuevo, Embalse de ⊜[1]	44	38.00 N	5.00 W
Puerco ≃	148	34.53 N	110.07 W
Puerco, Rio ≃	148	34.22 N	106.50 W
Puerto Aisén	120	45.24 S	72.42 W
Puerto Armuelles	108	8.17 N	82.52 W
Puerto Ayacucho	118	5.40 N	67.35 W
Puerto Barrios	108	15.43 N	88.36 W
Puerto Berrío	118	6.29 N	74.24 W
Puerto Cabello	118	10.28 N	68.01 W
Puerto Cabezas	108	14.02 N	83.23 W
Puerto Carreño	118	6.12 N	67.22 W
Puerto Chicama	118	7.42 S	79.27 W
Puerto Cortés, C.R.	108	8.58 N	83.32 W
Puerto Cortés, Hond.	108	15.48 N	87.56 W
Puerto Cumarebo	118	11.29 N	69.21 W
Puerto de Nutrias	118	8.05 N	69.18 W
Puerto de San José	108	13.55 N	90.49 W
Puerto Deseado	120	47.45 S	65.54 W
Puerto la Cruz	118	10.13 N	64.38 W
Puerto Leguízamo	118	0.12 S	74.46 W
Puertollano	44	38.41 N	4.07 W
Puerto Madryn	120	42.46 S	65.03 W
Puerto Maldonado	118	12.36 S	69.11 W
Puerto Montt	120	41.28 S	72.57 W
Puerto Morazán	108	12.51 N	87.11 W
Puerto Natales	120	51.44 S	72.31 W
Puerto Páez	118	6.13 N	67.28 W
Puerto Princesa	68	9.44 N	118.44 E
Puerto Real	44	36.32 N	6.11 W
Puerto Rico □[2]	108	18.15 N	66.30 W
Puerto Sastre	120	22.06 S	57.59 W
Puerto Suárez	118	18.57 S	57.51 W
Puerto Vallarta	108	20.37 N	105.15 W
Pueyrredón, Lago (Lago Cochrane) ⊜	120	47.20 S	72.00 W
Puget Sound ʊ	150	47.50 N	122.30 W
Puigcerdá	44	42.26 N	1.56 E
Puigmal ∧	44	42.23 N	2.07 E
Pukaki, Lake ⊜	98	44.07 S	170.10 E
Pukaskwa National Park ♦	138	48.20 N	85.50 W
Pukekohe	98	37.12 S	174.55 E
Pula	40	44.52 N	13.50 E
Pulaski, N.Y., U.S.	136	43.34 N	76.07 W
Pulaski, Tn., U.S.	144	35.11 N	87.01 W
Pulaski, Va., U.S.	142	37.02 N	80.46 W
Pulaski, Wi., U.S.	138	44.40 N	88.14 W
Puławy	30	51.25 N	21.57 E
Pullman	150	46.43 N	117.10 W
Pullo	118	15.14 S	73.50 W
Pulog, Mount ∧	68	16.36 N	120.54 E
Pułtusk	30	52.43 N	21.05 E
Puná, Isla I	118	2.50 S	80.08 W
Pune (Poona)	70	18.32 N	73.52 E
Pungo ≃	142	35.23 N	76.33 W
Punitaqui	120	30.50 S	71.16 W
Puno	118	15.50 S	70.02 W
Punta Alta	120	38.53 S	62.05 W
Punta Arenas	120	53.09 S	70.55 W
Punta del Este	120	34.58 S	54.57 W
Punta Gorda	142	26.55 N	82.02 W
Puntarenas	108	9.58 N	84.50 W
Punto Fijo	118	11.42 N	70.13 W
Punxsutawney	136	40.56 N	78.58 W
Purdy	144	36.49 N	93.55 W
Puri	70	19.48 N	85.51 E
Purus (Purús) ≃	118	3.42 S	61.28 W
Purwakarta	68	6.34 S	107.26 E
Purwokerto	68	7.25 S	109.14 E
Pusan	66	35.06 N	129.03 E
Puškin	20	59.43 N	30.25 E
Püspökladány	30	47.19 N	21.07 E
Putao	66	27.21 N	97.24 E
Putaruru	98	38.03 S	175.47 E
Puting, Tanjung ≻	68	3.31 S	111.46 E
Putnam	136	41.54 N	71.54 W
Putney	136	42.58 N	72.31 W
Putorana, plato ⚒[1]	54	69.00 N	95.00 E
Puttalam	70	8.02 N	79.49 E
Puttgarden	30	54.30 N	11.13 E
Putumayo (Içá) ≃	118	3.07 S	67.58 W
Puula ⊜	22	61.50 N	26.42 E
Pu'upu'a	93	13.34 S	172.09 W
Puyallup	150	47.11 N	122.17 W
Puymorens, Col de)(	36	42.30 N	1.50 E
Puysegur Point ≻	98	46.09 S	166.36 E
Pwllheli	26	52.53 N	4.25 W
Pyhäselkä ⊜	22	62.26 N	29.58 E
Pyhätunturi ∧	20	67.01 N	27.09 E
Pyinmana	68	19.44 N	96.13 E
Pymatuning Reservoir ⊜[1]	136	41.37 N	80.30 W
P'yŏngyang	66	39.01 N	125.45 E
Pyramid Lake ⊜	154	40.00 N	119.35 W
Pyrenees ⚒	44	42.40 N	1.00 E
Pyrzyce	30	53.10 N	14.55 E

Q

Name	Page	Lat.	Long.
Qacentina	82	36.22 N	6.37 E
Qaidam Pendi ≚[1]	66	37.00 N	95.00 E
Qalāt	70	32.07 N	66.54 E
Qalʿat Bīshah	70	20.01 N	42.36 E
Qamar, Ghubbat al- ⊂	70	16.00 N	52.30 E
Qamdo	66	31.11 N	97.15 E
Qandahār	70	31.32 N	65.30 E
Qārūn, Birkat ⊜	84	29.28 N	30.40 E
Qāsh, Nahr al- (Gash) ≃	84	16.48 N	35.51 E
Qaṣr al-Farāfirah	84	27.03 N	27.58 E
Qasr el-Boukhari	44	35.51 N	2.52 E
Qatar (Qaṭar) □[1]	70	25.00 N	51.10 E
Qattara Depression → Qaṭṭārah, Munkhafaḍ al- ≗[7]	84	30.00 N	27.30 E
Qaṭṭārah, Munkhafaḍ al- ≗[7]	84	30.00 N	27.30 E
Qazvīn	70	36.16 N	50.00 E
Qeqertaq I	130	71.55 N	55.30 W
Qeshm I	70	26.45 N	55.45 E
Qezel Owzan ≃	70	36.45 N	49.22 E
Qianyang	66	27.11 N	110.04 E
Qijiang	66	29.02 N	106.39 E
Qilian Shan ∧	66	39.12 N	98.35 E
Qilian Shan ⚒	66	39.06 N	98.40 E
Qinā	84	26.10 N	32.43 E
Qingdao (Tsingtao)	66	36.06 N	120.19 E
Qinghai Hu ⊜	66	36.50 N	100.20 E
Qinhuangdao	66	39.56 N	119.36 E
Qionglai	66	30.25 N	103.27 E
Qiongzhou Haixia ʊ	66	20.10 N	110.15 E
Qiqihar (Tsitsihar)	66	47.19 N	123.55 E
Qīzān	70	16.54 N	42.29 E

Symbols in the index entries are identified on page 162.

Symbols in the index entries are identified on page 162.

Rupe—Sant

Name	Page	Lat.	Long.
Rupert, W.V., U.S.	142	37.57 N	80.41 W
Rusape	86	18.32 S	32.07 E
Ruse	48	43.50 N	25.57 E
Rush City	138	45.41 N	92.57 W
Rushville, Il., U.S.	144	40.07 N	90.33 W
Rushville, In., U.S.	144	39.36 N	85.26 W
Rusken ⊜	22	57.17 N	14.20 E
Ruskin	142	27.43 N	82.26 W
Russell, Ky., U.S.	136	38.31 N	82.41 W
Russell, Pa., U.S.	136	41.56 N	79.08 W
Russell Islands II	94	9.04 S	159.12 E
Russell Springs	144	37.03 N	85.05 W
Russellville, Al., U.S.	144	34.30 N	87.43 W
Russellville, Ar., U.S.	144	35.16 N	93.08 W
Russellville, Ky., U.S.	144	36.50 N	86.53 W
Russellville, Mo., U.S.	144	38.30 N	92.26 W
Rüsselsheim	30	50.00 N	8.25 E
Russian ≃	154	38.27 N	123.08 W
Russian Soviet Federative Socialist Republic → Rossijskaja Sovetskaja Federativnaja Socialističeskaja Respublika □[3]	54	60.00 N	80.00 E
Russiaville	144	40.25 N	86.16 W
Russkij Zavorot, mys ≻	20	68.58 N	54.34 E
Rust	30	47.48 N	16.41 E
Rustavi	54	41.33 N	45.02 E
Rustenburg	86	25.37 S	27.08 E
Ruston	144	32.31 N	92.38 W
Rute	44	37.19 N	4.22 W
Ruteng	68	8.36 S	120.27 E
Ruth	144	31.22 N	90.18 W
Rutherfordton	142	35.22 N	81.57 W
Rutland	136	43.36 N	72.58 W
Rutledge, Ga., U.S.	142	33.37 N	83.36 W
Rutledge, Tn., U.S.	142	36.16 N	83.30 W
Ruvuma (Rovuma) ≃	86	10.29 S	40.28 E
Ružomberok	30	49.06 N	19.18 E
Rwanda □[1]	86	2.00 S	30.00 E
Ryan Peak ∧	150	43.54 N	114.25 W
Ryazan' → R'azan'	20	54.38 N	39.44 E
Rybačij, poluostrov ≻[1]	54	69.42 N	32.36 E
Rybinskoje vodochranilišče ⊜[1]	54	58.30 N	38.25 E
Rybnica	48	47.45 N	29.01 E
Rybnik	30	50.06 N	18.32 E
Rychwał	30	52.05 N	18.09 E
Ryde	26	50.44 N	1.10 W
Rye Patch Reservoir ⊜[1]	154	40.38 N	118.18 W
Rysy ∧	30	49.12 N	20.04 E
Ryukyu Islands → Nansei-shotō II	66	26.30 N	128.00 E
Rzeszów	30	50.03 N	22.00 E
Ržev	20	56.16 N	34.20 E
S			
Saale ≃	30	51.57 N	11.55 E
Saalfeld	30	50.39 N	11.22 E
Saar → Saarland □[3]	30	49.20 N	7.00 E
Saarbrücken	30	49.14 N	6.59 E
Saarburg	30	49.36 N	6.33 E
Saaremaa I	54	58.25 N	22.30 E
Saarland □[3]	30	49.20 N	7.00 E
Saarlouis	30	49.21 N	6.45 E
Şab, Tônlé ⊜	68	13.00 N	104.00 E
Šabac	48	44.45 N	19.42 E
Sabadell	44	41.33 N	2.06 E
Sabanalarga	118	10.38 N	74.55 W
Sābarmati ≃	70	22.18 N	72.22 E
Sabaudia	40	41.18 N	13.01 E
Şāberī, Hāmūn-e ⊜	70	31.30 N	61.20 E
Sabhā	84	27.03 N	14.26 E
Sabi (Save) ≃	86	21.00 S	35.02 E
Sabina	136	39.29 N	83.38 W
Sabina □[9]	40	42.15 N	12.42 E
Sabine ≃	144	30.00 N	93.45 W
Sabine Lake ⊜	144	29.50 N	93.50 W
Sabine Pass c	144	29.44 N	93.52 W
Sabini, Monti ⋏	40	42.13 N	12.50 E
Sabinov	30	49.06 N	21.06 E
Sable, Cape ≻	130	43.25 N	65.35 W
Sable, Cape ≻[1]	142	25.12 N	81.05 W
Sable Island I	130	43.55 N	59.50 W
Sabor ≃	44	41.10 N	7.07 W
Sabugal	44	40.21 N	7.05 W
Sabzevār	70	36.13 N	57.42 E
Sacajawea Peak ∧	150	45.15 N	117.17 W
Săcele	48	45.37 N	25.42 E
Sachalin, ostrov (Sakhalin) I	56	51.00 N	143.00 E
Sachalinskij zaliv c	56	53.45 N	141.30 E
Sachigo ≃	130	55.06 N	88.58 W
Sachsen □[9]	30	52.45 N	9.30 E
Šachty	54	47.42 N	40.13 E
Säckingen	30	47.33 N	7.56 E
Sackville	130	45.54 N	64.22 W
Saco	136	43.30 N	70.26 W
Saco Bay c	136	43.30 N	70.15 W
Sacramento	154	38.34 N	121.29 W
Sacramento ≃	154	38.03 N	121.56 W
Sacramento Mountains ⋏	148	32.45 N	105.30 W
Sacramento Valley V	154	39.15 N	122.00 W
Şa'dah	70	16.52 N	43.37 E
Saddle Mountain ∧	148	38.50 N	105.28 W
Sado I	66	38.00 N	138.25 E
Sado ≃	44	38.29 N	8.55 W
Šadrinsk	54	56.05 N	63.38 E
Säffle	22	59.08 N	12.56 E
Safford	148	32.50 N	109.42 W
Safi	82	32.20 N	9.17 W
Safīd Kūh, Selseleh-Ye ⋏	70	34.30 N	63.30 E
Saga	66	33.15 N	130.18 E
Sagaing	68	21.52 N	95.59 E
Saganaga Lake ⊜	132	48.14 N	90.52 W
Sāgar	70	23.50 N	78.43 E
Saginaw	138	43.25 N	83.56 W
Saginaw ≃	138	43.39 N	83.51 W
Saginaw Bay c	138	43.50 N	83.40 W
Sagra ∧	44	37.57 N	2.34 W
Şagu	48	46.03 N	21.17 E
Sagua la Grande	108	22.49 N	80.05 W
Saguaro National Monument ♦	148	32.12 N	110.38 W
Saguenay ≃	130	48.08 N	69.44 W
Sagunt	44	39.41 N	0.16 W
Sahagún	44	42.22 N	5.02 W
Sahara ◆[2]	82	26.00 N	13.00 E
Sahāranpur	70	29.58 N	77.33 E
Sahel → Sudan ◆[1]	82	10.00 N	20.00 E
Sahel, Oued ≃	44	36.26 N	4.33 E
Şahin	48	41.01 N	26.50 E
Şāhīwāl	70	30.40 N	73.06 E
Šahy	30	48.05 N	18.57 E
Saibai Island I	96	9.24 S	142.40 E
Sai Buri	68	6.42 N	101.37 E
Saïda	82	34.50 N	0.09 E
Saïdia	44	35.04 N	2.15 W
Saidpur	70	25.47 N	88.54 E
Sai-gon → Thanh-pho Ho Chi Minh	68	10.45 N	106.40 E
Saimaa ⊜	22	61.15 N	28.15 E
Saimaa Canal ≊	22	61.05 N	28.18 E
Sainte-Agathe-des-Monts	130	46.03 N	74.17 W
Saint Albans, Eng., U.K.	26	51.46 N	0.21 W
Saint Albans, Vt., U.S.	136	44.48 N	73.05 W
Saint Albans, W.V., U.S.	136	38.23 N	81.50 W
Saint Aldhelm's Head ≻	26	50.34 N	2.04 W
Saint-Amand-Montrond	36	46.44 N	2.30 E
Saint-André, Cap ≻	86	16.11 S	44.27 E
Saint Andrews, Scot., U.K.	26	56.20 N	2.48 W
Saint Andrews, S.C., U.S.	142	32.46 N	79.59 W
Saint Anne	138	41.01 N	87.42 W
Saint Anne's	26	53.45 N	3.02 W
Saint Ansgar	138	43.22 N	92.55 W
Saint Anthony	150	43.57 N	111.40 W
Saint-Auban	36	43.51 N	6.44 E
Saint Augustine	142	29.53 N	81.18 W
Saint-Augustin-Saguenay	130	51.14 N	58.39 W
Saint Austell	26	50.20 N	4.48 W
Saint-Avold	36	49.06 N	6.42 E
Saint Bathans, Mount ∧	98	44.44 S	169.46 E
Saint-Brieuc	36	48.31 N	2.47 W
Saint Catharines	130	43.10 N	79.15 W
Saint Catherines Island I	142	31.38 N	81.10 W
Saint Catherine's Point ≻	26	50.34 N	1.15 W
Saint-Chamond	36	45.28 N	4.30 E
Saint Charles, Il., U.S.	138	41.54 N	88.18 W
Saint Charles, Mi., U.S.	138	43.17 N	84.08 W
Saint Charles, Mn., U.S.	138	43.58 N	92.03 W
Saint Charles, Mo., U.S.	144	38.47 N	90.28 W
Saint Christopher I	108	17.20 N	62.45 W
Saint Christopher-Nevis □[1]	108	17.20 N	62.45 W
Saint Clair, Mi., U.S.	138	42.48 N	82.29 W
Saint Clair, Mo., U.S.	144	38.20 N	90.58 W
Saint Clair ≃	138	42.37 N	82.31 W
Saint Clair, Lake ⊜	138	42.25 N	82.41 W
Saint Clair Shores	138	42.29 N	82.53 W
Saint Clairsville	136	40.04 N	80.54 W
Saint-Claud	36	45.53 N	0.23 E
Saint-Claude	36	46.23 N	5.52 E
Saint Cloud, Fl., U.S.	142	28.14 N	81.16 W
Saint Cloud, Mn., U.S.	138	45.33 N	94.09 W
Saint Croix I	108	17.45 N	64.45 W
Saint Croix ≃, N.A.	136	45.10 N	67.10 W
Saint Croix ≃, U.S.	138	44.45 N	92.49 W
Saint Croix Falls	138	45.24 N	92.38 W
Saint Croix Island National Monument ♦	136	45.08 N	67.08 W
Saint David's	26	51.54 N	5.16 W
Saint David's Head ≻	26	51.55 N	5.19 W
Saint-Denis, Fr.	36	48.56 N	2.22 E
Saint-Denis, Réu.	86	20.52 S	55.28 E
Saint-Dié	36	48.17 N	6.57 E
Saint-Dizier	36	48.38 N	4.57 E
Saint Elias, Mount ∧	130	60.18 N	140.55 W
Saint Elmo	144	39.01 N	88.50 W
Saint-Étienne	36	45.26 N	4.24 E
Saint-Félicien	130	48.39 N	72.26 W
Saint Francis	138	42.58 N	87.52 W
Saint Francis ≃	144	34.38 N	90.35 W
Saint Francis, Cape ≻	86	34.14 S	24.49 E
Saint Francis, Lake ⊜	136	45.08 N	74.25 W
Saint-François, Lac ⊜	136	45.55 N	71.10 W
Saint Francois Mountains ⋏[2]	144	37.30 N	90.35 W
Saint-Gaudens National Historic Site ⊥	136	43.29 N	72.19 W
Sainte Genevieve	144	37.59 N	90.03 W
Saint George	148	37.06 N	113.34 W
Saint George, Cape ≻	142	29.35 N	85.04 W
Saint George, Point ≻	154	41.47 N	124.15 W
Saint George Island I	142	29.39 N	84.55 W
Saint George's	108	12.03 N	61.45 W
Saint George's Bay c	130	48.20 N	59.00 W
Saint George's Channel ᵕ	26	52.00 N	6.00 W
Saint George Sound ᵕ	142	29.47 N	84.42 W
Saint-Germain	36	48.54 N	2.05 E
Saint-Germain-du-Bois	36	46.45 N	5.15 E
Saint Helena Sound ᵕ	142	32.27 N	80.25 W
Saint Helens	150	45.51 N	122.48 W
Saint Helens, Mount ∧[1]	150	46.12 N	122.11 W
Saint Helier	26	49.11 N	2.06 W
Saint-Hyacinthe	130	45.37 N	72.57 W
Saint Ignace	138	45.52 N	84.43 W
Saint Ignace Island I	130	48.48 N	87.55 W
Saint Ives	26	50.12 N	5.29 W
Saint James, Mi., U.S.	138	45.45 N	85.30 W
Saint James, Mo., U.S.	144	37.59 N	91.36 W
Saint James, N.Y., U.S.	136	40.52 N	73.09 W
Saint James, Cape ≻	130	51.56 N	131.01 W
Saint-Jean, Lac ⊜	130	48.35 N	72.05 W
Saint-Jean-d'Angély	36	45.57 N	0.31 W
Saint-Jean-de-Luz	36	43.23 N	1.40 W
Saint-Jean-de-Monts	36	46.48 N	2.03 W
Saint-Jean-sur-Richelieu	130	45.19 N	73.16 W
Saint-Jérôme	130	45.47 N	74.00 W
Saint John, N.B., Can.	130	45.16 N	66.03 W
Saint John, Wa., U.S.	150	47.05 N	117.34 W
Saint John ≃	130	45.15 N	66.04 W
Saint John, Cape ≻	130	50.00 N	55.32 W
Saint Johns, Antig.	108	17.06 N	61.51 W
Saint John's, Nf., Can.	130	47.34 N	52.43 W
Saint Johns, Az., U.S.	148	34.30 N	109.21 W
Saint Johns, Mi., U.S.	138	43.00 N	84.33 W
Saint Johns ≃	142	30.24 N	81.24 W
Saint Johnsbury	136	44.25 N	72.00 W
Saint-Joseph, N. Cal.	92	20.27 S	166.36 E
Saint Joseph, Mi., U.S.	138	42.05 N	86.29 W
Saint Joseph, Mo., U.S.	144	39.46 N	94.50 W
Saint Joseph ≃, U.S.	138	41.05 N	85.08 W
Saint Joseph ≃, U.S.	138	42.07 N	86.29 W
Saint Joseph, Lake ⊜	130	51.05 N	90.35 W
Saint Joseph Bay c	142	29.47 N	85.21 W
Saint Joseph Island I	138	46.13 N	83.57 W
Saint-Junien	36	45.53 N	0.54 E
Saint Kilda	98	45.54 S	170.30 E
Saint Kilda I	26	57.49 N	8.36 W
Saint-Laurent-du-Maroni	118	5.30 N	54.02 W
Saint Lawrence ≃	130	49.30 N	67.00 W
Saint Lawrence, Gulf of c	130	48.00 N	62.00 W
Saint Lawrence Island I	132a	63.30 N	170.30 W
Saint-Lô	36	49.07 N	1.05 W
Saint-Louis, Sén.	82	16.02 N	16.30 W
Saint Louis, Mi., U.S.	138	43.24 N	84.36 W
Saint Louis, Mo., U.S.	144	38.37 N	90.11 W
Saint Louis ≃	138	46.45 N	92.06 W
Saint-Louis, Lac ⊜	136	45.24 N	73.48 W
Saint Louis Park	138	44.56 N	93.20 W
Saint-Loup-sur-Semouse	36	47.53 N	6.16 E
Saint Lucia □[1]	108	13.53 N	60.58 W
Saint Lucia, Lake ⊜	86	28.05 S	32.26 E
Saint Lucie Canal ≊	142	27.10 N	80.15 W
Saint Lucie Inlet c	142	27.10 N	80.10 W
Saint Magnus Bay c	26	60.24 N	1.34 W
Saint-Malo	36	48.39 N	2.01 W
Saint-Malo, Golfe de c	36	48.45 N	2.00 W
Saint-Marc	108	19.07 N	72.42 W
Sainte-Marguerite ≃	130	50.09 N	66.36 W
Sainte-Marie, Cap ≻	86	25.36 S	45.08 E
Saint Maries	150	47.18 N	116.33 W
Saint Marks	142	30.09 N	84.12 W
Saint Marks ≃	142	30.08 N	84.12 W
Saint-Martin I	108	18.04 N	63.04 W
Saint Martinville	144	30.07 N	91.49 W
Saint Mary Lake ⊜	150	48.40 N	113.30 W
Saint Mary Peak ∧	96	31.30 S	138.33 E
Saint Mary Reservoir ⊜[1]	150	49.19 N	113.12 W
Saint Marys, Austl.	96	41.35 S	148.10 E
Saint Marys, Ga., U.S.	142	30.43 N	81.32 W
Saint Marys, Oh., U.S.	136	40.32 N	84.23 W
Saint Marys, Pa., U.S.	136	41.25 N	78.33 W
Saint Marys, W.V., U.S.	136	39.23 N	81.12 W
Saint Marys ≃, N.A.	138	45.58 N	83.54 W
Saint Marys ≃, U.S.	142	30.43 N	81.27 W
Saint Mary's, Cape ≻	130	46.49 N	54.12 W
Saint Mary's Bay c	130	46.50 N	53.47 W
Saint-Mathieu, Pointe de ≻	36	48.20 N	4.46 W
Saint Matthews, Ky., U.S.	144	38.15 N	85.39 W
Saint Matthews, S.C., U.S.	142	33.39 N	80.46 W
Saint-Maur [-des-Fossés]	36	48.48 N	2.30 E
Saint Meinrad	144	38.10 N	86.48 W
Saint Michaels	136	38.47 N	76.13 W
Saint-Moritz → Sankt Moritz	36	46.30 N	9.50 E
Saint-Nazaire	36	47.17 N	2.12 W
Saint Nazianz	138	44.00 N	87.55 W
Saint Neots	26	52.14 N	0.17 W
Saint-Omer	36	50.45 N	2.15 E
Saint Paris	136	40.07 N	83.57 W
Saint Paul, Ab., Can.	130	53.59 N	111.17 W
Saint-Paul, Fr.	36	43.42 N	7.07 E
Saint-Paul, Réu.	86	21.00 S	55.16 E
Saint Paul, Mn., U.S.	138	44.57 N	93.05 W
Saint Paul ≃	82	6.23 N	10.48 W
Saint Pauls	142	34.48 N	78.58 W
Saint Peter	138	44.19 N	93.57 W
Saint Peter Port	26	49.27 N	2.32 W
Saint Petersburg	142	27.46 N	82.40 W
Saint-Pierre	86	21.19 S	55.29 E
Saint-Pierre, Lac ⊜	136	46.12 N	72.52 W
Saint Pierre and Miquelon (Saint-Pierre-et-Miquelon) □[2]	130	46.55 N	56.20 W
Saint-Quentin	36	49.51 N	3.17 E
Saint-Raphaël	36	43.25 N	6.46 E
Saintes	36	45.45 N	0.38 W
Saint-Savinien	36	45.53 N	0.41 W
Saint-Sébastien, Cap ≻	86	12.26 S	48.44 E
Saint Simons Island	142	31.09 N	81.22 W
Saint Simons Island I	142	31.14 N	81.21 W
Saint Stephen	130	45.12 N	67.17 W
Saint Thomas	130	42.47 N	81.12 W
Saint Thomas I	108	18.21 N	64.55 W
Saint-Tropez	36	43.16 N	6.38 E
Saint Vincent I	108	13.15 N	61.12 W
Saint-Vincent, Baie de c	92	22.00 S	166.05 E
Saint-Vincent, Cap ≻	86	21.57 S	43.16 E
Saint Vincent, Cape → São Vicente, Cabo de ≻	44	37.01 N	9.00 W
Saint Vincent, Gulf c	96	35.00 S	138.05 E
Saint Vincent and the Grenadines □[1]	108	13.15 N	61.12 W
Saint-Vith	30	50.17 N	6.08 E
Saipan I	68	15.12 N	145.45 E
Sairecábur, Cerro ∧	120	22.43 S	67.54 W
Sajama, Nevado ∧	118	18.06 S	68.54 W
Sajano-Sušenskoje vodochranilišče ⊜[1]	54	52.20 N	92.25 E
Sajnšand	66	44.52 N	110.09 E
Sajó ≃	30	47.56 N	21.08 E
Sajószentpéter	30	48.13 N	20.44 E
Sak ≃	86	30.02 S	20.40 E
Sakākah	70	29.59 N	40.06 E
Sakakawea, Lake ⊜[1]	132	47.50 N	102.20 W
Sakania	86	12.45 S	28.34 E
Sakata	66	38.55 N	139.50 E
Sakhalin → Sachalin, ostrov I	56	51.00 N	143.00 E
Sakishima-guntō II	66	24.46 N	124.00 E
Saks	144	33.42 N	85.52 W
Şal ≃	54	47.31 N	40.45 E
Šal'a, Česko.	30	48.09 N	17.52 E
Sala, Sve.	22	59.55 N	16.36 E
Salada, Laguna ⊜	154	32.20 N	115.40 W
Salado ≃, Arg.	120	38.05 S	65.48 W
Salado ≃, Arg.	120	31.42 S	60.44 W
Salado ≃, Méx.	108	26.52 N	99.19 W
Şalālah	70	17.00 N	54.06 E
Salamanca, Chile	120	31.47 S	70.58 W
Salamanca, Esp.	44	40.58 N	5.39 W
Salamanca, Méx.	108	20.34 N	101.12 W
Salamanca, N.Y., U.S.	136	42.09 N	78.42 W
Salamat, Bahr ≃	84	9.27 N	18.06 E
Salamís	48	37.59 N	23.28 E
Salamonie ≃	144	40.50 N	85.43 W
Salani	93	14.00 S	171.33 W
Salat ≃	36	43.10 N	0.58 E
Salatiga	68	7.19 S	110.30 E
Salavat	54	53.21 N	55.55 E
Saldaña	44	42.31 N	4.44 W
Saldanha	86	33.00 S	17.56 E
Salé	82	34.04 N	6.50 W
Salechard	54	66.33 N	66.40 E
Salem, India	70	11.39 N	78.10 E
Salem, Ar., U.S.	144	36.22 N	91.49 W
Salem, Il., U.S.	144	38.37 N	88.56 W
Salem, In., U.S.	144	38.03 N	86.15 W
Salem, Ky., U.S.	144	37.15 N	88.14 W
Salem, Ma., U.S.	136	42.31 N	70.53 W
Salem, Mo., U.S.	144	37.38 N	91.32 W
Salem, N.H., U.S.	136	42.47 N	71.12 W
Salem, N.J., U.S.	136	39.34 N	75.28 W
Salem, N.Y., U.S.	136	43.10 N	73.19 W
Salem, Oh., U.S.	136	40.54 N	80.51 W
Salem, Or., U.S.	150	44.56 N	123.02 W
Salem, Va., U.S.	142	37.17 N	80.03 W
Salem, W.V., U.S.	136	39.16 N	80.33 W
Salemi	40	37.49 N	12.48 E
Salentina, Penisola ≻[1]	40	40.25 N	18.00 E
Salerno	40	40.41 N	14.47 E
Salerno, Golfo di c	40	40.32 N	14.42 E
Salford	26	53.28 N	2.18 W
Salgótarján	30	48.07 N	19.48 E
Salida	148	38.32 N	105.59 W
Salignac-Eyvignes	36	44.59 N	1.19 E
Salihli	48	38.29 N	28.09 E
Salima	86	13.47 S	34.26 E
Salīmah, Wāḥat Ŧ[4]	84	21.22 N	29.19 E
Salina	132	38.50 N	97.36 W
Salina, Isola I	40	38.34 N	14.50 E
Salina Cruz	108	16.10 N	95.12 W
Salinas, Ec.	118	2.13 S	80.58 W
Salinas, Ca., U.S.	154	36.40 N	121.39 W
Salinas ≃	154	36.45 N	121.48 W
Saline, La., U.S.	144	32.09 N	92.58 W
Saline, Mi., U.S.	138	42.10 N	83.46 W
Saline ≃	144	33.44 N	93.58 W
Salisbury, Eng., U.K.	26	51.05 N	1.48 W
Salisbury, Md., U.S.	136	38.21 N	75.35 W
Salisbury, Mo., U.S.	144	39.25 N	92.48 W
Salisbury, N.C., U.S.	142	35.40 N	80.28 W
Salisbury, Pa., U.S.	136	39.45 N	79.04 W
Salisbury Plain ≚	26	51.12 N	1.55 W
Salish Mountains ⋏	150	48.15 N	114.45 W
Sallisaw	144	35.27 N	94.47 W
Salluit	130	62.14 N	75.38 W
Salmon	150	45.10 N	113.53 W
Salmon ≃	150	45.51 N	116.46 W
Salmon Mountains ⋏	154	41.00 N	123.00 W
Salmon River Mountains ⋏	150	44.45 N	115.30 W
Salo	22	60.23 N	23.08 E
Salon-de-Provence	36	43.38 N	5.06 E
Salonika → Thessaloníki	48	40.38 N	22.56 E
Salonta	48	46.48 N	21.40 E
Salor ≃	44	39.39 N	7.03 W
Saloum ≃	82	13.50 N	16.45 W
Salpausselkä ∧	22	61.00 N	26.30 E
Salso ≃	40	37.06 N	13.57 E
Salt ≃, Az., U.S.	148	33.23 N	112.18 W
Salt ≃, Ky., U.S.	144	38.00 N	85.57 W
Salt ≃, Mo., U.S.	144	39.28 N	91.04 W
Salta	120	24.47 S	65.25 W
Saltash	26	50.24 N	4.12 W
Saltcoats	26	55.38 N	4.47 W
Saltillo	108	25.25 N	101.00 W
Salt Lake City	148	40.45 N	111.53 W
Salto	120	31.23 S	57.58 W
Salto ≃	40	42.23 N	12.54 E
Salton City	154	33.19 N	115.59 W
Salton Sea ⊜	154	33.19 N	115.50 W
Saluda, S.C., U.S.	142	34.00 N	81.46 W
Saluda, Va., U.S.	142	37.36 N	76.35 W
Saluda ≃	142	34.00 N	81.04 W
Saluzzo	40	44.39 N	7.29 E
Salvador	118	12.59 S	38.31 W
Salvador, Lake ⊜	144	29.45 N	90.15 W
Salween (Nu) ≃	66	17.30 N	97.30 E
Salyersville	142	37.45 N	83.04 W
Salza ≃	30	47.40 N	14.43 E
Salzach ≃	30	48.12 N	12.56 E
Salzburg	30	47.48 N	13.02 E
Salzgitter	30	52.10 N	10.25 E
Salzkammergut ◆[1]	30	47.45 N	13.30 E
Salzwedel	30	52.51 N	11.09 E
Samālūt	84	28.18 N	30.42 E
Samar I	68	12.00 N	125.00 E
Samara ≃	54	53.10 N	50.04 E
Samarinda	68	0.30 S	117.09 E
Samarkand	54	39.40 N	66.48 E
Sambhal	70	28.35 N	78.33 E
Sambor	54	49.32 N	23.11 E
Sambre ≃	36	50.28 N	4.52 E
Same	86	4.04 S	37.44 E
Samoa → American Samoa □[2]	93	14.20 S	170.00 W
Samoa Islands II	93	14.00 S	171.00 W
Samokov	48	42.20 N	23.33 E
Sámos I	48	37.48 N	26.44 E
Samoset	142	27.28 N	82.32 W
Samothrace → Samothráki I	48	40.30 N	25.32 E
Samothráki I	48	40.30 N	25.32 E
Sampit	68	2.32 S	112.57 E
Sam Rayburn Reservoir ⊜[1]	144	31.27 N	94.37 W
Samsø I	22	55.52 N	10.37 E
Samson	144	31.06 N	86.02 W
Samsun	16	41.17 N	36.20 E
Samtown	144	31.16 N	92.26 W
Samui, Ko I	68	9.30 N	100.00 E
San	82	13.18 N	4.54 W
San ≃, Asia	68	13.32 N	105.58 E
San ≃, Europe	30	50.44 N	21.50 E
San'ā'	70	15.23 N	44.12 E
Sanaga ≃	82	3.35 N	9.38 E
San Agustin, Cape ≻	68	6.16 N	126.11 E
San Agustin, Plains of ≚	148	33.50 N	108.00 W
Sanandaj	70	35.19 N	47.00 E
San Andreas	154	38.11 N	120.40 W
San Andrés	118	12.35 N	81.42 W
San Andrés, Isla de I	118	12.32 N	81.42 W
San Andres Mountains ⋏	148	32.55 N	106.45 W
San Andrés Tuxtla	108	18.27 N	95.13 W
San Angelo	132	31.27 N	100.26 W
San Anselmo	154	37.58 N	122.33 W
San Antonio, Chile	120	33.35 S	71.38 W
San Antonio, Tx., U.S.	132	29.25 N	98.29 W
San Antonio, Cabo ≻, Arg.	120	36.40 S	56.42 W
San Antonio, Cabo ≻, Cuba	108	21.52 N	84.57 W
San Antonio, Lake ⊜[1]	154	35.55 N	121.00 W
San Antonio, Mount ∧	154	34.17 N	117.39 W
San Antonio Mountain ∧	148	36.52 N	106.02 W
San Antonio Oeste	120	40.44 S	64.56 W
San Augustin Pass)(	148	32.26 N	106.34 W
San Benedetto del Tronto	40	42.57 N	13.53 E
San Benito	108	16.55 N	89.54 W
San Bernardino	154	34.07 N	117.18 W
San Bernardino Mountains ⋏	154	34.10 N	116.45 W
San Bernardino Strait ᵕ	68	12.32 N	124.10 E
San Bernardo	120	33.36 S	70.43 W
San Blas, Cape ≻	142	29.40 N	85.22 W
San Borja	118	14.49 S	66.51 W
San Bruno	154	37.37 N	122.24 W
San Candido	40	46.44 N	12.17 E
San Carlos, Pil.	68	15.55 N	120.20 E
San Carlos, Az., U.S.	148	33.20 N	110.27 W
San Carlos, Ca., U.S.	154	37.29 N	122.15 W
San Carlos, Ven.	118	9.40 N	68.36 W
San Carlos de Bariloche	120	41.09 S	71.18 W
San Carlos Reservoir ⊜[1]	148	33.13 N	110.24 W
San Cataldo	40	37.29 N	13.59 E
Sánchez	108	19.14 N	69.36 W
San Clemente, Esp.	44	39.24 N	2.26 W
San Clemente, Ca., U.S.	154	33.25 N	117.36 W
San Clemente Island I	154	32.54 N	118.29 W
San Cristóbal	118	7.46 N	72.14 W
San Cristobal I	94	10.36 S	161.45 E
San Cristóbal de las Casas	108	16.45 N	92.38 W
Sancti-Spíritus	108	21.56 N	79.27 W
Sancy, Puy de ∧	36	45.32 N	2.49 E
Sandakan	68	5.50 N	118.07 E
Sanday I	26	59.15 N	2.35 W
Sanderson	132	30.08 N	102.23 W
Sandersville	142	32.58 N	82.48 W
Sandhammaren ≻	22	55.23 N	14.12 E
Sandia	118	14.17 S	69.26 W
San Diego	154	32.42 N	117.09 W
San Diego ≃	154	32.46 N	117.13 W
San Diego, Cabo ≻	120	54.38 S	65.07 W
San Diego Aqueduct ≊[1]	154	32.55 N	116.55 W
Sand Key I	142	27.53 N	82.51 W
Sandnes	22	58.51 N	5.44 E
Sandomierz	30	50.41 N	21.45 E
San Donà di Piave	40	45.38 N	12.34 E
Sandoway	68	18.28 N	94.22 E
Sandown	26	50.39 N	1.09 W
Sandpoint	150	48.16 N	116.33 W
Sandringham	26	52.50 N	0.30 W
Sandston	142	37.31 N	77.18 W
Sandstone	96	27.59 S	119.17 E
Sandu Ao c	66	26.35 N	119.50 E
Sandusky, Mi., U.S.	138	43.25 N	82.49 W
Sandusky, Oh., U.S.	136	41.26 N	82.42 W
Sandusky ≃	136	41.27 N	83.00 W
Sandviken	22	60.37 N	16.46 E
Sandwich, Il., U.S.	138	41.38 N	88.37 W
Sandwich, Ma., U.S.	136	41.45 N	70.29 W
Sandy	148	40.35 N	111.53 W
Sandy Cape ≻	96	24.42 S	153.17 E
Sandy Hook ≻[2]	136	40.27 N	74.00 W
Sandy Lake ⊜	130	53.02 N	93.00 W
Sandy Springs	142	33.55 N	84.22 W
Sandžak ◆[1]	48	43.10 N	19.30 E
San Felipe, Chile	120	32.45 S	70.44 W
San Felipe, Col.	118	1.55 N	67.06 W
San Felipe, Ven.	118	10.20 N	68.44 W
San Felipe de Puerto Plata	108	19.48 N	70.41 W
San Felipe Pueblo	148	35.27 N	106.28 W
San Félix, Isla I	120	26.17 S	80.05 W
San Fernando, Chile	120	34.35 S	71.00 W
San Fernando, Esp.	44	36.28 N	6.12 W
San Fernando, Pil.	68	15.01 N	120.41 E
San Fernando, Pil.	68	16.37 N	120.19 E
San Fernando, Trin.	108	10.17 N	61.28 W
San Fernando, Ca., U.S.	154	34.16 N	118.26 W
San Fernando de Apure	118	7.54 N	67.28 W
San Fernando de Atabapo	118	4.03 N	67.42 W
Sanford, Fl., U.S.	142	28.48 N	81.16 W
Sanford, Me., U.S.	136	43.26 N	70.46 W
Sanford, N.C., U.S.	142	35.28 N	79.10 W
San Francisco, Arg.	120	31.26 S	62.05 W
San Francisco, Ca., U.S.	154	37.46 N	122.25 W
San Francisco ≃	148	32.59 N	109.22 W
San Francisco Bay c	154	37.43 N	122.17 W
San Francisco de Macorís	108	19.18 N	70.15 W
San Gabriel Mountains ⋏	154	34.20 N	118.00 W
San Gallán, Isla I	118	13.51 S	76.28 W
Sangamon ≃	144	40.07 N	90.20 W
Sangay, Volcán ∧[1]	118	2.00 S	78.20 W
Sanger	154	36.42 N	119.33 W
Sangerhausen	30	51.28 N	11.17 E
Sangha ≃	86	1.13 S	16.49 E
Sangihe, Kepulauan II	68	3.00 N	125.30 E
San Gimignano	40	43.28 N	11.02 E
San Giovanni in Fiore	40	39.15 N	16.42 E
San Giovanni in Persiceto	40	44.38 N	11.11 E
San Giovanni Rotondo	40	41.42 N	15.44 E
San Giovanni Valdarno	40	43.34 N	11.32 E
Sāngli	70	16.52 N	74.34 E
San Gorgonio Mountain ∧	154	34.06 N	116.50 W
San Gottardo, Passo del)(	36	46.33 N	8.34 E
Sangre de Cristo Mountains ⋏	148	37.30 N	105.15 W
Sanibel Island I	142	26.27 N	82.06 W
San Isidro	120	34.27 S	58.30 W
San Jacinto	154	33.47 N	116.57 W
San Jacinto Peak ∧	154	33.49 N	116.41 W
San Joaquín ≃, Bol.	118	13.08 S	63.41 W
San Joaquin ≃, Ca., U.S.	154	38.03 N	121.50 W
San Joaquin Valley V	154	36.50 N	120.10 W
San Jorge, Golfo c	120	46.00 S	67.00 W
San José, C.R.	108	9.56 N	84.05 W
San Jose, Pil.	68	12.27 N	121.03 E
San Jose, Ca., U.S.	154	37.20 N	121.53 W
San Jose, Il., U.S.	144	40.18 N	89.36 W
San Jose, Rio ≃	148	34.52 N	107.01 W
San José del Guaviare	118	2.35 N	72.38 W
San José de Mayo	120	34.20 S	56.42 W
San Juan, Arg.	120	31.32 S	68.31 W
San Juan, P.R.	108	18.28 N	66.07 W
San Juan, Rep. Dom.	108	18.48 N	71.14 W
San Juan ≃, Arg.	120	32.17 S	67.22 W
San Juan ≃, N.A.	108	10.56 N	83.42 W
San Juan ≃, U.S.	148	37.18 N	110.28 W
San Juan Bautista	154	36.51 N	121.32 W
San Juan del Norte	108	10.55 N	83.42 W
San Juan de los Morros	118	9.55 N	67.21 W
San Juan del Sur	108	11.15 N	85.52 W
San Juan Island National Historical Park ♦	150	48.28 N	123.00 W
San Juan Islands II	150	48.36 N	122.50 W
San Juan Mountains ⋏	148	37.35 N	107.10 W
Sankt Gallen, Öst.	30	47.41 N	14.37 E
Sankt Gallen, Schw.	36	47.25 N	9.23 E
Sankt Goar	30	50.09 N	7.43 E
Sankt Ingbert	30	49.17 N	7.06 E
Sankt Johann im Pongau	30	47.21 N	13.12 E
Sankt Moritz	36	46.30 N	9.50 E
Sankt Pölten	30	48.12 N	15.37 E
Sankt Veit an der Glan	30	46.46 N	14.21 E
Sankuru ≃	86	4.17 S	20.25 E
San Lázaro, Cabo ≻	108	24.48 N	112.19 W
San Leandro	154	37.43 N	122.09 W
San Lorenzo, Arg.	120	32.45 S	60.44 W
San Lorenzo, Ec.	118	1.17 N	78.50 W
San Lorenzo, Isla I	118	12.05 S	77.15 W
San Lorenzo de El Escorial	44	40.35 N	4.09 W
Sanlúcar de Barrameda	44	36.47 N	6.21 W
San Lucas, Cabo ≻	108	22.52 N	109.53 W
San Luis, Arg.	120	33.18 S	66.21 W
San Luis, Guat.	108	16.14 N	89.27 W
San Luis, Laguna ⊜	118	13.45 S	64.00 W
San Luis Obispo	154	35.16 N	120.39 W
San Luis Peak ∧	148	37.59 N	106.56 W
San Luis Potosí	108	22.09 N	100.59 W
San Luis Reservoir ⊜[1]	154	37.07 N	121.05 W
San Luis Río Colorado	108	32.29 N	114.48 W
San Luis Valley V	148	37.25 N	106.00 W
Sanluri	40	39.34 N	8.54 E
San Manuel	148	32.35 N	110.37 W
San Marcos	132	29.52 N	97.56 W
San Marino	40	43.55 N	12.28 E
San Marino □[1]	40	43.56 N	12.25 E
San Martín ≃	118	13.08 S	63.43 W
San Martín, Lago (Lago O'Higgins) ⊜	120	49.00 S	72.40 W
San Martín de los Andes	120	40.10 S	71.21 W
San Mateo, Ca., U.S.	154	37.33 N	122.19 W
San Mateo, Fl., U.S.	142	29.36 N	81.35 W
San Matías, Golfo c	120	41.30 S	64.15 W
Sanmenxia	66	34.45 N	111.05 E
San Miguel	108	13.29 N	88.11 W
San Miguel ≃	118	13.52 S	63.56 W
San Miguel de Tucumán	120	26.49 S	65.13 W
San Miguel Island I	154	34.02 N	120.22 W
San Miniato	40	43.41 N	10.51 E
Sannār	84	13.33 N	33.38 E
Sannicandro Garganico	40	41.50 N	15.34 E
San Nicolás de los Arroyos	120	33.20 S	60.13 W
San Nicolas Island I	154	33.15 N	119.31 W
Sannikova, proliv ᵕ	56	74.30 N	140.00 E
Sanniquellie	82	7.22 N	8.43 W
Sanok	30	49.34 N	22.13 E
San Pablo	68	14.04 N	121.19 E
San Pablo Bay c	154	38.06 N	122.22 W
San-Pédro	82	4.44 N	6.37 W
San Pedro ≃	148	32.59 N	110.47 W
San Pedro, Punta ≻	120	25.30 S	70.38 W
San Pedro, Volcán ∧[1]	120	21.53 S	68.25 W
San Pedro Channel ᵕ	154	33.35 N	118.25 W
San Pedro de las Colonias	108	25.45 N	102.59 W
San Pedro de Macorís	108	18.27 N	69.18 W
San Pedro Sula	108	15.27 N	88.02 W
San Pietro, Isola di I	40	39.08 N	8.17 E
San Quintín, Cabo ≻	108	30.21 N	116.00 W
San Rafael, Arg.	120	34.36 S	68.20 W
San Rafael, Ca., U.S.	154	37.58 N	122.31 W
San Rafael ≃	148	38.47 N	110.07 W
San Remo	40	43.49 N	7.46 E
San Roque	44	36.13 N	5.24 W
San Roque, Punta ≻	108	27.11 N	114.26 W
San Salvador	108	13.42 N	89.12 W
San Salvador (Watling Island) I	108	24.02 N	74.28 W
San Salvador de Jujuy	120	24.11 S	65.18 W
San Sebastián → Donostia	44	43.19 N	1.59 W
Sansepolcro	40	43.34 N	12.08 E
San Severo	40	41.41 N	15.23 E
San Simon	148	32.16 N	109.13 W
San Simon ≃	148	32.50 N	109.39 W
Sanski Most	40	44.46 N	16.40 E
Santa Ana, Bol.	118	15.31 S	67.30 W
Santa Ana, El Sal.	108	13.59 N	89.34 W
Santa Ana, Ca., U.S.	154	33.44 N	117.52 W
Santa Bárbara, Méx.	108	26.48 N	105.49 W
Santa Barbara, Ca., U.S.	154	34.25 N	119.42 W

Symbols in the index entries are identified on page 162.

Name	Page	Lat.	Long.
Santa Barbara Channel ʊ	154	34.15N	119.55W
Santa Catalina, Gulf of c	154	33.20N	117.45W
Santa Catalina Island I	154	33.23N	118.24W
Santa Clara, Cuba	108	22.24N	79.58W
Santa Clara, Ca., U.S.	154	37.20N	121.56W
Santa Clara ≃	154	34.14N	119.16W
Santa Cruz, Bol.	118	17.48S	63.10W
Santa Cruz, Ca., U.S.	154	36.58N	122.01W
Santa Cruz ≃	148	32.42N	111.33W
Santa Cruz de la Palma	82	28.41N	17.45W
Santa Cruz de la Zarza	44	39.58N	3.10W
Santa Cruz del Sur	108	20.43N	78.00W
Santa Cruz de Tenerife	82	28.27N	16.14W
Santa Cruz Island I	154	34.01N	119.45W
Santa Eulalia	44	40.34N	1.19W
Santa Eulària del Riu	44	38.59N	1.31 E
Santa Fe, Arg.	120	31.38S	60.42W
Santa Fe, N.M., U.S.	148	35.41N	105.56W
Santa Fe Baldy ∧	148	35.50N	105.46W
Santai	66	31.10N	105.02 E
Santa Inés, Isla I	120	53.45S	72.45W
Santa Isabel → Malabo	82	3.45N	8.47 E
Santa Isabel I	94	8.00S	159.00 E
Santa Lucía	120	34.27S	56.24W
Santa Lucia Range ⋏	154	36.00N	121.20W
Santa Margarita	154	35.23N	120.36W
Santa Margherita Ligure	40	44.20N	9.12 E
Santa Maria, Bra.	120	29.41S	53.48W
Santa Maria, Ca., U.S.	154	34.57N	120.26W
Santa Maria I	92	14.15S	167.30 E
Santa Maria, Cabo de >, Ang.	86	13.25S	12.32 E
Santa Maria, Cabo de >, Port.	44	36.58N	7.54W
Santa Maria Capua Vetere	40	41.05N	14.15 E
Santa Maria di Leuca, Capo >	40	39.47N	18.22 E
Santa Marta	118	11.15N	74.13W
Santa Monica	154	34.01N	118.29W
Santa Monica Bay c	154	33.54N	118.25W
Santana do Livramento	120	30.53S	55.31W
Santander, Esp.	44	43.28N	3.48W
Santander, Pil.	68	9.25N	123.20 E
Santanilla, Islas II	108	17.25N	83.55W
Sant'Antioco, Isola di I	40	39.02N	8.25 E
Sant Antoni de Portmany	44	38.58N	1.18 E
Santa Paula	154	34.21N	119.03W
Sant'Arcangelo	40	40.15N	16.17 E
Santarém, Bra.	118	2.26S	54.42W
Santarém, Port.	44	39.14N	8.41W
Santa Rita	108	15.09N	87.53W
Santa Rosa, Arg.	120	32.20S	65.12W
Santa Rosa, Ca., U.S.	154	38.26N	122.42W
Santa Rosa Beach	144	30.23N	86.13W
Santa Rosa de Copán	108	14.47N	88.46W
Santa Rosa Island I, Ca., U.S.	154	33.58N	120.06W
Santa Rosa Island I, Fl., U.S.	144	30.22N	86.55W
Šantarskije ostrova II	56	55.00N	137.36 E
Santa Teresa, Embalse de ⊜[1]	44	40.40N	5.30W
Santa Ynez ≃	154	34.41N	120.36W
Santee	154	32.50N	116.58W
Santee ≃	142	33.14N	79.28W
Sant'Eufemia, Golfo di c	40	38.50N	16.00 E
Sant Feliu de Guíxols	44	41.47N	3.02 E
Santiago, Chile	120	33.27S	70.40W
Santiago, Pan.	108	8.06N	80.59W
Santiago, Rep. Dom.	108	19.27N	70.42W
Santiago I	82	15.05N	23.40W
Santiago de Compostela	44	42.53N	8.33W
Santiago de Cuba	108	20.01N	75.49W
Santiago del Estero	120	27.47S	64.16W
Santiago Peak ∧	154	33.42N	117.32W
Santiam Pass)(	150	44.25N	121.51W
Säntis ∧	36	47.15N	9.21 E
Santisteban del Puerto	44	38.15N	3.12W
Sant Jordi, Golf de c	44	40.53N	1.00 E
Santo	92	15.32S	167.08 E
Santo André	118	23.40S	46.31W
Santo Ângelo	120	28.18S	54.16W
Santo Antão I	82	17.05N	25.10W
Santo António	86	1.39N	7.26 E
Santo Domingo	108	18.28N	69.54W
Santo Domingo Pueblo	148	35.30N	106.21W
Santop, Pic ∧	92	18.39S	169.03 E
Santorini → Thíra I	48	36.24N	25.29 E
Santos	118	23.57S	46.20W
San Valentín, Cerro ∧	120	46.36S	73.20W
San Vicente	108	13.38N	88.48W
San Vicente de Alcántara	44	39.21N	7.08W
San Vito	40	39.26N	9.32 E
San Vito, Capo >	40	38.11N	12.44 E
San Vito dei Normanni	40	40.39N	17.42 E
São Borja	120	28.39S	56.00W
São Carlos	118	22.01S	47.54W
São Francisco ≃	118	10.30S	36.24W
São Gabriel	120	30.20S	54.19W
São Jerônimo	120	29.58S	51.43W
São João da Boa Vista	118	21.58S	46.47W
São João da Madeira	44	40.54N	8.30W
São João del Rei	118	21.09S	44.16W
São José do Rio Prêto	118	20.48S	49.23W
São José dos Campos	118	23.11S	45.53W
São Leopoldo	120	29.46S	51.09W
São Lourenço ≃	118	17.53S	57.27W
São Lourenço, Pantanal de ≋	118	17.30S	56.30W
São Luís	118	2.31S	44.16W
São Manuel ≃	118	7.21S	58.03W
Saône ≃	36	45.44N	4.50 E
São Nicolau I	82	16.35N	24.15W
São Paulo	118	23.32S	46.37W
São Roque, Cabo de >	118	5.29S	35.16W
São Sebastião, Ponta >	86	22.07S	35.30 E
São Tomé	86	0.20N	6.44 E
São Tomé I	86	0.12N	6.39 E
São Tomé, Cabo de >	118	21.59S	40.59W
Sao Tome and Principe □[1]	86	1.00N	7.00 E
Saoura, Oued V	82	29.00N	0.55W
São Vicente	118	23.58S	46.23W
São Vicente I	82	16.50N	25.00W
São Vicente, Cabo de (Cape Saint Vincent) >	44	37.01N	9.00W
Sapele	82	5.54N	5.41 E
Sapelo Island I	142	31.28N	81.15W
Sapitwa ∧	86	15.57S	35.36 E
Sapporo	66	43.03N	141.21 E
Sapt Kosi ≃	70	26.31N	86.58 E
Sapulpa	132	35.59N	96.06W
Sarajevo	48	43.52N	18.25 E
Saraland	144	30.49N	88.04W
Saranac	138	42.55N	85.12W
Saranac ≃	136	44.42N	73.27W
Saranac Lake	136	44.19N	74.07W
Saransk	20	54.11N	45.11 E
Sarapul	20	56.28N	53.48 E
Sarasota	142	27.20N	82.31W
Saratoga, Ca., U.S.	154	37.15N	122.01W
Saratoga, Wy., U.S.	148	41.27N	106.48W
Saratoga National Historical Park ♦	136	43.00N	73.38W
Saratoga Springs	136	43.04N	73.47W
Saratov	54	51.34N	46.02 E
Saratovskoje vodochranilišče ⊜[1]	54	52.45N	48.30 E
Sarayköy	48	37.55N	28.58 E
Sarcidano ◆[1]	40	39.55N	9.05 E
Sardegna (Sardinia) I	40	40.00N	9.00 E
Sardinia → Sardegna I	40	40.00N	9.00 E
Sardis, Al., U.S.	144	32.17N	86.59W
Sardis, Ga., U.S.	142	32.58N	81.45W
Sardis, Ms., U.S.	144	34.26N	89.55W
Sardis, Tn., U.S.	144	35.27N	88.18W
Sardis Lake ⊜[1]	144	34.27N	89.43W
Sarek ∧	20	67.25N	17.46 E
Sarepta	144	32.53N	93.26W
Sargans	36	47.03N	9.26 E
Sargent	142	33.25N	84.52W
Sargodha	70	32.05N	72.40 E
Sarh	84	9.09N	18.23 E
Sārī	70	36.34N	53.04 E
Sarina	96	21.26S	149.13 E
Sariwŏn	66	38.31N	125.44 E
Sark I	26	49.26N	2.21W
Sármellék	30	46.44N	17.10 E
Sarmiento, Cerro ∧	120	54.27S	70.50W
Sârnena ⋏	48	42.35N	25.10 E
Sarnia	130	42.58N	82.23W
Sarno	40	40.49N	14.37 E
Saronikós Kólpos c	48	37.54N	23.12 E
Saronno	40	45.38N	9.02 E
Saros Körfezi c	48	40.30N	26.20 E
Sárospatak	30	48.19N	21.34 E
Šar Planina ⋏	48	42.05N	20.50 E
Sarpsborg	22	59.17N	11.07 E
Sarrath, Oued V	40	35.59N	8.23 E
Sarreguemines	36	49.06N	7.03 E
Sarria	44	42.47N	7.24W
Sartène	40	41.36N	8.59 E
Sarthe ≃	36	47.30N	0.32W
Saruhanlı	48	38.44N	27.34 E
Sárvár	30	47.15N	16.57 E
Sárvíz ≃	30	46.24N	18.41 E
Sarzana	40	44.07N	9.58 E
Sasebo	66	33.10N	129.43 E
Saskatchewan □[4]	130	54.00N	105.00W
Saskatchewan ≃	130	53.12N	99.16W
Saskatoon	130	52.07N	106.38W
Sassafras	142	37.14N	83.06W
Sassafras Mountain ∧	142	35.03N	82.48W
Sassandra	82	4.58N	6.05W
Sassandra ≃	82	4.58N	6.05W
Sassari	40	40.44N	8.33 E
Sassnitz	30	54.31N	13.38 E
Sasso Marconi	40	44.24N	11.15 E
Sassuolo	40	44.33N	10.47 E
Sata-misaki >	66	30.59N	130.40 E
Sātāra	70	17.41N	73.59 E
Satellite Beach	142	28.10N	80.35W
Satilla ≃	142	30.59N	81.28W
Sátoraljaújhely	30	48.24N	21.39 E
Sātpura Range ⋏	70	22.00N	78.00 E
Satsuma	144	30.51N	88.03W
Satsunan-shotō II	66	29.00N	130.00 E
Sattahip	68	12.40N	100.54 E
Satu Mare	48	47.48N	22.53 E
Saucier	144	30.38N	89.08W
Saudi Arabia (Al-'Arabīyah as-Sa'ūdīyah) □[1]	70	25.00N	45.00 E
Sauerland ◆[1]	30	51.10N	8.00 E
Saugatuck	138	42.39N	86.12W
Saugerties	136	42.04N	73.57W
Sauk City	138	43.16N	89.43W
Sauk Rapids	138	45.35N	94.09W
Saukville	138	43.22N	87.56W
Saül	118	3.37N	53.12W
Sault Sainte Marie, On., Can.	130	46.31N	84.20W
Sault Sainte Marie, Mi., U.S.	138	46.29N	84.20W
Saumur	36	47.16N	0.05W
Sauquoit	136	43.00N	75.16W
Sausalito	154	37.51N	122.29W
Sauwald ◆[3]	30	48.28N	13.40 E
Sava	40	40.24N	17.34 E
Sava ≃	16	44.50N	20.26 E
Savage	136	39.08N	76.49W
Savai'i I	93	13.35S	172.25W
Savanna	138	42.05N	90.09W
Savannah, Ga., U.S.	142	32.05N	81.06W
Savannah, Mo., U.S.	144	39.56N	94.49W
Savannah, Tn., U.S.	144	35.13N	88.14W
Savannah ≃	142	32.02N	80.53W
Savannakhét	68	16.33N	104.45 E
Savanna-la-Mar	108	18.13N	78.08W
Save (Sabi) ≃, Afr.	86	21.00S	35.02 E
Save ≃, Fr.	36	43.47N	1.17 E
Savenay	36	47.22N	1.57W
Săveni	48	47.57N	26.52 E
Saverne	36	48.44N	7.22 E
Savigliano	40	44.38N	7.40 E
Šavnik	48	42.57N	19.05 E
Savona	40	44.17N	8.30 E
Savonlinna	22	61.52N	28.53 E
Savusavu	91	16.16S	179.21 E
Savu Sea → Sawu, Laut ⊤[2]	68	9.40S	122.00 E
Sawākin	84	19.07N	37.20 E
Sawatch Range ⋏	148	39.10N	106.25W
Sawdā', Jabal as- ⋏[2]	84	28.40N	15.30 E
Sawdā', Qurnat as- ∧	70	34.18N	36.07 E
Sawel Mountain ∧	26	54.49N	7.02W
Sawhāj	84	26.33N	31.42 E
Sawqarah, Dawḥat c	70	18.35N	57.15 E
Sawtooth National Recreation Area ♦	150	44.00N	114.55W
Sawu, Laut (Savu Sea) ⊤[2]	68	9.40S	122.00 E
Saxony → Sachsen □[9]	30	52.45N	9.30 E
Saxton	136	40.12N	78.14W
Sayan Mountains (Sajany) ⋏	54	52.45N	96.00 E
Şaydā	70	33.33N	35.22 E
Saylorville Lake ⊜[1]	138	41.48N	93.46W
Sayre	136	41.58N	76.30W
Sayreville	136	40.27N	74.21W
Say'ūn	70	15.56N	48.47 E
Sazanit I	48	40.30N	19.16 E
Sazlijka ≃	48	42.02N	25.52 E
Sbeïtla	40	35.14N	9.08 E
Sbiba	40	35.33N	9.05 E
Scafell Pikes ∧	26	54.27N	3.12W
Scalea	40	39.49N	15.48 E
Scapa Flow c	26	58.55N	3.06W
Scarborough, Trin.	108	11.11N	60.44W
Scarborough, Eng., U.K.	26	54.17N	0.24W
Scărişoara	48	44.00N	24.35 E
Schaffhausen	36	47.42N	8.38 E
Schefferville	130	54.48N	66.50W
Schelde (Escaut) ≃	30	51.22N	4.15 E
Schell Creek Range ⋏	154	39.10N	114.40W
Schenectady	136	42.48N	73.56W
Schesslitz	30	49.59N	11.01 E
Schiedam	30	51.55N	4.24 E
Schiermonnikoog I	30	53.28N	6.15 E
Schiltigheim	36	48.36N	7.45 E
Schio	40	45.43N	11.21 E
Schkeuditz	30	51.24N	12.13 E
Schleswig	30	54.31N	9.33 E
Schleswig-Holstein □[3]	30	54.20N	9.40 E
Schlitz	30	50.40N	9.33 E
Schmalkalden	30	50.43N	10.26 E
Schmölln	30	50.53N	12.20 E
Schneeberg	30	50.36N	12.38 E
Schneeberg ∧	36	50.03N	11.51 E
Schofield	138	44.54N	89.36W
Schoharie	136	42.39N	74.18W
Schönebeck	30	52.01N	11.44 E
Schongau	30	47.49N	10.54 E
Schoolcraft	138	42.06N	85.38W
Schorndorf	30	48.48N	9.31 E
Schouwen I	30	51.43N	3.50 E
Schramberg	30	48.13N	8.23 E
Schreiber	130	48.48N	87.15W
Schrobenhausen	30	48.33N	11.17 E
Schuylkill ≃	136	39.53N	75.12W
Schuylkill Haven	136	40.37N	76.10W
Schwabach	30	49.20N	11.01 E
Schwaben □[9]	30	48.10N	9.25 E
Schwäbische Alb ⋏	30	48.25N	9.30 E
Schwäbisch Gmünd	30	48.48N	9.47 E
Schwäbisch Hall	30	49.07N	9.44 E
Schwandorf	30	49.20N	12.08 E
Schwarza ≃	30	47.43N	16.13 E
Schwarzwald (Black Forest) ⋏	30	48.00N	8.15 E
Schwechat	30	48.08N	16.29 E
Schwedt	30	53.03N	14.17 E
Schweinfurt	30	50.03N	10.14 E
Schwerin	30	53.38N	11.25 E
Schweriner See ⊜	30	53.45N	11.28 E
Schwetzingen	30	49.23N	8.34 E
Schwyz	36	47.02N	8.40 E
Sciacca	40	37.31N	13.03 E
Scicli	40	36.47N	14.42 E
Scilly, Isles of II	26	49.55N	6.20W
Ścinawa	30	51.25N	16.27 E
Scio	136	40.23N	81.05W
Scioto ≃	136	38.44N	83.01W
Ščokino	54	54.01N	37.31 E
Scooba	144	32.49N	88.28W
Scordia	40	37.18N	14.51 E
Scotia	136	42.49N	73.57W
Scotland □[8]	26	57.00N	4.00W
Scotland Neck	142	36.07N	77.25W
Scotlandville	144	30.31N	91.10W
Scott, Mount ∧	150	42.56N	122.01W
Scott City	144	37.13N	89.31W
Scottdale	136	40.06N	79.35W
Scott Peak ∧	150	44.21N	112.50W
Scottsbluff	132	41.52N	103.40W
Scottsboro	144	34.40N	86.02W
Scottsburg	144	38.41N	85.46W
Scottsdale	148	33.30N	111.53W
Scottsville	144	36.45N	86.11W
Scranton	136	41.24N	75.39W
Scugog, Lake ⊜	138	44.10N	78.51W
Scunthorpe	26	53.36N	0.38W
Scuol	36	46.48N	10.18 E
Scutari, Lake ⊜	48	42.12N	19.18 E
Seaboard	142	36.29N	77.26W
Seaford	136	38.38N	75.36W
Seaham	26	54.52N	1.21W
Seahorse Point >	130	63.47N	80.09W
Sea Islands II	142	31.20N	81.20W
Sea Isle City	136	39.09N	74.41W
Seal ≃	130	59.04N	94.48W
Seale	144	32.17N	85.10W
Sealevel	142	34.51N	76.23W
Searcy	144	35.15N	91.44W
Searles Lake ⊜	154	35.43N	117.20W
Searsport	136	44.27N	68.55W
Seaside, Ca., U.S.	154	36.36N	121.51W
Seaside, Or., U.S.	150	45.59N	123.55W
Seaside Park	136	39.55N	74.04W
Seattle	150	47.36N	122.19W
Sebago Lake ⊜	136	43.50N	70.35W
Sebastián Vizcaíno, Bahía c	108	28.00N	114.30W
Sebastopol, Ca., U.S.	154	38.24N	122.49W
Sebastopol, Ms., U.S.	144	32.34N	89.20W
Sebec Lake ⊜	136	45.18N	69.18W
Sebeş	48	45.58N	23.34 E
Sebes Körös (Crişul Repede) ≃	48	46.55N	20.59 E
Sebewaing	138	43.43N	83.27W
Sebnitz	30	50.58N	14.16 E
Sebree	144	37.36N	87.31W
Sebring	142	27.29N	81.26W
Sechura, Bahía de c	118	5.42S	81.00W
Secretary Island I	98	45.15S	166.55 E
Séd ≃	30	47.00N	18.31 E
Sedalia	144	38.42N	93.13W
Sedan	36	49.42N	4.57 E
Sedlčany	30	49.40N	14.26 E
Sedona	148	34.52N	111.45W
Sedova, pik ∧	54	73.29N	54.58 E
Sedro Woolley	150	48.30N	122.14W
Sędziszów	30	50.04N	21.41 E
Seeheim	86	26.50S	17.45 E
Sefton, Mount ∧	98	43.41S	170.03 E
Segama ≃	68	5.27N	118.48 E
Segangane	44	35.09N	3.00W
Şegarcea	48	44.06N	23.45 E
Segeža	20	63.44N	34.19 E
Segorbe	44	39.51N	0.29W
Ségou	82	13.27N	6.16W
Segovia	44	40.57N	4.07W
Segre ≃	44	41.40N	0.43 E
Segura	44	39.50N	6.59W
Segura ≃	44	38.06N	0.38W
Segura, Sierra de ⋏	44	38.00N	2.43W
Seiland I	20	70.25N	23.15 E
Sein, Île de I	36	48.02N	4.51W
Seinäjoki	22	62.47N	22.50 E
Seine ≃, On., Can.	130	48.40N	92.49W
Seine ≃, Fr.	36	49.26N	0.26 E
Seine, Baie de la c	36	49.30N	0.30W
Sejerø I	22	55.53N	11.09 E
Sejm ≃	54	51.27N	32.34 E
Sejny	30	54.07N	23.20 E
Sekondi-Takoradi	82	4.59N	1.43W
Šelagskij, mys >	56	70.06N	170.26 E
Selah	150	46.39N	120.31W
Selatan, Tanjung >	68	4.10S	114.38 E
Selb	30	50.10N	12.08 E
Selbusjøen ⊜	22	63.14N	10.54 E
Selby	26	53.48N	1.04W
Selbyville	136	38.27N	75.13W
Selçuk	48	37.56N	27.22 E
Selenga (Selenge) ≃	56	52.16N	106.16 E
Selenge (Selenga) ≃	56	52.16N	106.16 E
Selenicë	48	40.32N	19.38 E
Sélestat	36	48.16N	7.27 E
Šelichova, zaliv c	56	60.00N	158.00 E
Seliger, ozero ⊜	54	57.13N	33.05 E
Seligman	148	35.19N	112.52W
Selinsgrove	136	40.47N	76.51W
Selkirk	130	50.09N	96.52W
Sellers	142	34.17N	79.28W
Sellersburg	144	38.23N	85.45W
Selm	30	51.42N	7.28 E
Selma, Al., U.S.	144	32.24N	87.01W
Selma, Ca., U.S.	154	36.34N	119.36W
Selma, N.C., U.S.	142	35.32N	78.17W
Selmer	144	35.10N	88.35W
Selmont	144	32.23N	87.01W
Selouane	44	35.04N	2.58W
Selvagens, Ilhas II	82	30.05N	15.55W
Selvas ◆[3]	118	5.00S	68.00W
Selwyn, Passage ʊ	92	16.03S	168.12 E
Selwyn Mountains ⋏	130	63.10N	130.20W
Seman ≃	48	40.56N	19.24 E
Semarang	68	6.58S	110.25 E
Semenicului, Munţii ⋏	48	45.05N	22.05 E
Semeru, Gunung ∧	68	8.06S	112.55 E
Seminoe Reservoir ⊜[1]	148	42.00N	106.50W
Seminole, Lake ⊜[1]	142	30.46N	84.50W
Semipalatinsk	56	50.28N	80.13 E
Semporna	68	4.28N	118.36 E
Semuliki ≃	86	1.14N	30.28 E
Seňa, Česko.	30	48.34N	21.15 E
Sena, Moç.	86	17.27S	35.00 E
Senath	144	36.08N	90.09W
Senatobia	144	34.37N	89.58W
Sendai	66	38.15N	140.53 E
Seneca, Il., U.S.	138	41.18N	88.36W
Seneca, Mo., U.S.	144	36.50N	94.36W
Seneca, S.C., U.S.	142	34.41N	82.57W
Seneca Falls	136	42.54N	76.47W
Seneca Lake ⊜	136	42.40N	76.57W
Senegal (Sénégal) □[1]	82	14.00N	14.00W
Sénégal ≃	82	15.48N	16.32W
Senetosa, Capu di >	40	41.33N	8.47 E
Senftenberg	30	51.31N	14.00 E
Senica	30	48.41N	17.22 E
Senigallia	40	43.43N	13.13 E
Senj	40	44.59N	14.54 E
Senja I	20	69.20N	17.30 E
Senlis	36	49.12N	2.35 E
Senneterre	130	48.23N	77.15W
Sennori	40	40.48N	8.35 E
Sens	36	48.12N	3.17 E
Senta	48	45.56N	20.04 E
Seo de Urgel	44	42.21N	1.28 E
Seoul → Sŏul	66	37.33N	126.58 E
Separation Point >	98	40.47S	173.00 E
Sepi	94	8.33S	159.50 E
Sepik ≃	96a	3.51S	144.34 E
Sępólno Krajeńskie	30	53.28N	17.32 E
Sept-Îles (Seven Islands)	130	50.12N	66.23W
Sequatchie ≃	142	35.02N	85.38W
Sequim	150	48.04N	123.06W
Sequoia National Park ♦	154	36.30N	118.30W
Seraing	30	50.36N	5.29 E
Seram (Ceram) I	68	3.00S	129.00 E
Seram, Laut (Ceram Sea) ⊤[2]	68	2.30S	128.00 E
Serang	68	6.07S	106.09 E
Serbia → Srbija □[3]	48	44.00N	21.00 E
Séré'ama, Mont ∧	92	13.47S	167.29 E
Sered'	30	48.17N	17.44 E
Seremban	68	2.43N	101.56 E
Serengeti Plain ≚	86	2.50S	35.00 E
Serenje	86	13.15S	30.14 E
Sergeja Kirova, ostrova II	54	77.12N	89.30 E
Seria	68	4.39N	114.23 E
Sérifos I	48	37.11N	24.31 E
Sermilik c[2]	130	65.37N	38.03W
Serov	54	59.29N	60.31 E
Serowe	86	22.25S	26.44 E
Serpuchov	20	54.55N	37.25 E
Sérrai	48	41.05N	23.32 E
Serrat, Cap >	40	37.14N	9.13 E
Serres	36	44.26N	5.43 E
Servi Burnu >	48	41.40N	28.06 E
Sesia ≃	40	45.05N	8.37 E
Sessa Aurunca	40	41.14N	13.56 E
Ses Salines, Cap de >	44	39.16N	3.03 E
Sestao	44	43.18N	3.00W
Sestri Levante	40	44.16N	9.24 E
Sestroreck	20	60.06N	29.58 E
Sète	36	43.24N	3.41 E
Sete Lagoas	118	19.27S	44.14W
Seto-naikai ⊤[2]	66	34.20N	133.30 E
Settat	82	33.04N	7.37W
Sette-Daban, chrebet ⋏	56	62.00N	138.00 E
Setúbal	44	38.32N	8.54W
Setúbal, Baía de c	44	38.27N	8.53W
Seui	40	39.50N	9.19 E
Seul, Lac ⊜	130	50.20N	92.30W
Seul Choix Point >	138	45.56N	85.52W
Sevan, ozero ⊜	54	40.20N	45.20 E
Sevastopol'	54	44.36N	33.32 E
Ševčenko	54	43.35N	51.05 E
Severn ≃, On., Can.	130	56.02N	87.36W
Severn ≃, U.K.	26	51.35N	2.40W
Severnaja Dvina ≃	54	64.32N	40.30 E
Severnaja Zeml'a II	56	79.30N	98.00 E
Severna Park	136	39.04N	76.32W
Severnyje uvaly ⋏[2]	54	59.30N	49.00 E
Severodvinsk	20	64.34N	39.50 E
Severomorsk	20	69.05N	33.24 E
Severo-Sibirskaja nizmennost' ≚	54	73.00N	100.00 E
Severskij Donec ≃	54	47.35N	40.54 E
Sevier ≃	148	39.04N	113.06W
Sevier Lake ⊜	148	38.55N	113.09W
Sevierville	142	35.52N	83.33W
Sevilla, Col.	118	4.16N	75.57W
Sevilla (Seville), Esp.	44	37.23N	5.59W
Seville → Sevilla, Esp.	44	37.23N	5.59W
Seville, Oh., U.S.	136	41.00N	81.51W
Sevlievo	48	43.01N	25.06 E
Sewanee	144	35.04N	85.55W
Seward, Ak., U.S.	132a	60.06N	149.26W
Seward, Ne., U.S.	132	40.54N	97.05W
Seward, Pa., U.S.	136	40.25N	79.01W
Seychelles □[1]	86	4.35S	55.40 E
Seylac	84	11.21N	43.29 E
Seymour, Ct., U.S.	136	41.23N	73.04W
Seymour, In., U.S.	144	38.57N	85.53W
Seymour, Mo., U.S.	144	37.08N	92.46W
Seymour, Wi., U.S.	138	44.30N	88.19W
Seymourville	144	30.27N	91.29W
Sežana	40	45.42N	13.52 E
Sezimovo Ústí	30	49.23N	14.42 E
Sfax	82	34.44N	10.46 E
Sfîntu-Gheorghe	48	45.52N	25.47 E
Sfîntu Gheorghe, Braţul ≃[1]	48	44.53N	29.36 E
Sfîntu Gheorghe, Ostrovul I	48	45.07N	29.22 E
's-Gravenhage (The Hague)	30	52.06N	4.18 E
Shabeelle (Shebele) ≃	84	0.50N	43.10 E
Shache	66	38.25N	77.16 E
Shadyside	136	39.58N	80.45W
Shag ≃	98	45.29S	170.49 E
Shag Rocks II[1]	120	53.33S	42.02W
Shahdād, Namakzār-e ≚	70	30.30N	58.30 E
Shāhjahānpur	70	27.53N	79.55 E
Shakawe	86	18.23S	21.50 E
Shaker Heights	136	41.28N	81.32W
Shakhty → Šachty	54	47.42N	40.13 E
Shaki	82	8.39N	3.25 E
Shakopee	138	44.47N	93.31W
Shala, Lake ⊜	84	7.25N	38.30 E
Shām, Bādiyat ash- ◆[2]	70	32.00N	40.00 E
Shām, Jabal ash- ∧	70	23.13N	57.16 E
Shamokin	136	40.47N	76.33W
Shandī	84	16.42N	33.26 E
Shandong Bandao >[1]	66	37.00N	121.00 E
Shangani ≃	86	18.41S	27.10 E
Shanghai	66	31.14N	121.28 E
Shangqiu	66	34.27N	115.42 E
Shangrao	66	28.26N	117.58 E
Shangshui	66	33.33N	114.34 E
Shannon	142	34.20N	85.04W
Shannon ≃	26	52.36N	9.41W
Shannontown	142	33.53N	80.21W
Shantou (Swatow)	66	23.23N	116.41 E
Shantung Peninsula → Shandong Bandao >[1]	66	37.00N	121.00 E
Shanxian	66	34.48N	116.03 E
Shaoguan	66	24.50N	113.37 E
Shaoxing	66	30.00N	120.35 E
Shaoyang	66	27.15N	111.28 E
Sharbatāt, Ra's ash- >	70	17.52N	56.22 E
Sharjah → Ash-Shāriqah	70	25.22N	55.23 E
Shark Bay c	96	25.30S	113.30 E
Sharon	136	41.13N	80.29W
Sharqīyah, Aṣ-Ṣaḥrā' ash- (Arabian Desert) ◆[2]	84	28.00N	32.00 E
Shashe ≃	86	22.14S	29.20 E
Shashi	66	30.19N	112.14 E
Shasta	154	40.36N	122.29W
Shasta ≃	154	41.50N	122.35W
Shasta, Mount ∧[1]	154	41.20N	122.20W
Shasta Lake ⊜[1]	154	40.50N	122.25W
Shaunavon	130	49.40N	108.25W
Shaw	144	33.36N	90.46W
Shawano	138	44.46N	88.36W
Shawinigan	130	46.33N	72.45W
Shawnee, Oh., U.S.	136	39.36N	82.12W
Shawnee, Ok., U.S.	132	35.19N	96.55W
Shawneetown	144	37.42N	88.11W
Shaybārā I	70	25.27N	36.48 E
Shay Gap	96	20.25S	120.03 E
Shaykh, Jabal ash- ∧	70	33.26N	35.51 E
Shaykh 'Uthmān	70	12.52N	44.59 E
Shebele (Shabeelle) ≃	84	0.50N	43.10 E
Sheberghān	70	36.41N	65.45 E
Sheboygan	138	43.45N	87.42W
Sheboygan Falls	138	43.43N	87.48W
Sheep Mountain ∧	150	43.33N	110.32W
Sheffield, Eng., U.K.	26	53.23N	1.30W
Sheffield, Al., U.S.	144	34.45N	87.41W
Sheffield, Pa., U.S.	136	41.42N	79.02W
Shekhūpura	70	31.42N	73.59 E
Shelbina	144	39.41N	92.02W
Shelburn	144	39.11N	87.24W
Shelburne	130	43.46N	65.19W
Shelburne Falls	136	42.36N	72.44W
Shelby, Ms., U.S.	144	33.57N	90.46W
Shelby, Mt., U.S.	150	48.30N	111.51W
Shelby, N.C., U.S.	142	35.17N	81.32W
Shelby, Oh., U.S.	136	40.52N	82.39W
Shelbyville, Il., U.S.	144	39.24N	88.47W
Shelbyville, In., U.S.	144	39.31N	85.46W
Shelbyville, Ky., U.S.	144	38.12N	85.13W
Shelbyville, Tn., U.S.	144	35.29N	86.27W
Shelbyville, Lake ⊜[1]	144	39.30N	88.40W
Sheldon	144	37.39N	94.17W
Shellbrook	130	53.13N	106.24W
Shelley	150	43.22N	112.07W
Shell Rock ≃	138	42.38N	92.30W
Shelton, Ct., U.S.	136	41.18N	73.05W
Shelton, Wa., U.S.	150	47.13N	123.06W
Shenandoah, Pa., U.S.	136	40.49N	76.12W
Shenandoah, Va., U.S.	136	38.29N	78.37W
Shenandoah ≃	136	39.19N	77.44W
Shenandoah National Park ♦	136	38.48N	78.12W
Shenyang (Mukden)	66	41.48N	123.27 E
Shepherd, Îles II	92	16.55S	168.36 E
Shepherdsville	144	37.59N	85.42W
Sheppey, Isle of I	26	51.24N	0.50 E
Sherbro Island I	82	7.45N	12.55W
Sherbrooke	130	45.25N	71.54W
Sheridan, Ar., U.S.	144	34.18N	92.24W
Sheridan, In., U.S.	144	40.08N	86.13W
Sheridan, Wy., U.S.	150	44.47N	106.57W
Sherman	136	42.09N	79.35W
's-Hertogenbosch	30	51.41N	5.19 E
Sherwood	144	34.48N	92.13W
Shetland Islands II	26	60.30N	1.15W
Sheyenne ≃	132	47.05N	96.50W
Shibām	70	15.56N	48.38 E
Shickshinny	136	41.09N	76.09W
Shijiazhuang	66	38.03N	114.28 E
Shikārpur	70	27.57N	68.38 E
Shikoku I	66	33.45N	133.30 E
Shillelagh	26	52.45N	6.32W
Shillington	136	40.18N	75.57W
Shillong	70	25.34N	91.53 E
Shiloh	136	39.49N	84.13W
Shiloh National Military Park ♦	144	35.06N	88.21W
Shimber Berris ∧	84	10.44N	47.15 E
Shimoga	70	13.55N	75.34 E
Shimonoseki	66	33.57N	130.57 E
Shin, Loch ⊜	26	58.06N	4.34W
Shinglehouse	136	41.57N	78.11W
Shinkolobwe	86	11.02S	26.35 E
Shinnston	136	39.23N	80.18W
Shinyanga	86	3.40S	33.26 E
Shiocton	138	44.26N	88.34W
Shiono-misaki >	66	33.26N	135.45 E
Shippensburg	136	40.03N	77.31W
Shiprock	148	36.47N	108.41W
Ship Rock ∧	148	36.42N	108.50W
Shire ≃	86	17.42S	35.19 E
Shiretoko-misaki >	66	44.14N	145.17 E
Shirley	144	39.53N	85.34W
Shively	144	38.12N	85.49W
Shizuoka	66	34.58N	138.23 E
Shkodër	48	42.05N	19.30 E
Shkumbin ≃	48	41.01N	19.26 E
Sholāpur	70	17.41N	75.55 E
Shorewood	138	43.05N	87.53W
Shortland Islands II	94	6.55S	155.53 E
Shoshone ≃	150	44.52N	108.11W
Shoshone Lake ⊜	150	44.22N	110.43W
Shoshone Mountains ⋏	154	39.00N	117.30W
Shoshone Range ⋏	154	40.20N	116.50W
Shoshoni	150	43.14N	108.06W
Show Low	148	34.15N	110.01W
Shreve	136	40.40N	82.01W
Shreveport	144	32.30N	93.44W
Shrewsbury, Eng., U.K.	26	52.43N	2.45W
Shrewsbury, Ma., U.S.	136	42.17N	71.42W
Shropshire □[6]	26	52.40N	2.40W
Shuangcheng	66	45.21N	126.17 E
Shuangliao	66	43.31N	123.30 E
Shuangyashan	66	46.37N	131.22 E
Shubrā al-Khaymah	84	30.06N	31.15 E
Shuksan, Mount ∧	150	48.50N	121.36W
Shullsburg	138	42.34N	90.13W
Shuqrah	70	13.21N	45.42 E
Shūshtar	70	32.03N	48.51 E
Shwebo	68	22.34N	95.42 E
Shyok ≃	70	35.13N	75.53 E
Siālkot	70	32.30N	74.31 E
Siam, Gulf of → Thailand, Gulf of c	68	10.00N	101.00 E
Siasconset	136	41.15N	69.58W
Šiauliai	20	55.56N	23.19 E
Šibenik	40	43.44N	15.54 E
Siberia → Sibir' ◆[1]	56	65.00N	110.00 E
Sibérie Occidental, Dépression de la → Zapadno-Sibirskaja ravnina ≚	54	60.00N	75.00 E
Siberut, Pulau I	68	1.20S	98.55 E
Sibir' (Siberia) ◆[1]	56	65.00N	110.00 E
Sibiu	48	45.48N	24.09 E
Sibley, La., U.S.	144	32.33N	93.18W
Sibley, Ms., U.S.	144	31.22N	91.23W
Sibolga	68	1.45N	98.48 E
Sibu	68	2.18N	111.49 E
Sibuyan Sea ⊤[2]	68	12.50N	122.40 E
Sichote-Alin' ⋏	56	48.00N	138.00 E
Sicié, Cap >	36	43.03N	5.51 E
Sicilia (Sicily) I	40	37.30N	14.00 E
Sicily → Sicilia I	40	37.30N	14.00 E
Sicily, Strait of ʊ	40	37.20N	11.20 E
Sicily Island	144	31.50N	91.39W
Sicuani	118	14.16S	71.13W
Sídheros, Ákra >	48	35.19N	26.19 E
Sidi Aïch	44	36.37N	4.42 E
Sidi bel Abbès	82	35.13N	0.10W
Sidi Bennour	82	32.30N	8.30W
Sidi el Hani, Sebkhet ⊜	40	35.33N	10.25 E
Sidi Ifni	82	29.24N	10.12W
Sidmouth	26	50.41N	3.15W
Sidnaw	138	46.30N	88.42W
Sidney, Mt., U.S.	132	47.43N	104.09W
Sidney, Ne., U.S.	132	41.08N	102.58W
Sidney, N.Y., U.S.	136	42.18N	75.23W
Sidney, Oh., U.S.	136	40.17N	84.09W
Sidney Lanier, Lake ⊜[1]	142	34.15N	83.57W
Sidra, Gulf of → Surt, Khalīj c	84	31.30N	18.00 E
Siedlce	30	52.11N	22.16 E
Siegburg	30	50.47N	7.12 E
Siegen	30	50.52N	8.02 E
Siemianowice Śląskie	30	50.19N	19.01 E
Siemiatycze	30	52.26N	22.53 E
Siĕmréab	68	13.22N	103.51 E
Siena	40	43.19N	11.21 E
Sieradz	30	51.36N	18.45 E
Sieraków	30	52.39N	16.04 E
Sierpc	30	52.52N	19.41 E
Sierra Blanca	148	31.11N	105.21W
Sierra Blanca Peak ∧	148	33.23N	105.48W
Sierra de Outes	44	42.51N	8.54W
Sierra Leone □[1]	82	8.30N	11.30W
Sierra Vista	148	31.33N	110.18W
Sierre	36	46.18N	7.32 E
Siesta Key	142	27.19N	82.34W
Sífnos I	48	36.59N	24.40 E
Sighetu Marmaţiei	48	47.56N	23.54 E
Sighişoara	48	46.13N	24.48 E
Siglufjörður	20a	66.10N	18.56W
Sigmaringen	30	48.05N	9.13 E
Signal Mountain	144	35.07N	85.20W
Sigourney	138	41.20N	92.12W
Sigsig	118	3.01S	78.45W
Siguiri	82	11.25N	9.10W
Sikanni Chief ≃	130	58.20N	121.50W
Sīkar	70	27.37N	75.09 E
Sikasso	82	11.19N	5.40W
Sikéai	48	36.46N	22.56 E
Sikeston	144	36.52N	89.35W
Sikiang → Xi ≃	66	22.25N	113.23 E
Síkinos I	48	36.39N	25.06 E
Silchar	70	24.49N	92.48 E
Şile	48	41.11N	29.36 E
Šiler City	142	35.43N	79.27W
Silesia □[9]	30	51.00N	16.45 E
Siletz ≃	150	44.54N	124.00W
Siliana, Oued ≃	40	36.33N	9.25 E
Silīguri	70	26.42N	88.26 E
Silistra	48	44.07N	27.16 E
Siljan ⊜	22	60.50N	14.45 E
Šilka ≃	56	53.22N	121.32 E
Silkeborg	22	56.10N	9.34 E
Sillon de Talbert >[1]	36	48.53N	3.05W
Siloam Springs	144	36.11N	94.32W
Silsbee	144	30.20N	94.10W
Silver Bay	138	47.17N	91.15W

Symbols in the index entries are identified on page 162.

Name	Page	Lat.	Long.
Silver City, N.M., U.S.	148	32.46N	108.16W
Silver City, N.C., U.S.	142	35.00N	79.12W
Silver Creek	136	42.32N	79.10W
Silverdale	150	47.38N	122.41W
Silver Spring	136	38.59N	77.01W
Silver Star Mountain ∧	150	48.33N	120.35W
Silverton, Co., U.S.	148	37.48N	107.39W
Silverton, Or., U.S.	150	45.00N	122.46W
Silves	44	37.11N	8.26W
Simav ≃	48	40.23N	28.31 E
Simbach	30	48.34N	12.45 E
Simcoe, Lake ⊜	138	44.20N	79.20W
Simeria	48	45.51N	23.01 E
Simeto ≃	40	37.24N	15.06 E
Simeulue, Pulau I	68	2.35N	96.00 E
Simferopol'	54	44.57N	34.06 E
Simi I	48	36.35N	27.52 E
Simi Valley	154	34.16N	118.47W
Simla	70	22.47N	88.16 E
Simmesport	144	30.59N	91.48W
Simojoki ≃	20	65.37N	25.03 E
Simon's Town	86	34.14S	18.26 E
Simplon Pass)(	36	46.15N	8.02 E
Simpson	144	31.14N	93.00W
Simpson Desert ◆ 2	96	25.00S	137.00 E
Simpsonville	142	34.44N	82.15W
Simrishamn	22	55.33N	14.20 E
Simsbury	136	41.52N	72.48W
Sīnā', Shibh Jazīrat (Sinai Peninsula) > 1	84	29.30N	34.00 E
Sinaia	48	45.21N	25.33 E
Sinai Peninsula → Sīnā', Shibh Jazīrat > 1	84	29.30N	34.00 E
Sincelejo	118	9.18N	75.24W
Sinclair	150	41.46N	107.06W
Sinclair, Lake ⊜ 1	142	33.11N	83.16W
Sindelfingen	30	48.42N	9.00 E
Sine ∨	82	14.10N	16.28W
Singapore	68	1.17N	103.51 E
Singapore □ 1	68	1.22N	103.48 E
Singaraja	68	8.07S	115.06 E
Singatoka	91	18.08S	177.30 E
Singen [Hohentwiel]	30	47.46N	8.50 E
Singkang	68	4.08S	120.01 E
Singkawang	68	0.54N	109.00 E
Sining → Xining	66	36.38N	101.55 E
Siniscola	40	40.34N	9.41 E
Sinjah	84	13.09N	33.56 E
Sinkāt	84	18.50N	36.50 E
Sinnamahoning	136	41.19N	78.06W
Sinnamary	118	5.23N	52.57W
Sinni ≃	40	40.09N	16.42 E
Sînnicolau Mare	48	46.05N	20.38 E
Sinnūris	84	29.25N	30.52 E
Sinoie, Lacul ⊜	48	44.38N	28.53 E
Sint-Niklaas	30	51.10N	4.08 E
Sint-Truiden	30	50.48N	5.12 E
Sinú ≃	118	9.24N	75.49W
Sinŭiju	66	40.05N	124.24 E
Sió ≃	30	46.20N	18.55 E
Siófok	30	46.54N	18.04 E
Sion	36	46.14N	7.21 E
Sioule ≃	36	46.22N	3.19 E
Sioux City	132	42.30N	96.24W
Sioux Falls	132	43.33N	96.42W
Sioux Lookout	130	50.06N	91.55W
Šipčenski prohod)(	48	42.46N	25.19 E
Siping	66	43.12N	124.20 E
Sipsey ≃	144	33.00N	88.10W
Siracusa	40	37.04N	15.17 E
Sirājganj	70	24.27N	89.43 E
Sirdalsvatn ⊜	22	58.33N	6.41 E
Sir Edward Pellew Group II	96	15.40S	136.48 E
Siret ≃	48	45.24N	28.01 E
Sirhān, Wādī as- ∨	70	30.30N	38.00 E
Sirino, Monte ∧	40	40.08N	15.50 E
Sir James MacBrien, Mount ∧	130	62.07N	127.41W
Siros I	48	37.26N	24.54 E
Sirrī, Jazīreh-ye I	70	25.55N	54.32 E
Sirte, Gulf of → Surt, Khalīj c	84	31.30N	18.00 E
Sir Wilfrid Laurier's Birthplace National Historic Site ı	136	45.51N	73.45W
Sisaba ∧	86	6.09S	29.48 E
Sisak	40	45.29N	16.23 E
Sisaket	68	15.07N	104.20 E
Sishen	86	27.55S	22.59 E
Siskiyou Mountains ∧	150	41.55N	123.15W
Siskiyou Pass)(	150	42.03N	122.36W
Sissach	36	47.28N	7.49 E
Sīstān, Daryācheh-ye ⊜	70	31.00N	61.15 E
Sister Bay	138	45.11N	87.07W
Sisters	150	44.17N	121.32W
Sistersville	136	39.33N	80.59W
Sītāpur	70	27.34N	80.41 E
Sithoniá > 1	48	40.10N	23.47 E
Sitna ≃	48	47.37N	27.08 E
Sitnica ≃	48	42.45N	21.01 E
Sittang ≃	68	17.10N	96.58 E
Sittard	30	51.00N	5.53 E
Sittwe (Akyab)	68	20.09N	92.54 E
Sivas	16	39.45N	37.02 E
Šiveluč, vulkan ∧ 1	56	56.39N	161.18 E
Sjælland I	22	55.30N	11.45 E
Sjællands Odde > 1	22	55.58N	11.22 E
Sjeništa ∧	48	43.42N	18.37 E
Skagen	22	57.44N	10.36 E
Skagerrak u	22	57.45N	9.00 E
Skagit ≃	150	48.20N	122.25W
Skalbmierz	30	50.19N	20.25 E
Skalka ⊜	20	66.50N	18.46 E
Skamlingsbanke ∧ 2	22	55.25N	9.34 E
Skåne □ 9	22	55.59N	13.30 E
Skārdu	70	35.18N	75.37 E
Skarżysko-Kamienna	30	51.08N	20.53 E
Skaugum	22	59.51N	10.26 E
Skawina	30	49.59N	19.49 E
Skeena ≃	130	54.09N	130.02W
Skegness	26	53.10N	0.21 E
Skellefteå	22	64.46N	20.57 E
Skellefteälven ≃	20	64.42N	21.06 E
Skiddaw ∧	26	54.38N	3.08W
Skien	22	59.12N	9.36 E
Skierniewice	30	51.58N	20.08 E
Skiftet u	22	60.15N	21.05 E
Skikda	82	36.50N	6.58 E
Skiros I	48	38.53N	24.32 E
Skive	22	56.34N	9.02 E
Skoki	30	52.41N	17.10 E
Skokie	138	42.02N	87.44W
Skópelos I	48	39.10N	23.40 E
Skopje	48	41.59N	21.26 E
Skövde	22	58.24N	13.50 E
Skowhegan	136	44.45N	69.43W
Skunk ≃	138	40.42N	91.07W
Skurup	22	55.28N	13.30 E
Skye, Island of I	26	57.18N	6.15W
Skyland	142	35.29N	82.31W
Skyring, Seno u	120	52.35S	72.00W
Slagelse	22	55.24N	11.22 E
Slamet, Gunung ∧	68	7.14S	109.12 E
Slancy	20	59.06N	28.04 E
Slanské vrchy ∧	30	48.50N	21.30 E
Slaný	30	50.11N	14.04 E
Slater	144	39.13N	93.04W
Slatina	48	44.26N	24.22 E
Slav'ansk	54	48.52N	37.37 E
Slave ≃	130	61.18N	113.39W
Slavkov u Brna	30	49.09N	16.52 E
Slavonska Požega	40	45.20N	17.41 E
Slavonski Brod	48	45.10N	18.01 E
Sławno	30	54.22N	16.40 E
Sleat, Sound of u	26	57.06N	5.49W
Sledge	144	34.25N	90.13W
Sleeping Bear Dunes National Lakeshore ♦	138	44.50N	86.08W
Slidell	144	30.16N	89.46W
Slide Mountain ∧	136	42.00N	74.23W
Sliedrecht	30	51.49N	4.45 E
Sligo, Ire.	26	54.17N	8.28W
Sligo, Pa., U.S.	136	41.06N	79.29W
Sligo □ 6	26	54.10N	8.40W
Sligo Bay c	26	54.20N	8.40W
Slinger	138	43.20N	88.17W
Slippery Rock	136	41.03N	80.03W
Sliven	48	42.40N	26.19 E
Slobozia, Rom.	48	43.51N	25.54 E
Slobozia, Rom.	48	44.34N	27.23 E
Slocomb	144	31.06N	85.35W
Slovakia → Slovensko □ 9	30	48.50N	20.00 E
Slovenia → Slovenija □ 3	40	46.15N	15.10 E
Slovenija □ 3	40	46.15N	15.10 E
Slovenska Bistrica	40	46.23N	15.34 E
Slovenské rudohorie ∧	30	48.45N	20.00 E
Slovensko □ 9	30	48.50N	20.00 E
Słupia ≃	30	54.35N	16.50 E
Słupsk (Stolp)	30	54.28N	17.01 E
Smackover	144	33.21N	92.43W
Smallwood Reservoir ⊜ 1	130	54.05N	64.30W
Smara	82	26.44N	11.41W
Smederevo	48	44.40N	20.56 E
Smethport	136	41.48N	78.26W
Smethwick	26	52.30N	1.58W
Śmigiel	30	52.01N	16.32 E
Smith ≃	154	41.56N	124.12W
Smithers, B.C., Can.	130	54.47N	127.10W
Smithers, W.V., U.S.	136	38.10N	81.18W
Smithfield, N.C., U.S.	142	35.30N	78.20W
Smithfield, Ut., U.S.	148	41.50N	111.49W
Smith Island I	142	33.52N	77.59W
Smithland	144	37.08N	88.24W
Smith Mountain Lake ⊜ 1	142	37.10N	79.40W
Smiths Falls	136	44.54N	76.01W
Smiths Fork ≃	150	41.23N	110.12W
Smithton	96	40.51S	145.07 E
Smithville, Mo., U.S.	144	39.23N	94.34W
Smithville, Tn., U.S.	144	35.57N	85.48W
Smithville Lake ⊜ 1	144	39.25N	94.30W
Smokey Dome ∧	150	43.29N	114.56W
Smoky ≃	130	56.10N	117.21W
Smøla I	20	63.24N	8.00 E
Smolensk	20	54.47N	32.03 E
Smólikas ∧	48	40.06N	20.52 E
Smoljan	48	41.35N	24.41 E
Smygehuk >	22	55.21N	13.23 E
Smyrna → İzmir	48	38.25N	27.09 E
Smyrna, De., U.S.	136	39.17N	75.36W
Smyrna, Ga., U.S.	142	33.53N	84.30W
Smyrna, Tn., U.S.	144	35.58N	86.31W
Smythe, Mount ∧	130	57.54N	124.53W
Snaefell ∧	26	54.16N	4.27W
Snag	130	62.24N	140.22W
Snake ≃, Yk., Can.	130	65.58N	134.10W
Snake ≃, U.S.	150	46.12N	119.02W
Snasahögarna ∧	22	63.13N	12.21 E
Sneads	142	30.42N	84.55W
Sneek	30	53.02N	5.40 E
Snežnik ∧	40	45.35N	14.27 E
Śniardwy, Jezioro ⊜	30	53.46N	21.44 E
Snina	30	48.59N	22.07 E
Snøhetta ∧	22	62.20N	9.17 E
Snohomish	150	47.54N	122.05W
Snoqualmie Pass)(	150	47.25N	121.25W
Snøtinden ∧	20	66.38N	14.00 E
Snowdon ∧	26	53.04N	4.05W
Snow Hill, Md., U.S.	136	38.10N	75.23W
Snow Hill, N.C., U.S.	142	35.27N	77.40W
Snowmass Mountain ∧	148	39.07N	107.04W
Snow Mountain ∧	154	39.23N	122.45W
Snowy Mountain ∧	136	43.42N	74.23W
Snowy Mountains ∧	96	36.30S	148.20 E
Snowyside Peak ∧	150	43.57N	114.58W
Soalala	86	16.06S	45.20 E
Soap Lake	150	47.23N	119.29W
Sobat ≃	84	9.22N	31.33 E
Sobernheim	30	49.47N	7.38 E
Sobral	118	3.42S	40.21W
Sochaczew	30	52.14N	20.14 E
Sochi → Soči	54	43.35N	39.45 E
Soči	54	43.35N	39.45 E
Société, Îles de la (Society Islands) II	8	17.00S	150.00W
Society Hill	142	34.30N	79.51W
Socorro, N.M., U.S.	148	34.03N	106.53W
Socorro, Tx., U.S.	148	31.39N	106.18W
Socotra → Suquṭrā I	70	12.30N	54.00 E
Socuéllamos	44	39.17N	2.48W
Soda Lake ⊜	154	35.08N	116.04W
Sodankylä	20	67.29N	26.32 E
Soda Springs	150	42.39N	111.36W
Soddy-Daisy	144	35.16N	85.10W
Söderhamn	22	61.18N	17.03 E
Södertälje	22	59.12N	17.37 E
Sodo	84	6.52N	37.47 E
Södra Kvarken u	22	60.15N	19.05 E
Sodražica	40	45.46N	14.38 E
Sodus	136	43.14N	77.03W
Soe	68	9.52S	124.17 E
Soela väin u	22	58.40N	22.35 E
Soest, B.R.D.	30	51.34N	8.07 E
Soest, Ned.	30	52.09N	5.18 E
Sofia → Sofija	48	42.41N	23.19 E
Sofia ≃	86	15.27S	47.23 E
Sofija (Sofia)	48	42.41N	23.19 E
Sogamoso	118	5.43N	72.56W
Sognafjorden c 2	22	61.06N	5.10 E
Søgne	22	58.05N	7.49 E
Sogne Fjord → Sognafjorden c 2	22	61.06N	5.10 E
Sohano	94	5.27S	154.40 E
Soignies	30	50.35N	4.04 E
Soissons	36	49.22N	3.20 E
Sŏjosŏn-man c	66	39.20N	124.50 E
Šokal'skogo, proliv u	54	79.00N	100.25 E
Sokch'o	66	38.12N	128.36 E
Söke	48	37.45N	27.24 E
Sokodé	82	8.59N	1.08 E
Sokol	20	59.28N	40.10 E
Sokółka	30	53.25N	23.31 E
Sokolov	30	50.09N	12.40 E
Sokołów	30	50.14N	22.07 E
Sokołów Podlaski	30	52.25N	22.15 E
Sokoto	82	13.04N	5.16 E
Sokoto ≃	82	11.20N	4.10 E
Sol, Costa del ◆ 2	44	36.40N	4.00W
Sola	92	13.53S	167.33 E
Soła ≃	30	50.04N	19.13 E
Solana	142	26.56N	82.01W
Solec Kujawski	30	53.06N	18.14 E
Soledad, Col.	118	10.55N	74.46W
Soledad, Ca., U.S.	154	36.25N	121.19W
Soledad Pass)(	154	34.30N	118.07W
Solihull	26	52.25N	1.45W
Solikamsk	20	59.39N	56.47 E
Solingen	30	51.10N	7.05 E
Sollentuna	22	59.28N	17.54 E
Solna	22	59.22N	18.01 E
Sologne ◆ 1	36	47.50N	2.00 E
Solomon Islands □ 1	94	8.00S	159.00 E
Solomon Sea ᵀ 2	96	8.00S	155.00 E
Solon	136	44.56N	69.51W
Solon Springs	138	46.21N	91.49W
Solothurn	36	47.13N	7.32 E
Solsona	44	41.59N	1.31 E
Šolt	30	46.48N	19.00 E
Solta, Otok I	40	43.23N	16.15 E
Soltau	30	52.59N	9.49 E
Solvang	154	34.36N	120.08W
Solvay	136	43.03N	76.12W
Solway Firth c 1	26	54.50N	3.35W
Soma	48	39.10N	27.36 E
Somalia (Somaliya) □ 1	84	6.00N	48.00 E
Sombor	48	45.46N	19.07 E
Şomcuta-Mare	48	47.31N	23.29 E
Somerset, Ky., U.S.	142	37.05N	84.36W
Somerset, Ma., U.S.	136	41.46N	71.07W
Somerset, Pa., U.S.	136	40.00N	79.04W
Somerset □ 6	26	51.08N	3.00W
Somerset Island I	130	73.15N	93.30W
Somers Point	136	39.19N	74.35W
Somersworth	136	43.15N	70.51W
Somerton	148	32.35N	114.42W
Somerville	136	40.34N	74.36W
Someş (Szamos) ≃	48	48.07N	22.22 E
Someşu Cald ≃	48	46.44N	23.22 E
Someşul Mare ≃	48	47.12N	24.12 E
Someşul Mic ≃	48	47.09N	23.55 E
Somme ≃	36	50.11N	1.39 E
Sommen ⊜	22	58.01N	15.15 E
Sömmerda	30	51.10N	11.07 E
Somosomo Strait u	91	16.47S	179.58 E
Sompolno	30	52.24N	18.31 E
Somport, Puerto de)(	44	42.48N	0.31W
Sønderborg	22	54.55N	9.47 E
Sondershausen	30	51.22N	10.52 E
Søndre Strømfjord	130	66.59N	50.40W
Søndre Strømfjord c 2	130	66.30N	52.15W
Sondrio	40	46.10N	9.52 E
Songea	86	10.41S	35.39 E
Songhua ≃	66	47.44N	132.32 E
Songhua Hu ⊜ 1	66	43.20N	127.07 E
Songkhla	68	7.12N	100.36 E
Songnim	66	38.44N	125.38 E
Sonmiāni Bay c	70	25.15N	66.30 E
Sonneberg	30	50.22N	11.10 E
Sonoma	154	38.17N	122.27W
Sonora ≃	108	28.48N	111.33W
Sonsón	118	5.42N	75.18W
Sonsonate	108	13.43N	89.44W
Sontag	144	31.39N	90.12W
Son-tay	68	21.08N	105.30 E
Sonthofen	30	47.31N	10.17 E
Soo → Sault Sainte Marie	138	46.29N	84.20W
Sopchoppy	142	30.03N	84.29W
Soperton	142	32.22N	82.35W
Sopot	30	54.28N	18.34 E
Sopron	30	47.41N	16.36 E
Sora	40	41.43N	13.37 E
Söråker	22	62.31N	17.30 E
Sorel	130	46.02N	73.07W
Sorell, Cape >	96	42.12S	145.10 E
Sorgues	36	44.00N	4.52 E
Soria	44	41.46N	2.28W
Sorocaba	118	23.29S	47.27W
Soroki	48	48.09N	28.17 E
Sorol I 1	68	8.08N	140.23 E
Soroti	86	1.43N	33.37 E
Sørøya I	20	70.36N	22.46 E
Sorraia ≃	44	38.56N	8.53W
Sorrento, It.	40	40.37N	14.22 E
Sorrento, La., U.S.	144	30.11N	90.51W
Sorsatunturi ∧	20	67.24N	29.38 E
Sortavala	20	61.42N	30.41 E
Sos del Rey Católico	44	42.30N	1.13W
Sösjöfjällen ∧	22	63.53N	13.15 E
Sosnogorsk	20	63.37N	53.51 E
Sosnowiec	30	50.18N	19.08 E
Sotteville	36	49.25N	1.06 E
Souderton	136	40.18N	75.19W
Souk-Khemis-Du-Sahel	44	35.17N	6.05W
Sŏul (Seoul)	66	37.33N	126.58 E
Soummam, Oued ≃	44	36.45N	5.04 E
Souq Ahras	40	36.23N	8.00 E
Souris ≃	130	49.39N	99.34W
Sourland Mountain ∧ 2	136	40.29N	74.43W
Sousse	82	35.49N	10.38 E
South Africa (Suid-Afrika) □ 1	86	30.00S	26.00 E
South America ◆ 1	8	15.00S	60.00W
Southampton, Eng., U.K.	26	50.55N	1.25W
Southampton, N.Y., U.S.	136	40.53N	72.23W
Southampton Island I	130	64.20N	84.40W
South Andaman I	70	11.45N	92.45 E
South Australia □ 3	96	30.00S	135.00 E
Southaven	144	34.59N	90.02W
South Bay	142	26.39N	80.42W
South Beloit	138	42.29N	89.02W
South Bend, In., U.S.	144	41.41N	86.15W
South Bend, Wa., U.S.	150	46.40N	123.48W
South Boston	142	36.41N	78.54W
Southbridge	136	42.04N	72.02W
South Bruny Island I	96	43.23S	147.17 E
South Burlington	136	44.28N	73.10W
South Carolina □ 3	132	34.00N	81.00W
South Charleston	136	38.22N	81.41W
South China Sea ᵀ 2	68	10.00N	113.00 E
South Dakota □ 3	132	44.15N	100.00W
South Downs ∧ 1	26	50.55N	0.25W
South East Cape >	96	43.39S	146.50 E
South East Point >	96	39.00S	146.20 E
Southend-on-Sea	26	51.33N	0.43 E
Southern Alps ∧	98	43.30S	170.30 E
Southern Cross	96	31.13S	119.19 E
Southern Indian Lake ⊜	130	57.10N	98.40W
Southern Ocean ᵀ 1	8	50.00S	135.00 E
Southern Pines	142	35.10N	79.23W
Southern Yemen → Yemen, People's Democratic Republic of □ 1	70	15.00N	48.00 E
Southfield	138	42.28N	83.13W
South Foreland >	26	51.09N	1.23 E
South Fulton	144	36.30N	88.52W
Southgate	138	42.12N	83.11W
South Georgia I	120	54.15S	36.45W
South Glamorgan □ 6	26	51.30N	3.25W
South Hadley	136	42.15N	72.34W
South Haven	138	42.24N	86.16W
South Head >	98	36.26S	174.14 E
South Henderson	142	36.17N	78.25W
South Hero	136	44.38N	73.18W
South Hill	142	36.43N	78.07W
South Holston Lake ⊜ 1	142	36.35N	82.00W
Southington	136	41.35N	72.52W
South International Falls	138	48.35N	93.23W
South Island I	98	43.00S	171.00 E
South Kenosha	138	42.32N	87.50W
South Lake Tahoe	154	38.56N	119.58W
South Lyon	138	42.27N	83.39W
South Medford	150	42.18N	122.50W
South Miami	142	25.42N	80.17W
South Milwaukee	138	42.54N	87.51W
South Ogden	148	41.11N	111.58W
South Orkney Islands II	8	60.35S	45.30W
South Paris	136	44.13N	70.30W
South Pass)(	150	42.22N	108.55W
South Pekin	144	40.29N	89.39W
South Pittsburg	144	35.00N	85.42W
South Platte ≃	132	41.07N	100.42W
Southport, Austl.	96	27.58S	153.25 E
Southport, Eng., U.K.	26	53.39N	3.01W
Southport, In., U.S.	144	39.39N	86.07W
Southport, N.Y., U.S.	136	42.03N	76.49W
Southport, N.C., U.S.	142	33.55N	78.01W
South Portland	136	43.38N	70.14W
South River	136	45.50N	79.23W
South Ronaldsay I	26	58.46N	2.58W
South San Francisco	154	37.39N	122.24W
South Saskatchewan ≃	130	53.15N	105.05W
South Shields	26	55.00N	1.25W
South Tucson	148	32.11N	110.58W
South Uist I	26	57.15N	7.21W
South West Africa → Namibia □ 2	86	22.00S	17.00 E
South West Cape >, Austl.	96	43.34S	146.02 E
South West Cape >, N.Z.	98	47.17S	167.28 E
South Whitley	144	41.05N	85.37W
Sovetsk	20	55.05N	21.53 E
Soviet Union → Union of Soviet Socialist Republics □ 1	54	60.00N	80.00 E
Spa	30	50.30N	5.52 E
Spain (España) □ 1	44	40.00N	4.00W
Spalding	26	52.47N	0.10W
Spanish ≃	138	46.11N	82.19W
Spanish Fork	148	40.06N	111.39W
Spanish North Africa □ 2	44	35.53N	5.19W
Spanish Sahara → Western Sahara □ 2	82	24.30N	13.00W
Spanish Town	108	17.59N	76.57W
Sparks, Ga., U.S.	142	31.10N	83.26W
Sparks, Nv., U.S.	154	39.32N	119.45W
Sparrows Point	136	39.13N	76.28W
Sparta → Spárti, Ellás	48	37.05N	22.27 E
Sparta, Ga., U.S.	142	33.16N	82.58W
Sparta, Il., U.S.	144	38.07N	89.42W
Sparta, Ky., U.S.	144	38.40N	84.54W
Sparta, Mi., U.S.	138	43.09N	85.42W
Sparta, N.J., U.S.	136	41.02N	74.38W
Sparta, N.C., U.S.	142	36.30N	81.07W
Sparta, Tn., U.S.	144	35.55N	85.27W
Sparta, Wi., U.S.	138	43.56N	90.48W
Spartanburg	142	34.56N	81.55W
Spartel, Cap >	44	35.48N	5.56W
Spárti (Sparta)	48	37.05N	22.27 E
Spartivento, Capo >	40	38.53N	8.50 E
Spátha, Ákra >	48	35.42N	23.44 E
Spear, Cape >	130	47.32N	52.32W
Spearfish	132	44.29N	103.51W
Spednic Lake ⊜	136	45.36N	67.35W
Speedway	144	39.48N	86.16W
Spello	40	42.59N	12.40 E
Spencer, In., U.S.	144	39.17N	86.45W
Spencer, Ma., U.S.	136	42.14N	71.59W
Spencer, N.C., U.S.	142	35.41N	80.26W
Spencer, Tn., U.S.	142	35.44N	85.28W
Spencer, W.V., U.S.	136	38.48N	81.21W
Spencer, Cape >	96	35.18S	136.53 E
Spencer Gulf c	96	34.00S	137.00 E
Spey ≃	26	57.40N	3.06W
Speyer	30	49.19N	8.26 E
Spickard	144	40.14N	93.35W
Spiekeroog I	30	53.46N	7.42 E
Spillville	138	43.12N	91.57W
Spindale	142	35.21N	81.55W
Spiro	144	35.14N	94.37W
Spišská Nová Ves	30	48.57N	20.34 E
Spittal an der Drau	30	46.48N	13.30 E
Split	40	43.31N	16.27 E
Spokane	150	47.39N	117.25W
Spokane ≃	150	47.54N	118.20W
Spoleto	40	42.44N	12.44 E
Spoon ≃	144	40.18N	90.04W
Spooner	138	45.49N	91.53W
Spotsylvania	136	38.12N	77.35W
Sprague	150	47.18N	117.58W
Sprague ≃	150	42.34N	121.51W
Spratly Island I	68	8.38N	111.55 E
Spreča ≃	48	44.45N	18.06 E
Spremberg	30	51.34N	14.22 E
Spring ≃	144	36.52N	94.44W
Spring Bay c	148	41.40N	112.50W
Springdale, Nf., Can.	130	49.30N	56.04W
Springdale, Ar., U.S.	144	36.11N	94.07W
Springdale, S.C., U.S.	142	33.57N	81.06W
Springfield, Fl., U.S.	144	30.09N	85.36W
Springfield, Ga., U.S.	142	32.22N	81.18W
Springfield, Il., U.S.	144	39.48N	89.38W
Springfield, Ky., U.S.	144	37.41N	85.13W
Springfield, Ma., U.S.	136	42.06N	72.35W
Springfield, Mo., U.S.	144	37.12N	93.17W
Springfield, Oh., U.S.	136	39.55N	83.48W
Springfield, Or., U.S.	150	44.02N	123.01W
Springfield, S.D., U.S.	132	42.51N	97.53W
Springfield, Tn., U.S.	144	36.30N	86.53W
Springfield, Vt., U.S.	136	43.17N	72.28W
Springfield, Lake ⊜ 1	144	39.40N	89.36W
Springfontein	86	30.19S	25.36 E
Spring Green	138	43.10N	90.04W
Springhill, N.S., Can.	130	45.39N	64.03W
Springhill, La., U.S.	144	33.00N	93.28W
Spring Hill, Tn., U.S.	144	35.45N	86.55W
Spring Lake	142	35.10N	78.58W
Springs	86	26.13S	28.25 E
Springvale	136	43.28N	70.47W
Spring Valley, Ca., U.S.	154	32.44N	116.59W
Spring Valley, Il., U.S.	138	41.19N	89.11W
Spring Valley, Mn., U.S.	138	43.41N	92.23W
Spring Valley, N.Y., U.S.	136	41.06N	74.02W
Spring Valley, Wi., U.S.	138	44.50N	92.14W
Spring Valley ∨	154	39.15N	114.25W
Springville, Ca., U.S.	154	36.08N	118.49W
Springville, N.Y., U.S.	136	42.30N	78.40W
Springville, Ut., U.S.	148	40.09N	111.36W
Spruce Knob ∧	136	38.42N	79.32W
Spruce Knob-Seneca Rocks National Recreation Area ♦	136	38.50N	79.20W
Spruce Mountain ∧	148	34.28N	112.24W
Spruce Pine, Al., U.S.	144	34.23N	87.43W
Spruce Pine, N.C., U.S.	142	35.54N	82.03W
Spulico, Capo >	40	39.58N	16.39 E
Spurn Head >	26	53.34N	0.07 E
Squamish	130	49.42N	123.09W
Squillace, Golfo di c	40	38.50N	16.50 E
Squinzano	40	40.26N	18.03 E
Squire	142	37.14N	81.36W
Srbija (Serbia) □ 3	48	44.00N	21.00 E
Srbobran	48	45.33N	19.48 E
Srednij chrebet ∧	56	56.00N	158.00 E
Sredna Gora ∧	48	42.30N	25.00 E
Srednerusskaja vozvyšennost' ∧ 1	54	52.00N	38.00 E
Srednesibirskoje ploskogorje ∧ 1	54	65.00N	105.00 E
Śrem	30	52.08N	17.01 E
Sremska Mitrovica	48	44.58N	19.37 E
Sremski Karlovci	48	45.12N	19.57 E
Sri Gangānagar	70	29.55N	73.53 E
Sri Lanka □ 1	70	7.00N	81.00 E
Srīnagar	70	34.05N	74.49 E
Środa Wielkopolski	30	52.14N	17.17 E
Stachanov	54	48.34N	38.40 E
Stade	30	53.36N	9.28 E
Stadskanaal	30	53.00N	6.55 E
Stadtoldendorf	30	51.53N	9.37 E
Stafford	26	52.48N	2.07W
Staffordshire □ 6	26	52.50N	2.00W
Stafford Springs	136	41.57N	72.18W
Staffordsville	142	37.49N	82.50W
Staines	26	51.26N	0.31W
Stalin (Kuçovë)	48	40.48N	19.54 E
Stalingrad → Volgograd	54	48.44N	44.25 E
Stalowa Wola	30	50.35N	22.02 E
Stamford, Eng., U.K.	26	52.39N	0.29W
Stamford, Ct., U.S.	136	41.03N	73.32W
Stamford, N.Y., U.S.	136	42.24N	74.36W
Stamford, Tx., U.S.	132	32.56N	99.48W
Stamps	144	33.21N	93.29W
Stanberry	144	40.13N	94.32W
Standerton	86	26.58S	29.07 E
Standish	138	43.58N	83.57W
Stanfield	148	32.52N	111.57W
Stanford	142	37.31N	84.39W
Stanislaus ≃	154	37.40N	121.14W
Stanke Dimitrov	48	42.16N	23.07 E
Stanley, Falk. Is.	120	51.42S	57.51W
Stanley, N.C., U.S.	142	35.21N	81.05W
Stanley, Wi., U.S.	138	44.57N	90.56W
Stanley Falls ⌊	86	0.30N	25.12 E
Stanleyville → Kisangani	86	0.30N	25.12 E
Stann Creek	108	16.58N	88.13W
Stanovoj chrebet ∧	56	56.20N	126.00 E
Stanovoje nagorje (Stanovoy Mountains) ∧	56	56.00N	114.00 E
Stanovoy Mountains → Stanovoje nagorje ∧	56	56.00N	114.00 E
Stanton	142	37.50N	83.51W
Stanwood	150	48.14N	122.22W
Star	142	35.24N	79.47W
Stará Boleslav	30	50.12N	14.42 E
Starachowice	30	51.03N	21.04 E
Staraja Russa	20	58.00N	31.23 E
Stara Planina (Balkan Mountains) ∧	48	42.45N	25.00 E
Stara Zagora	48	42.25N	25.38 E
Star City, Ar., U.S.	144	33.56N	91.50W
Star City, In., U.S.	144	40.58N	86.33W
Stargard Szczeciński (Stargard in Pommern)	30	53.20N	15.02 E
Star Harbour c	94	10.47S	162.18 E
Stari Grad	40	43.11N	16.36 E
Stari Vlah ◆ 1	48	43.35N	20.15 E
Starke	142	29.56N	82.06W
Starkville	144	33.27N	88.49W
Starnberg	30	48.00N	11.20 E
Starnberger See ⊜	30	47.55N	11.18 E
Starogard Gdański	30	53.59N	18.33 E
Start Point >	26	50.13N	3.38W
Staryj Oskol	54	51.19N	37.51 E
Stassfurt	30	51.51N	11.34 E
State College	136	40.47N	77.51W
State Line, Ms., U.S.	144	31.26N	88.28W
Stateline, Nv., U.S.	154	38.58N	119.56W
Statenville	142	30.42N	83.02W
Statesboro	142	32.26N	81.47W
Statesville	142	35.46N	80.53W
Staunton, Il., U.S.	144	39.00N	89.47W
Staunton, Va., U.S.	136	38.08N	79.04W
Stavanger	22	58.58N	5.45 E
Stavropol'	54	45.02N	41.59 E
Stawiski	30	53.23N	22.09 E
Stawiszyn	30	51.55N	18.07 E
Stayton	150	44.48N	122.47W
Steamboat Springs	148	40.29N	106.49W
Stębark	30	53.30N	20.08 E
Steele	144	36.05N	89.49W
Steels Point >	93	29.02S	168.00 E
Steenbergen	30	51.35N	4.19 E
Steens Mountain ∧	150	42.35N	118.40W
Steep Point >	96	26.08S	113.08 E
Steinfurt	30	52.09N	7.21 E
Steinkjer	20	64.01N	11.30 E
Stellarton	130	45.34N	62.40W
Stellenbosch	86	33.58S	18.50 E
Stelvio, Passo dello)(	40	46.32N	10.27 E
Stendal	30	52.36N	11.51 E
Stephens, Cape >	98	40.42S	173.57 E
Stephenson	138	45.24N	87.36W
Stephenville	130	48.33N	58.35W
Steps Point >	93	14.22S	170.45W
Sterling, Co., U.S.	132	40.37N	103.12W
Sterling, Il., U.S.	138	41.47N	89.41W
Sterlitamak	54	53.37N	55.58 E
Šternberk	30	49.44N	17.18 E
Stęszew	30	52.18N	16.42 E
Stettin → Szczecin	30	53.24N	14.32 E
Steubenville	136	40.22N	80.38W
Stevenage	26	51.55N	0.14W
Stevenson	144	34.52N	85.50W
Stevens Pass)(	150	47.45N	121.04W
Stevens Point	138	44.31N	89.34W
Stewart ≃	130	63.18N	139.25W
Stewart Island I	98	47.00S	167.50 E
Stewartstown	136	39.45N	76.35W
Stewartville	138	43.51N	92.29W
Steyr	30	48.03N	14.25 E
Štiavnické vrchy ∧	30	48.40N	18.45 E
Stif	82	36.09N	5.26 E
Stikine ≃	130	56.40N	132.30W
Stillmore	142	32.26N	82.12W
Stillwater, Mn., U.S.	138	45.03N	92.48W
Stillwater, Ok., U.S.	132	36.06N	97.03W
Stillwell	144	35.49N	94.38W
Stilo, Punta >	40	38.28N	16.36 E
Stimson, Mount ∧	150	48.31N	113.36W
Stînişoarei, Munţii ∧	48	47.10N	26.00 E
Štip	48	41.44N	22.12 E
Stirling	26	56.07N	3.57W
Stockach	30	47.51N	9.00 E
Stockerau	30	48.23N	16.13 E
Stockholm	22	59.20N	18.03 E
Stockport	26	53.25N	2.10W
Stockton, Al., U.S.	144	30.59N	87.51W
Stockton, Ca., U.S.	154	37.57N	121.17W
Stockton, Mo., U.S.	144	37.41N	93.47W
Stockton Reservoir ⊜ 1	144	37.40N	93.45W
Stœng Trêng	68	13.31N	105.58 E
Stoke-on-Trent	26	53.00N	2.10W
Stolberg	30	50.46N	6.13 E
Stonefort	144	37.37N	88.42W
Stone Harbor	136	39.03N	74.45W
Stone Mountain	142	33.48N	84.10W
Stone Mountain Memorial State Park ♦	142	33.49N	84.06W
Stonewall	144	32.16N	93.49W
Stony Rapids	130	59.16N	105.50W
Stopnica	30	50.27N	20.57 E
Storå ≃	22	56.19N	8.19 E
Stora Alvaret ◆	22	56.30N	16.30 E
Stora Lulevatten ⊜	20	67.10N	19.16 E
Storavan ⊜	20	65.40N	18.15 E
Storebælt u	22	55.30N	11.00 E
Storfjorden c 2	22	62.25N	6.30 E
Storm Bay c	96	43.10S	147.32 E
Stornoway	26	58.12N	6.23W
Storrs	136	41.48N	72.15W
Storsjön ⊜	22	63.12N	14.18 E
Storsteinsfjellet ∧	20	68.14N	17.52 E
Storstrømmen u	22	54.58N	11.55 E
Storuman	20	65.06N	17.06 E
Storvätteshågna ∧	22	62.07N	12.27 E
Storvindeln ⊜	20	65.43N	17.05 E
Story City	138	42.11N	93.35W
Stoughton, Ma., U.S.	136	42.07N	71.06W
Stoughton, Wi., U.S.	138	42.55N	89.13W
Stour ≃	26	50.43N	1.46W
Stover	144	38.26N	92.59W
Stow	136	41.10N	81.27W
Stowe	136	44.27N	72.41W
Strabane	26	54.49N	7.27W
Stradella	40	45.05N	9.18 E
Strakonice	30	49.16N	13.55 E
Stralsund	30	54.19N	13.05 E
Strangford Lough ⊜	26	54.28N	5.35W
Stranraer	26	54.55N	5.02W
Strasbourg	36	48.35N	7.45 E
Strasburg	136	40.35N	81.31W
Stratford, N.Z.	98	39.20S	174.17 E
Stratford, Ct., U.S.	136	41.11N	73.08W
Stratford, Wi., U.S.	138	44.48N	90.04W
Stratford-upon-Avon	26	52.12N	1.41W
Strathy Point >	26	58.35N	4.02W
Stratton Mountain ∧	136	43.05N	72.56W
Straubing	30	48.53N	12.34 E
Strausberg	30	52.35N	13.53 E
Strawberry ≃	148	40.10N	110.24W
Strawberry Mountain ∧	150	44.19N	118.43W
Strážske	30	48.53N	21.50 E
Streator	144	41.07N	88.50W
Streetsboro	136	41.14N	81.20W
Strehaia	48	44.37N	23.12 E
Stresa	40	45.53N	8.32 E
Strimón (Struma) ≃	48	40.47N	23.51 E
Strjama ≃	48	42.10N	24.56 E
Stromboli, Isola I	40	38.47N	15.13 E
Stromness	26	58.57N	3.18W
Strong	144	33.06N	92.20W
Stronghurst	144	40.44N	90.54W
Strongoli	40	39.15N	17.03 E
Stronsay I	26	59.07N	2.37W
Stroud	26	51.45N	2.12W
Stroudsburg	136	40.59N	75.11W
Strum	138	44.32N	91.23W
Struma (Strimón) ≃	48	40.47N	23.51 E
Strumble Head >	26	52.02N	5.04W
Strumica	48	41.26N	22.38 E
Struthers	136	41.03N	80.36W
Stryker	136	41.30N	84.24W
Strzegom	30	50.57N	16.21 E
Strzelce Opolskie	30	50.31N	18.19 E
Strzelecki Creek ≃	96	29.37S	139.59 E
Strzelin	30	50.47N	17.03 E
Stuart	142	27.11N	80.15W
Stuarts Draft	136	38.01N	79.02W
Studen Kladenec, jazovir ⊜ 1	48	41.37N	25.30 E
Stupino	20	54.53N	38.05 E

Symbols in the index entries are identified on page 162.

Symbols in the index entries are identified on page 162.

Symbols in the index entries are identified on page 162.

Name	Page	Lat.	Long.
Usumbura → Bujumbura	86	3.23 S	29.22 E
Utah □³	132	39.30 N	111.30 W
Utah Lake	148	40.13 N	111.49 W
Utembo ≃	86	17.06 S	22.01 E
Utersum	30	54.43 N	8.24 E
Utete	86	7.59 S	38.47 E
Utica, Mi., U.S.	138	42.37 N	83.02 W
Utica, N.Y., U.S.	136	43.06 N	75.13 W
Utica, Oh., U.S.	138	40.14 N	82.27 W
Utrecht	30	52.05 N	5.08 E
Utrera	44	37.11 N	5.47 W
Utsunomiya	66	36.33 N	139.52 E
Uttaradit	68	17.38 N	100.06 E
Uusimaa ◆¹	22	60.30 N	25.00 E
Uvá ≃	118	3.57 N	68.24 W
Uvalda	142	33.41 N	83.25 W
Uvalde	132	29.12 N	99.47 W
Uvinza	86	5.06 S	30.22 E
Uvs nuur ⊜	54	50.20 N	92.45 E
Uwajima	66	33.13 N	132.34 E
'Uwaynāt, Jabal al- ʌ	84	21.54 N	24.58 E
Uyuni	118	20.28 S	66.50 W
Uyuni, Salar de ≃	118	20.20 S	67.42 W
Už (Uh) ≃	30	48.34 N	22.00 E
Uzbekskaja Sovetskaja Socialističeskaja Respublika □³	54	41.00 N	64.00 E
Užgorod	48	48.37 N	22.18 E
Uzunköprü	48	41.16 N	26.41 E
Uzunkuyu	48	38.17 N	26.33 E
V			
Vaal ≃	86	29.04 S	23.38 E
Vaasa (Vasa)	22	63.06 N	21.36 E
Vác	30	47.47 N	19.08 E
Vacaville	154	38.21 N	121.59 W
Vaccarès, Étang de ⊂	36	43.32 N	4.34 E
Väddö I	22	60.00 N	18.50 E
Vädeni	48	45.22 N	27.56 E
Vadsø	20	70.05 N	29.46 E
Vaduz	30	47.09 N	9.31 E
Værøy I	20	67.40 N	12.39 E
Vaga ≃	54	62.48 N	42.56 E
Váh ≃	30	47.55 N	18.00 E
Vaigat U	130	70.11 N	53.00 W
Vail	148	39.38 N	106.22 W
Vaimali	92	16.34 S	168.11 E
Vajgač, ostrov I	54	70.00 N	59.30 E
Vākhān ▪¹	70	37.00 N	73.00 E
Valašské Meziříčí	30	49.28 N	17.58 E
Valatie	136	42.24 N	73.40 W
Valdagno	40	45.39 N	11.18 E
Valdai Hills → Valdajskaja vozvyšennosť ʌ²	20	57.00 N	33.30 E
Valdajskaja vozvyšennosť ʌ²	54	57.00 N	33.30 E
Valdavia ≃	44	42.24 N	4.16 W
Valdecañas, Embalse de ⊜¹	44	39.45 N	5.30 W
Valdepeñas	44	38.46 N	3.23 W
Valderaduey ≃	44	41.31 N	5.42 W
Valderas	44	42.05 N	5.27 W
Valders	138	44.03 N	87.53 W
Valdés, Península ʌ¹	120	42.30 S	64.00 W
Valdese	142	35.44 N	81.33 W
Valdivia	120	39.48 S	73.14 W
Valdobbiadene	40	45.54 N	12.00 E
Val-d'Or	130	48.07 N	77.47 W
Valdosta	142	30.49 N	83.16 W
Valdoviño	44	43.36 N	8.08 W
Valence	36	44.56 N	4.54 E
Valencia, Esp.	44	39.28 N	0.22 W
Valencia, Ven.	118	10.11 N	68.00 W
València, Golf de ⊂	44	39.50 N	0.30 E
Valencia de Alcántara	44	39.25 N	7.14 W
Valencia de Don Juan	44	42.18 N	5.31 W
Valencia Island I	26	51.52 N	10.20 W
Valenciennes	36	50.21 N	3.32 E
Valentine	132	42.52 N	100.33 W
Valenza	40	45.01 N	8.38 E
Valera	118	9.19 N	70.37 W
Valjevo	48	44.16 N	19.53 E
Valkeakoski	22	61.16 N	24.02 E
Valkenswaard	30	51.21 N	5.28 E
Valladolid	44	41.39 N	4.43 W
Vallecitos	148	36.05 N	106.20 W
Valle de la Pascua	118	9.13 N	66.00 W
Valledolmo	40	37.45 N	13.49 E
Valledupar	118	10.29 N	73.15 W
Vallejo	154	38.06 N	122.15 W
Vallenar	120	28.35 S	70.46 W
Vallentuna	22	59.32 N	18.05 E
Valles Caldera ≃⁶	148	35.52 N	106.33 W
Valletta	40	35.54 N	14.31 E
Valley City	132	46.55 N	97.59 W
Valley Forge National Historical Park ◆	136	40.06 N	75.27 W
Valley of Fire State Park ◆	154	36.26 N	114.30 W
Valley Station	144	38.06 N	85.52 W
Vallgrund I	22	63.12 N	21.14 E
Valls	44	41.17 N	1.15 E
Valmaseda	44	43.12 N	3.12 W
Valparaíso, Chile	120	33.02 S	71.38 W
Valparaiso, Fl., U.S.	142	30.29 N	86.29 W
Valparaiso, In., U.S.	144	41.28 N	87.03 W
Valpovo	48	45.39 N	18.26 E
Vals, Tanjung ⊁	68	8.26 S	137.38 E
Valsbaai ⊂	86	34.12 S	18.40 E
Valverde del Camino	44	37.34 N	6.45 W
Van	16	38.28 N	43.20 E
Van Buren, Ar., U.S.	144	35.26 N	94.20 W
Van Buren, Mo., U.S.	144	36.59 N	91.00 W
Vancouver, B.C., Can.	130	49.16 N	123.07 W
Vancouver, Wa., U.S.	150	45.38 N	122.39 W
Vancouver, Cape ⊁	96	35.01 S	118.12 E
Vancouver Island I	130	49.45 N	126.00 W
Vandalia, Il., U.S.	144	38.57 N	89.05 W
Vandalia, Mo., U.S.	144	39.18 N	91.29 W
Vandalia, Oh., U.S.	136	39.53 N	84.11 W
Vanderbijlpark	86	26.42 S	27.54 E
Vanderbilt	138	45.08 N	84.39 W
Vandergrift	136	40.36 N	79.33 W
Van Diemen Gulf ⊂	96	11.50 S	132.00 E
Vänern ⊜	22	58.55 N	13.30 E
Vänersborg	22	58.22 N	12.19 E
Van Gölü ⊜	16	38.33 N	42.46 E
Vangunu Island I	94	8.38 S	158.00 E
Vanna I	22	70.09 N	19.51 E
Vännäs	22	63.55 N	19.45 E
Vannes	36	47.39 N	2.46 W
Vanoise, Massif de la ʌ	36	45.23 N	6.40 E
Vanrhynsdorp	86	31.36 S	18.42 E
Vantaa ≃	22	60.13 N	24.59 E
Vanua Lava I	91	13.48 S	167.28 E
Vanua Levu I	91	16.33 S	179.15 E
Vanua Mbalavu Island I	91	17.40 S	178.57 W
Vanuatu ▫¹	92	16.00 S	167.00 E
Van Wert	136	40.52 N	84.35 W
Vārānasi (Benares)	70	25.20 N	83.00 E
Varangerfjorden c²	20	70.00 N	30.00 E
Varangerhalvøya ʌ¹	20	70.25 N	29.30 E
Varaždin	40	46.19 N	16.20 E
Varazze	40	44.22 N	8.34 E
Varberg	22	57.06 N	12.15 E
Vardar (Axiós) ≃	48	40.35 N	22.52 E
Vardø	20	70.21 N	31.02 E
Varel	30	53.22 N	8.10 E
Vareš	48	44.09 N	18.19 E
Varese	40	45.48 N	8.48 E
Varese Ligure	40	44.22 N	9.37 E
Varginha	118	21.33 S	45.26 W
Varkaus	22	62.19 N	27.55 E
Värmeln ⊜	22	59.32 N	12.54 E
Varna	48	43.13 N	27.55 E
Värnamo	22	57.11 N	14.02 E
Varnenski zaliv c	48	43.11 N	27.55 E
Varnsdorf	30	50.52 N	14.40 E
Varnville	142	32.51 N	81.04 W
Várpalota	30	47.12 N	18.09 E
Vârșui ≃	48	43.12 N	23.17 E
Varsinais-Suomi ◆¹	22	60.40 N	22.30 E
Vascău	48	46.28 N	22.28 E
Vashon Island I	150	47.24 N	122.27 W
Vaslui	48	46.38 N	27.44 E
Vass	142	35.15 N	79.16 W
Vassar	138	43.22 N	83.35 W
Västerås	22	59.37 N	16.33 E
Västerdalälven ≃	22	60.33 N	15.08 E
Västervik	22	57.45 N	16.38 E
Vasto	40	42.07 N	14.42 E
Vas'uganje ⊞	54	58.00 N	77.00 E
Vasvár	30	47.03 N	16.49 E
Vathi	48	37.45 N	26.59 E
Vatican City (Città del Vaticano) □¹	40	41.54 N	12.27 E
Vaticano, Capo ⊁	40	38.38 N	15.50 E
Vat'ka ≃	54	55.36 N	51.30 E
Vatnajökull ⊠	20a	64.25 N	16.50 W
Vatoa Island I	91	19.50 S	178.13 W
Vatra Dornei	48	47.21 N	25.21 E
Vättern ⊜	22	58.24 N	14.36 E
Vatu Ira Channel ⋃	91	17.17 S	178.31 E
Vatukoula	91	17.31 S	177.51 E
Vaughn	148	34.36 N	105.12 W
Vaupés (Uaupés) ≃	118	0.02 N	67.16 W
Väjxö	22	56.52 N	14.49 E
Vaz'ma	20	55.13 N	34.18 E
Veazie	136	44.50 N	68.42 W
Vechta	30	52.43 N	8.16 E
Vecsés	30	47.25 N	19.16 E
Veddige	22	57.16 N	12.19 E
Vedea ≃	48	43.43 N	25.32 E
Veenendaal	30	52.02 N	5.34 E
Veendam	30	53.06 N	6.58 E
Vefsna ≃	20	65.50 N	13.12 E
Vega I	20	65.39 N	11.50 E
Vegreville	130	53.30 N	112.03 W
Vejer de la Frontera	44	36.15 N	5.58 W
Vejle	22	55.42 N	9.32 E
Vela Luka	40	42.58 N	16.43 E
Velbert	30	51.20 N	7.02 E
Velebitski Kanal ⋃	40	45.00 N	14.50 E
Velencei-tó ⊜	30	47.12 N	18.35 E
Velez de la Gomera, Peñón de I	44	35.11 N	4.21 W
Vélez-Málaga	44	36.47 N	4.06 W
Vélez Rubio	44	37.39 N	2.04 W
Velikaja ≃	54	57.48 N	28.20 E
Velika Morava ≃	48	44.43 N	21.03 E
Velikije Luki	20	56.20 N	30.32 E
Veliki Ust'ug	20	60.48 N	46.18 E
Veliki kanal ≃	48	45.45 N	18.50 E
Veliki Vitorog ʌ	48	44.07 N	17.03 E
Veliko Tŭrnovo	48	43.04 N	25.39 E
Veli Lošinj	40	44.31 N	14.30 E
Velingrad	48	42.04 N	24.00 E
Velino, Monte ʌ	40	42.09 N	13.23 E
Vella Lavella I	94	7.45 S	156.40 E
Velletri	40	41.41 N	12.47 E
Venado Tuerto	120	33.45 S	61.58 W
Venda □¹	86	23.00 S	30.30 E
Vendéen, Bocage ◆¹	36	46.40 N	1.30 W
Vendôme	36	47.48 N	1.04 E
Venezia (Venice)	40	45.27 N	12.21 E
Venezuela □¹	118	8.00 N	66.00 W
Venezuela, Golfo de c	118	11.30 N	71.00 W
Venice → Venezia, It.	40	45.27 N	12.21 E
Venice, Fl., U.S.	142	27.05 N	82.27 W
Venice, La., U.S.	144	29.16 N	89.21 W
Venice, Gulf of c	40	45.15 N	13.00 E
Vénissieux	36	45.41 N	4.53 E
Venlo	30	51.24 N	6.10 E
Venosa	40	40.57 N	15.49 E
Ventimiglia	40	43.47 N	7.36 E
Ventspils	20	57.24 N	21.36 E
Ventura	154	34.16 N	119.17 W
Venus	142	27.04 N	81.21 W
Veracruz	108	19.12 N	96.08 W
Verāval	70	20.54 N	70.22 E
Verbania	40	45.56 N	8.33 E
Vercelli	40	45.19 N	8.25 E
Verchojansk	56	67.00 N	129.00 E
Verchojanskij chrebet ʌ	56	67.00 N	129.00 E
Verde ≃	148	33.33 N	111.40 W
Verden	30	52.55 N	9.13 E
Verdigris ≃	144	35.48 N	95.19 W
Verdon ≃	36	43.43 N	5.46 E
Verdun-sur-Meuse	36	49.10 N	5.23 E
Vereeniging	86	26.38 S	27.57 E
Vergennes	136	44.10 N	73.15 W
Vermilion ≃, Il., U.S.	136	41.25 N	82.21 W
Vermilion Bay c	144	29.40 N	92.00 W
Vermilion Lake ⊜	138	47.53 N	92.25 W
Vermillion	132	42.46 N	96.55 W
Vermont □³	136	43.50 N	72.45 W
Vernal	148	40.27 N	109.31 W
Verneukpan ⊜	86	30.00 S	21.10 E
Vernon, B.C., Can.	130	49.05 N	1.29 E
Vernon, Fr.	36	49.05 N	1.29 E
Vernon, Al., U.S.	144	33.45 N	88.06 W
Vernon, Ct., U.S.	136	41.49 N	72.28 W
Vernon, Fl., U.S.	144	30.37 N	85.42 W
Vernon, Tx., U.S.	144	34.09 N	99.16 W
Vero Beach	142	27.38 N	80.23 W
Véroia	48	40.31 N	22.12 E
Verona, It.	40	45.27 N	11.00 E
Verona, Wi., U.S.	138	42.59 N	89.31 W
Versailles, Fr.	36	48.48 N	2.08 E
Versailles, In., U.S.	144	39.04 N	85.15 W
Versailles, Ky., U.S.	144	38.03 N	84.43 W
Versailles, Mo., U.S.	144	38.26 N	92.50 W
Versailles, Oh., U.S.	136	40.13 N	84.29 W
Vert, Cap ⊁	82	14.43 N	17.32 W
Vertou	36	47.10 N	1.29 W
Verviers	30	50.35 N	5.52 E
Vesoul	36	47.38 N	6.10 E
Vestavia Hills	144	33.26 N	86.46 W
Vesterålen II	20	68.45 N	15.00 E
Vestfjorden c²	20	68.08 N	15.00 E
Vestmannaeyjar	20a	63.26 N	20.12 W
Vestvågøya I	20	68.15 N	13.50 E
Vesuvius → Vesuvio ʌ¹	40	40.49 N	14.26 E
Vesuvio ʌ¹	40	40.49 N	14.26 E
Veszprém	30	47.06 N	17.55 E
Vésztő	30	46.55 N	21.16 E
Vetlanda	22	57.26 N	15.04 E
Vetren	48	42.16 N	24.03 E
Vettore, Monte ʌ	40	42.49 N	13.16 E
Veurne	30	51.04 N	2.40 E
Vevay	144	38.44 N	85.04 W
Vevey	36	46.28 N	6.51 E
Vézère ≃	36	44.53 N	0.53 E
Viacha	118	16.39 S	68.18 W
Viadana	40	44.56 N	10.31 E
Viana del Bollo	44	42.11 N	7.06 W
Viana do Castelo	44	41.42 N	8.50 W
Viangchan (Vientiane)	68	17.58 N	102.36 E
Viareggio	40	43.52 N	10.14 E
Viaur ≃	36	44.08 N	2.23 E
Viborg	22	56.26 N	9.24 E
Vibo Valentia	40	38.40 N	16.06 E
Vic (Vich)	44	41.56 N	2.15 E
Vicco	142	37.12 N	83.03 W
Vicenza	40	45.33 N	11.33 E
Vichada ≃	118	4.55 N	67.50 W
Vichadero	120	31.48 S	54.43 W
Vichy	36	46.08 N	3.26 E
Vicksburg	144	32.21 N	90.52 W
Vicksburg National Military Park ◆	144	32.24 N	90.52 W
Victoria, Cam.	82	4.01 N	9.12 E
Victoria, B.C., Can.	130	48.25 N	123.22 W
Victoria (Xianggang), H.K.	66	22.17 N	114.09 E
Victoria, Malay.	68	5.17 N	115.15 E
Victoria, Sey.	86	4.38 S	55.27 E
Victoria, Tx., U.S.	132	28.48 N	97.00 W
Victoria □³	96	38.00 S	145.00 E
Victoria, Lake ⊜	86	1.00 S	33.00 E
Victoria, Mount ʌ	68	21.14 N	93.55 E
Victoria de las Tunas	108	20.58 N	76.57 W
Victoria Falls ⌐	86	17.55 S	25.51 E
Victoria Island I	130	71.00 N	110.00 W
Victoria Nile ≃	84	2.14 N	31.26 E
Victoria Peak ʌ	108	16.48 N	88.37 W
Victoriaville	130	46.03 N	71.57 W
Victoria West	86	31.25 S	23.04 E
Victorville	154	34.32 N	117.17 W
Vičuga	20	57.13 N	41.56 E
Vidalia, Ga., U.S.	142	32.13 N	82.24 W
Vidalia, La., U.S.	144	31.33 N	91.25 W
Vidin	48	43.59 N	22.52 E
Vidor	144	30.07 N	94.00 W
Viedma, Lago ⊜	120	49.35 S	72.35 W
Viella	44	42.42 N	0.48 E
Vienna → Wien, Öst.	30	48.13 N	16.20 E
Vienna, Ga., U.S.	142	32.05 N	83.47 W
Vienna, Il., U.S.	144	37.25 N	88.54 W
Vienna, Md., U.S.	136	38.29 N	75.49 W
Vienna, W.V., U.S.	144	39.19 N	81.32 W
Vienne	36	45.31 N	4.52 E
Vienne ≃	36	47.13 N	0.05 E
Vieques, Isla de I	108	18.08 N	65.25 W
Viersen	30	51.15 N	6.23 E
Vierwaldstätter See ⊜	36	47.00 N	8.28 E
Vierzon	36	47.13 N	2.05 E
Vieste	40	41.53 N	16.10 E
Vietnam □¹	68	16.00 N	108.00 E
Vigan	68	17.34 N	120.23 E
Vigevano	40	45.19 N	8.51 E
Vignola	40	44.29 N	11.00 E
Vigo	44	42.14 N	8.43 W
Vigo, Ría de c¹	44	42.15 N	8.45 W
Vihren ʌ	48	41.46 N	23.24 E
Vijayawāda	70	16.31 N	80.37 E
Vila de Manica	86	18.56 S	32.53 E
Vila do Conde	44	41.21 N	8.45 W
Vila Fontes	86	17.50 S	35.21 E
Vila Franca de Xira	44	38.57 N	8.59 W
Vilaine ≃	36	47.30 N	2.27 W
Vila Nova de Gaia	44	41.08 N	8.37 W
Vila-real	44	39.56 N	0.06 W
Vila Real, Port.	44	41.18 N	7.45 W
Vila Velha	118	20.20 S	40.17 W
Vil'kickogo, proliv ⋃	56	77.55 N	103.00 E
Villa Bella	118	10.23 S	65.24 W
Villablino	44	42.56 N	6.19 W
Villacañas	44	39.38 N	3.20 W
Villacarrillo	44	38.07 N	3.05 W
Villach	30	46.36 N	13.50 E
Villacidro	40	39.27 N	8.44 E
Villafranca de los Barros	44	38.34 N	6.20 W
Villafranca di Verona	40	45.21 N	10.50 E
Villa Grove	144	39.51 N	88.09 W
Villa Hayes	120	25.06 S	57.34 W
Villahermosa	108	17.59 N	92.55 W
Villalba	44	43.18 N	7.41 W
Villa Maria	120	32.25 S	63.15 W
Villa Montes	118	21.15 S	63.30 W
Villanova Monteleone	40	40.30 N	8.28 E
Villanueva	120	32.54 S	68.47 W
Villanueva de Córdoba	44	38.20 N	4.37 W
Villanueva de la Serana	44	38.58 N	5.48 W
Villanueva de la Sierra	44	40.12 N	6.24 W
Villanueva del Río y Minas	44	37.39 N	5.42 W
Villardefrades	44	41.43 N	5.15 W
Villar del Arzobispo	44	39.44 N	0.49 W
Villa Rica	142	33.43 N	84.55 W
Villarrica, Chile	120	39.16 S	72.13 W
Villarrica, Para.	120	25.45 S	56.26 W
Villarrobledo	44	39.16 N	2.36 W
Villas	136	39.01 N	74.56 W
Villasor	40	39.23 N	8.56 E
Villavicencio	118	4.09 N	73.37 W
Villazón	118	22.06 S	65.36 W
Villefranche	36	44.21 N	4.43 E
Villefranche-de-Rouergue	36	44.21 N	2.02 E
Villena	44	38.38 N	0.51 W
Villeneuve-Saint-Georges	36	48.44 N	2.27 E
Villeneuve-sur-Lot	36	44.25 N	0.42 E
Ville Platte	144	30.41 N	92.16 W
Villerupt	36	49.28 N	5.56 E
Villeurbanne	36	45.46 N	4.53 E
Villingen-Schwenningen	30	48.04 N	8.28 E
Vilna → Vilnius	20	54.41 N	25.19 E
Vilnius	20	54.41 N	25.19 E
Vilsbiburg	30	48.27 N	12.12 E
Vil'uj ≃	56	64.24 N	126.26 E
Vil'ujsk	56	63.46 N	121.37 E
Vil'ujskoje vodochranilišče ⊜¹	56	62.30 N	111.00 E
Vilvoorde	30	50.56 N	4.26 E
Viña ≃	82	7.45 N	15.36 E
Viña del Mar	120	33.02 S	71.34 W
Vinalhaven	136	44.02 N	68.49 W
Vinalhaven Island I	136	44.05 N	68.52 W
Vinarós	44	40.28 N	0.29 E
Vincennes	144	38.40 N	87.31 W
Vincent	144	33.22 N	86.22 W
Vincent, Point ⊁	93	29.00 S	167.55 E
Vindelälven ≃	20	63.54 N	19.52 E
Vindhya Range ʌ	70	23.00 N	77.00 E
Vine Grove	144	37.48 N	85.58 W
Vineland	136	39.29 N	75.01 W
Vineyard Haven	136	41.27 N	70.36 W
Vineyard Sound ⋃	136	41.25 N	70.46 W
Vinh	68	18.40 N	105.40 E
Vinh-long	68	10.15 N	105.58 E
Vinica	48	45.28 N	15.15 E
Vinita	144	36.38 N	95.09 W
Vinkovci	48	45.17 N	18.49 E
Vinnitsa → Vinnica	54	49.14 N	28.29 E
Vinnica	54	49.14 N	28.29 E
Vinson Massif ʌ	8	78.35 S	85.25 W
Vinton, Ia., U.S.	138	42.10 N	92.01 W
Vinton, La., U.S.	144	30.11 N	93.34 W
Vinton, Va., U.S.	142	37.16 N	79.53 W
Virden	144	39.30 N	89.46 W
Vire	36	48.50 N	0.53 W
Vire ≃	36	49.20 N	1.07 W
Virgin ≃	148	36.31 N	114.20 W
Virginia, S. Afr.	86	28.12 S	26.49 E
Virginia, Il., U.S.	144	39.57 N	90.12 W
Virginia, Mn., U.S.	138	47.31 N	92.32 W
Virginia □³	132	37.30 N	78.45 W
Virginia Beach	142	36.51 N	75.58 W
Virginia City, Mt., U.S.	148	45.17 N	111.56 W
Virginia City, Nv., U.S.	154	39.18 N	119.38 W
Virginia Falls ⌐	130	61.38 N	125.42 W
Virgin Islands □²	108	18.20 N	64.50 W
Virihaure ⊜	20	67.20 N	16.35 E
Virojoki	22	60.35 N	27.42 E
Viroqua	138	43.33 N	90.53 W
Virovitica	48	45.50 N	17.23 E
Virtopu	48	44.03 N	23.43 E
Vis, Otok I	40	43.02 N	16.11 E
Visalia	154	36.19 N	119.17 W
Visayan Sea ⊜	68	11.35 N	123.51 E
Visby	22	57.38 N	18.18 E
Viseu	44	40.39 N	7.55 W
Vişeu ≃	48	47.55 N	24.09 E
Vishākhapatnam	70	17.42 N	83.18 E
Viskafors	22	57.38 N	12.50 E
Vislinskij zaliv c	30	54.27 N	19.40 E
Viso, Monte ʌ	40	44.40 N	7.07 E
Visoko	48	43.59 N	18.11 E
Vista	154	33.12 N	117.14 W
Vistula → Wisła ≃	30	54.22 N	18.55 E
Vitarte	118	12.02 S	76.56 W
Viterbo	40	42.25 N	12.06 E
Vitigudino	44	41.01 N	6.26 W
Viti Levu I	91	18.00 S	178.00 E
Vitim ≃	56	59.26 N	112.34 E
Vitória, Bra.	118	20.19 S	40.21 W
Vitoria (Gasteiz), Esp.	44	42.51 N	2.40 W
Vitória da Conquista	118	14.51 S	40.51 W
Vitré	36	48.08 N	1.12 W
Vitry-le-François	36	48.44 N	4.35 E
Vittoria	40	36.57 N	14.32 E
Vittorio Veneto	40	45.59 N	12.18 E
Vivero	44	43.40 N	7.35 W
Vizianagaram	70	18.07 N	83.25 E
Vizzini	40	37.10 N	14.53 E
Vlaardingen	30	51.54 N	4.21 E
Vládeasa, Vírful ʌ	48	46.45 N	22.48 E
Vladičin Han	48	42.42 N	22.04 E
Vladimir	20	56.10 N	40.25 E
Vladivostok	20	43.10 N	131.56 E
Vlieland I	30	53.15 N	5.00 E
Vlissingen (Flushing)	30	51.26 N	3.35 E
Vlorë	48	40.27 N	19.30 E
Vlorës, Gji i c	48	40.25 N	19.25 E
Vltava ≃	30	50.21 N	14.30 E
Vočin	40	45.37 N	17.32 E
Vogelkop → Doberai, Jazirah ʌ¹	68	1.30 S	132.30 E
Vogel Peak → Dimlang ʌ	82	8.24 N	11.47 E
Vogelsberg ʌ	30	50.30 N	9.15 E
Voghera	40	44.59 N	9.01 E
Vohibinany	86	18.49 S	49.04 E
Vohimarina	86	13.21 S	50.02 E
Voiron	36	45.22 N	5.35 E
Vojmsjön ⊜	22	64.55 N	16.40 E
Volchov	20	59.55 N	32.20 E
Volchov ≃	54	60.08 N	32.20 E
Volga ≃, S.S.S.R.	54	45.55 N	47.52 E
Volga, Ia., U.S.	138	42.45 N	91.17 W
Volga-Baltic Canal → Volgo-Baltijskij kanal ⋿	20	59.00 N	38.00 E
Volgo-Baltijskij kanal ⋿	20	59.00 N	38.00 E
Volgograd (Stalingrad)	54	48.44 N	44.25 E
Volgogradskoje vodochranilišče ⊜¹	54	49.20 N	45.00 E
Vólos	48	39.21 N	22.56 E
Volsk	54	52.02 N	47.23 E
Volta ≃¹	82	7.30 N	0.15 E
Volta Blanche (White Volta) ≃	82	8.41 N	1.33 E
Volta Noire (Black Volta) ≃	82	8.41 N	1.33 E
Volta Redonda	118	22.32 S	44.07 W
Volterra	40	43.24 N	10.51 E
Volturno ≃	40	41.01 N	13.55 E
Volyně	30	49.10 N	13.53 E
Volžsk	54	55.53 N	48.21 E
Volžskij	54	48.50 N	44.44 E
Vonavona Island I	94	8.15 S	157.05 E
Vorderrhein ≃	36	46.49 N	9.25 E
Voria Sporádhes II	48	39.17 N	23.23 E
Vórios Evvoïkós Kólpos c	48	38.40 N	23.15 E
Vorkuta	54	67.27 N	63.58 E
Voronež	54	51.40 N	39.10 E
Vorošilovgrad	54	48.34 N	39.20 E
Vosges ʌ	36	48.30 N	7.10 E
Voskresensk	20	55.19 N	38.42 E
Voss	22	60.39 N	6.26 E
Vostočno-Sibirskoje more (East Siberian Sea) ⊜²	56	74.00 N	166.00 E
Votkinsk	56	57.03 N	53.59 E
Vouga ≃	44	40.41 N	8.40 W
Voyageurs National Park ◆	138	48.30 N	93.00 W
Vraca	48	43.12 N	23.33 E
Vrancei, Munţii ʌ	48	46.00 N	26.30 E
Vrangel'a, ostrov I	56	71.00 N	179.30 W
Vranje	48	42.33 N	21.54 E
Vrbas	48	45.35 N	19.39 E
Vrbas ≃	48	45.06 N	17.31 E
Vrbovsko	40	45.23 N	15.05 E
Vrchlabí	30	50.38 N	15.37 E
Vredenburgh	144	31.49 N	87.19 W
Vršac	48	45.07 N	21.18 E
Vryburg	86	26.55 S	24.45 E
Vryheid	86	27.46 S	30.48 E
Vsetín	30	49.21 N	17.59 E
Vsevoložsk	20	60.01 N	30.40 E
Vught	30	51.40 N	5.17 E
Vukovar	48	45.21 N	19.00 E
Vulcan, Rom.	48	45.23 N	23.17 E
Vulcan, Mi., U.S.	138	45.46 N	87.51 W
Vulcano, Isola ʌ	40	38.24 N	14.58 E
Vung-tau	68	10.21 N	107.04 E
Vuoksenniska	22	61.13 N	28.47 E
Vyborg	20	60.42 N	28.45 E
Vyborgskij zaliv c	22	60.33 N	28.24 E
Vyčegda ≃	54	61.18 N	46.36 E
Vygozero, ozero ⊜	54	63.35 N	34.42 E
Vyškov	30	49.16 N	17.00 E
Vyšnij Voločok	20	57.35 N	34.34 E
Vysoké Tatry ʌ	30	49.12 N	20.05 E
Vyšší Brod	30	48.37 N	14.19 E
W			
Waal ≃	30	51.49 N	4.58 E
Waalwijk	30	51.41 N	5.04 E
Wabana	130	47.38 N	52.57 W
Wabasca ≃	130	58.22 N	115.20 W
Wabash	144	40.47 N	85.49 W
Wabash ≃	144	37.46 N	88.02 W
Wabasha	138	44.23 N	92.01 W
Wabasso	142	27.44 N	80.26 W
Wabe Gestro ≃	84	4.12 N	42.02 E
Wabeno	138	45.26 N	88.39 W
Wabrzeźno	30	53.17 N	18.57 E
Waccamaw ≃	142	33.21 N	79.16 W
Waccamaw, Lake ⊜	142	34.17 N	78.30 W
Wachau ◆¹	30	48.18 N	15.24 E
Wachusett Mountain ʌ	136	42.29 N	71.53 W
Waco	132	31.33 N	97.08 W
Waconia	138	44.51 N	93.47 W
Waddenilanden II	30	53.26 N	5.30 E
Waddenzee ⫲²	30	53.15 N	5.15 E
Waddington, Mount ʌ	130	51.23 N	125.15 W
Wadena	130	51.57 N	103.47 W
Wädenswil	36	47.14 N	8.40 E
Wadesboro	142	34.58 N	80.04 W
Wādī Ḥalfā'	84	21.56 N	31.20 E
Wadley	142	32.52 N	82.24 W
Wad Madanī	84	14.25 N	33.28 E
Wadsworth, Oh., U.S.	136	41.01 N	81.43 W
Wadsworth, Nv., U.S.	154	39.38 N	119.17 W
Wageningen	30	51.58 N	5.40 E
Wagga Wagga	96	35.07 S	147.22 E
Waging am See	30	47.56 N	12.43 E
Wagner	132	43.04 N	98.17 W
Wagoner	144	35.57 N	95.22 W
Wagontire Mountain ʌ	150	43.19 N	119.53 W
Wagrien ◆¹	30	54.15 N	10.45 E
Wągrowiec	30	52.49 N	17.11 E
Wahiawa	132b	21.30 N	158.01 W
Wahpeton	132	46.16 N	96.36 W
Wahran (Oran)	82	35.43 N	0.43 W
Waiau ≃	98	46.12 S	167.38 E
Waiblingen	30	48.50 N	9.19 E
Waigeo, Pulau I	68	0.14 S	130.45 E
Waiheke Island I	98	36.48 S	175.06 E
Waikare, Lake ⊜	98	37.24 S	175.11 E
Waikaremoana, Lake ⊜	98	38.46 S	177.07 E
Waikato ≃	98	37.23 S	174.43 E
Waimakariri ≃	98	43.23 S	172.42 E
Waimate	98	44.45 S	171.03 E
Waingapu	68	9.39 S	120.16 E
Wainuiomata	98	41.16 S	174.57 E
Wainwright	130	52.49 N	110.52 W
Waipa ≃	98	37.41 S	175.09 E
Waipukurau	98	40.00 S	176.34 E
Wairarapa, Lake ⊜	98	41.10 S	175.15 E
Wairoa	98	39.02 S	177.25 E
Wairoa ≃	98	39.03 S	177.25 E
Waitaki ≃	98	44.57 S	171.09 E
Waitara	98	38.59 S	174.14 E
Waite Park	138	45.33 N	94.14 W
Wajir	84	1.45 N	40.04 E
Wakarusa	144	41.32 N	86.03 W
Wakatipu, Lake ⊜	98	45.05 S	168.34 E
Wakayama	66	34.13 N	135.11 E
Wakefield, Eng., U.K.	26	53.42 N	1.29 W
Wakefield, R.I., U.S.	136	41.26 N	71.30 W
Wake Forest	142	35.58 N	78.30 W
Wake Island I	8	19.17 N	166.36 E
Wakhān → Vākhān ▪¹	70	37.00 N	73.00 E
Wakkanai	66	45.25 N	141.40 E
Wałbrzych (Waldenburg)	30	50.46 N	16.17 E
Wałcz	30	53.17 N	16.28 E
Waldbröl	30	50.53 N	7.37 E
Walden	136	41.33 N	74.11 W
Waldenburg → Wałbrzych	30	50.46 N	16.17 E
Waldmünchen	30	49.23 N	12.43 E
Waldorf	136	38.37 N	76.56 W
Waldron, Ar., U.S.	144	34.53 N	94.05 W
Waldshut	30	47.37 N	8.13 E
Waldviertel ◆¹	30	48.40 N	15.40 E
Wales □⁸	26	52.30 N	3.30 W
Walgett	96	30.01 S	148.07 E
Walhalla, N.D., U.S.	132	48.55 N	97.55 W
Walhalla, S.C., U.S.	142	34.45 N	83.03 W
Walla ≃	30	49.03 N	12.14 E
Walker	138	47.06 N	94.35 W
Walker ≃	154	39.08 N	118.47 W
Walker Lake ⊜	154	38.44 N	118.43 W
Walkerton	144	41.28 N	86.29 W
Wallace, Id., U.S.	150	47.28 N	115.55 W
Wallace, N.C., U.S.	142	34.44 N	77.59 W
Wallaceburg	136	42.36 N	82.23 W
Wallachia ▪⁹	48	44.00 N	25.00 E
Walla Walla	150	46.03 N	118.20 W
Wallingford, Ct., U.S.	136	41.27 N	72.49 W
Wallis and Futuna □²	8	14.00 S	177.00 W
Wallowa, Lake ⊜	150	45.17 N	117.12 W
Walnut	144	41.10 N	89.35 W
Walnut ≃, N.C., U.S.	142	35.26 N	77.01 W
Walnut Cove	142	36.17 N	80.08 W
Walnut Ridge	144	36.04 N	90.57 W
Walpole	136	42.09 N	71.15 W
Walsall	26	52.35 N	1.58 W
Walsenburg	148	37.37 N	104.46 W
Walsrode	30	52.52 N	9.35 E
Walterboro	142	32.54 N	80.40 W
Walter F. George Lake ⊜¹	142	31.49 N	85.08 W
Waltershausen	30	50.53 N	10.33 E
Waltham	136	42.22 N	71.14 W
Walton, Ky., U.S.	136	38.52 N	84.36 W
Walton, N.Y., U.S.	136	42.10 N	75.07 W
Walvisbaai (Walvis Bay)	86	22.59 S	14.31 E
Walvis Bay → Walvisbaai	86	22.59 S	14.31 E
Walworth	138	42.31 N	88.35 W
Wamba ≃	86	3.56 S	17.12 E
Wami ≃	86	6.08 S	38.49 E
Wampum	136	40.53 N	80.20 W
Wamsutter	150	41.40 N	107.58 W
Wanaka, Lake ⊜	98	44.30 S	169.08 E
Wanamingo	138	44.18 N	92.47 W
Wanchese	142	35.50 N	75.38 W
Wanganui	98	39.56 S	175.03 E
Wangen [im Allgäu]	30	47.41 N	9.50 E
Wangerooge I	30	53.46 N	7.55 E
Wanne-Eickel	30	51.32 N	7.09 E
Wanxian	66	30.52 N	108.22 E
Wapakoneta	136	40.34 N	84.11 W
Wapato	150	46.26 N	120.25 W
Wapello	138	41.11 N	91.11 W
Wappapello, Lake ⊜¹	144	36.58 N	90.20 W
Wappingers Falls	136	41.35 N	73.54 W
Wapsipinicon ≃	138	41.44 N	90.20 W
Warangal	70	18.00 N	79.35 E
Warburg	30	51.29 N	9.08 E
Warburton Creek ≃	96	27.55 S	137.28 E
Ward, Mount ʌ	98	43.52 S	169.50 E
Warden	86	27.51 S	28.58 E
Wardha	70	20.45 N	78.37 E
Ward Hill ʌ²	26	58.54 N	3.20 W
Ware	136	42.15 N	72.14 W
Wareham, Eng., U.K.	26	50.41 N	2.07 W
Wareham, Ma., U.S.	136	41.45 N	70.43 W
Waremme	30	50.41 N	5.15 E
Waren	30	53.31 N	12.40 E
Warendorf	30	51.57 N	7.59 E
Ware Shoals	142	34.23 N	82.14 W
Warka	30	51.47 N	21.10 E
Warmbad	86	28.25 S	18.44 E
Warminster, Eng., U.K.	26	51.13 N	2.12 W
Warminster, Pa., U.S.	136	40.12 N	75.06 W
Warm Springs, Ga., U.S.	142	32.53 N	84.40 W
Warm Springs, Or., U.S.	150	44.45 N	121.15 W
Warm Springs Reservoir ⊜¹	150	43.38 N	118.14 W
Warner ≃	136	43.16 N	71.49 W
Warner Mountains ʌ	154	41.40 N	120.20 W
Warner Peak ʌ	150	42.28 N	119.44 W
Warner Robins	142	32.37 N	83.36 W
Warnow ≃	30	54.06 N	12.09 E
Warrego ≃	96	30.24 S	145.21 E
Warren, Ar., U.S.	144	33.36 N	92.03 W
Warren, Mi., U.S.	136	42.28 N	83.01 W
Warren, Oh., U.S.	136	41.14 N	80.49 W
Warren, Pa., U.S.	136	41.50 N	79.08 W
Warrenpoint	26	54.06 N	6.15 W
Warrensburg, Mo., U.S.	144	38.45 N	93.44 W
Warrensburg, N.Y., U.S.	136	43.29 N	73.46 W
Warrenton, S. Afr.	86	28.09 S	24.47 E
Warrenton, Ga., U.S.	142	33.24 N	82.39 W
Warrenton, Mo., U.S.	144	38.49 N	91.08 W
Warrenton, Va., U.S.	136	38.42 N	77.47 W
Warri	82	5.31 N	5.45 E
Warrington, Eng., U.K.	26	53.24 N	2.37 W
Warrington, Fl., U.S.	144	30.23 N	87.16 W
Warrior	144	33.48 N	86.48 W
Warrnambool	96	38.23 S	142.29 E
Warsaw → Warszawa, Pol.	30	52.15 N	21.00 E
Warsaw, In., U.S.	144	41.14 N	85.51 W
Warsaw, Ky., U.S.	144	38.46 N	84.54 W
Warsaw, Mo., U.S.	144	38.14 N	93.22 W
Warsaw, N.Y., U.S.	136	42.44 N	78.07 W
Warsaw, N.C., U.S.	142	34.59 N	78.05 W
Warsaw, Oh., U.S.	136	40.20 N	82.00 W
Warszawa (Warsaw)	30	52.15 N	21.00 E
Warta	30	51.43 N	18.38 E
Warta ≃	30	52.35 N	14.39 E
Wartburg	142	36.06 N	84.35 W
Warwick, Austl.	96	28.13 S	152.02 E
Warwick, Eng., U.K.	26	52.17 N	1.34 W
Warwick, R.I., U.S.	136	41.41 N	71.22 W
Warwick Channel ⋃	96	13.51 S	136.16 E
Warwickshire ◆⁶	26	52.13 N	1.37 W
Wasatch Range ʌ	148	40.40 N	111.35 W
Wasco	154	35.35 N	119.20 W
Waseca	138	44.04 N	93.30 W
Washburn	138	46.40 N	90.53 W
Washington, D.C., U.S.	136	38.53 N	77.02 W
Washington, Ga., U.S.	142	33.44 N	82.44 W
Washington, Il., U.S.	144	40.42 N	89.24 W
Washington, In., U.S.	144	38.39 N	87.10 W
Washington, Ia., U.S.	144	41.17 N	91.41 W
Washington, Mo., U.S.	144	38.33 N	91.01 W
Washington, N.C., U.S.	142	35.33 N	77.03 W
Washington, Pa., U.S.	136	40.10 N	80.14 W
Washington □³	132	47.30 N	120.30 W
Washington, Mount ʌ	136	44.15 N	71.15 W
Washington Court House	136	39.32 N	83.26 W
Washington Island I	138	45.23 N	86.55 W
Washington Terrace	148	41.10 N	111.58 W
Washoe Lake ⊜	154	39.12 N	119.49 W
Wasilków	30	53.12 N	23.12 E
Waskom	144	32.28 N	94.03 W
Wassaw Sound ⊜	142	31.56 N	80.58 W
Wasserkuppe ʌ	30	50.30 N	9.56 E
Watampone	68	4.32 S	120.20 E
Watatic, Mount ʌ	136	42.42 N	71.53 W
Waterbury, Ct., U.S.	136	41.33 N	73.02 W
Waterbury, Vt., U.S.	136	44.20 N	72.45 W

Symbols in the index entries are identified on page 162.

Symbols in the index entries are identified on page 162.

Symbols in the index entries are identified on page 162.